Mr. Versatility

An Adoption, An Ambition:
Cheeky moves and memories from a basketball journeyman

By Delme Herriman (with Kirstie Herriman)

For
Ray 'Ozzie' Osborne.
For everything.

ISBN: 978-0-9566543-0-4

Published by Delme Herriman.

Design and layout by Tangent Design Ltd.

Cover photo by Nick Falzerano. Buzzer beater against No. 25 ranked Xavier, 1995 MCC tournament.

Printed in the United Kingdom

Acknowledgements

Firstly thanks go to all my basketball friends and coaches who contributed to this work, specifically Jim Brown, Jim Riley, Dean Lockwood, Bill Edwards, Nhamo Shire, Sam Stiller, Steve Bucknall, Laszlo Nemeth, Rick Brooks, Peter Scantlebury and of course my boy Allan Houston.

To all my friends from Claymont High School who helped to make my year with them one of the greatest I experienced. Thanks to the Dennison and Widnes branches of the International Rotary Club, the Carrothers family, the Pattersons and my Claymont guidance counsellor Pam Swinderman.

Thanks are also due to all those at Wright State University who have helped me in the production and promotion of this book; a special thank you to Bob Noss, Nick Falzerano, Bob Grant and also Tom Archdeacon from Dayton Daily News. A big Thank You to Larry Buckley and his wife for looking after my mum and Gideon during their visit to WSU. I would also like to say what's up to all my friends from WSU. It's a tribute to you all that you're too numerous to mention and you know who you are. Some of you feature in this book: Eric Wills, Femi Abodunde, Jon Ramey and Mike Nahar, others don't but are no less thought of.

I also want to thank Jane Rhodes and all the other sports development officers from Halton Council who helped me set up Halton Basketball Club, and to Rob Warburton and the people from Halton Youthbank for funding us.

I wanted to give a mention to my physio Alex from National team who helped keep my injuries down to a minimum over my ten-year stint.

To all of my teammates around the globe who have shared in and helped to create these cheeky memories, I say one word...........Meeeooooooww!

Thanks to my website and book designer, Adam Slater, for being a great friend and doing a terrific job. I really appreciate your work. Thanks to Dave Bergin from the Widnes Weekly News for his keen eye on the proofreading.

Thanks to Andrew Donaldson and Neil Kelly for believing in me!

I would also like to mention Brian Dobson who passed away in April 2010.

There are some people without whom this book wouldn't have come to fruition at all. Firstly my really hard working and special girlfriend, Yasmin, who has stuck by and supported me through the good and the really tough times over the past few years, thanks go to you and a big hug to your beautiful girls, Yalkin and Layla, who are like daughters to me. Thanks for all your support and love.

Also a special thank you to my sister Kirstie who had the great idea for us to write this book together, thanks for all your hard work and thanks to Mark and Elkie for their patience.

A huge thanks goes out to my big brother Gideon, who helped my whole dream come to light by befriending Coach Jim Riley at the Villanova camp. Thanks for looking after us all especially after Dad, 'Ozzie', passed away.

I just wanted to mention my three other lovely sisters Kimberley, Hayley and Hannah who have always stood by and supported our 'basketball lifestyle' and probably felt left out at times, thanks for your love and support.

I also want to thank my dad Dave Herriman, who along with my mum adopted me in the first place, all those years ago, and gave me the happy family home that any adopted kid would hope for.

My final thank you goes to my mum, Kay Jefferson, who adopted me when I was just five weeks old and has stood by me since day one. Who has listened to my outlandish dreams with patience, support and unerring faith, and has been my biggest fan. Thanks mum, without you, I wouldn't be me.

Explanatory Notes

i   Red Shirt - a player who is 'sitting out' of competition in spite of practicing and training with a team and being considered part of a squad.

ii   Swole' - really mad / as vexed as Hell.

iii   Scallies - scallywags/rascals, usually young and tough and often from an economically and socially deprived area.

iv   'give me toes' - chase after a person really quickly, usually with a malicious intent.

v   'a champion mitherer' - someone who persists incessantly.

vi   Rusholme - an area of South Manchester famed for having the UK's largest number of South Asian restraurants, commonly known as 'The Curry Mile'.

vii   The Vol's - abbreviation: Tennessee Volunteers, University of Tennessee's Division One Basketball team.

viii   'what the rass' - what on Earth / what the Hell.

ix   Tough-necks - fools, usually used in a light-hearted or affectionate way.

x   BBL - British Basketball League, the UK's top division.

xi   Bleachers - the stands / seating rows within a sports arena.

xii   'walk-on guy' - a player who is accepted to play on a team, who practices each day, but who isn't in receipt of a scholarship from the College.

xiii   Mrs Overall - comedy character created by English comedian Victoria Wood.

xiv   Crumpsall - a suburb of Northern Manchester.

xv   Aigburth - a suburb of Liverpool South of the city centre.

xvi   Scran - food

Photographs

1. Kimberley, Kirstie, Gid and me in back yard in 1976.

2. The adopted three, I was 5 months old.

3. 'Little cheeky' about six years old.

4. A wannabe soldier, age two in 1975.

5. A family day out with step-sister, Rachel, 2nd from right.

6. Farnworth C. of E. primary school, 1978.

7. Leeds basketball camp with Dean Lockwood stood behind me, in 1989.

8. Gid and I spent many hours in our back yard working on our dreams.

9. I was just dreaming about dunking then.

10. Hayley, Kirstie, Kimberley and Hannah my sisters in 1990.

11. In Manchester with Dr J , Trevor Campbell and Jeff Glover after I had a dunk contest with the legend (Julius Irving).

12. The type of gyms we grew up in were no match for the ones stateside.

13. The last farewell before I was supposed to go to the states in 1989.

14. My old friend Chris Wilson blocking my shot in my back yard.

15. The day I returned home from my great year at Claymont High in 1991.

16. Claymont Mustangs 1990-91 in Uhrichsville, Ohio.

17. Gid finding it hard that I actually did a real days work, helping my dad.

18. My high school Coach and his family came to visit me and my family in Widnes, 1991.

19. Standing proud in my England National Team blazer in Widnes, 1992.

20. England Under 19's National Team in Portugal, 1991.

21. Steve Hansell, Sean Mckie and me in 1991.

22. Gid hooping with some of my boys at Wright State in 1995.

23. Nice flat-top!

24. A great moment with Dick Vitale. (A legendary basketball commentator.)

25. Gid disguised as Coach Underhill giving me some pointers during the summer in Manchester.

26. WSU's No.1 fan and my mum in 1995.

27. The Shot.

28. Chilling in practice the day before the Xavier game.

29. One second after The Shot!

30. Instant National/International recognition, Fairborn, Ohio, 1995.

31. Tom Archdeacon (Dayton Daily News), Vitaly Potapenko and Gideon, 1996.

32. A very proud moment seeing my No.32 for sale in Dayton, Oh.

33. My biggest fan, Ozzie, my step-dad.

34. Mummy's Boy!

35. Just back in Widnes after signing my big contract for Genertel Trieste in Italy.

36. Handling my business in 1997 in Italy.

37. All of us in suits, Den Helder 1998.

38. My proudest moment after receiving our Bronze Medal at the 2006 Melbourne Commonwealth Games.

39. In action in the Bronze Medal game against Nigeria.

40. Nhamo Shire (founder of Midnight Madness, UK) and me chilling at the Quai 54 Tournament in Paris, 2007.

41. Allan and Wade Houston

42. Just home from the Commonwealth Games in Melbourne with my medal. 2006

43. My boy Sean Mckie, Mum and me at a Blackburn Rovers Football Game.

44. Chester Jets League Champions 2005.

45. Still getting up at the tender age of 35!

46. Everton Tigers, BBL Cup winners 2009.

47. In action with Everton.

48. Hollywood beware, Midnight Madness team in the window of Niketown.

49. Midnight Madness Finals at Crystal Palace 2007 with Dave Aliu.

50. Reifnitz, Austria. I lived right on the lake! Woerthersse Piraten, 2004.

51. Gid and his wife Ester and Me and Yasmin out for my 37th birthday.

52. The grave where I find it too difficult to visit. His commitment helped me achieve my dreams. I love you dad!

Contents

Foreword

When our Assistant Coach, Dean Lockwood, brought a light-skinned teenager into the University of Tennessee Basketball Office as part of the kid's introduction to the world of American basketball, I had no idea it would seal the beginning of a life-long friendship.

When Delme Herriman introduced himself to me and my father (UT Head Coach Wade Houston) the first thing that struck me was that he was definitely not from here. From his clothing to his shoes, his haircut and the look in his eyes, he was surely away from home. I soon found that the surface differences quickly changed into similarities in our personalities as I got to know him better.

Within days I had given Delme his first American haircut; he was sceptical about its success and smart enough to realise it wasn't the best he could have got, even if it was free. We found an immediate similarity in our appreciation of life's simple laughs and it was amazing to me how Del became like family right away.

When Delme secured a Full Ride Scholarship to Wright State University I was extremely excited for him. Always a hard worker, Del maintained a humility that I knew would allow him to have success in whatever he decided to do. With his size and athletic ability I knew that Del would add value to any team he'd play on. For his size he was a great ball-handler and was a great partner for me to go against in my workouts as he defended me tough and we challenged one another to make the most of the opportunity.

Delme and I would spend a lot of time in our younger days talking about the psychology of basketball, about our mutual need to be assertive on court so that our laid-back personalities weren't misinterpreted as a willingness to back down. Delme showed great character in his career and took every challenge that faced him head on.

I believe God blesses us with a few friends who are truly like family. When I got drafted by the Detroit Pistons, Del was part of a select group of friends I deliberately surrounded myself with; grateful to have people around me I knew I could trust. There are some friends who are there regardless of what might separate you in terms of time or distance. My man Delme is exactly that.

Allan Houston
(Former 2-Time NBA All Star & Olympic Gold Medallist)
Asst. President of Basketball Operations
New York Knicks

A Shot

We ended up with the last possession of the game. The crowd, 8,500 strong, were seething every ounce of their energy, channelling electricity, onto the court. Every basket had sent them through the roof and now we stood, five young men, proud underdogs, poised to claim the biggest scalp in our college's history. The last possession and it was ours. Xavier 70, Wright State Raiders 69 and just two small issues standing between us and Wright State history, national recognition, the greatest night of all our lives: only 1.1 seconds left in the game, and the fact that the ball was on the sideline, at the opposite end of the court, with 93' still to travel.

Coach called a last-second 'Hail Mary' play we'd practised only once, prophetically called 'Home Run'. No problem, except the plan had been that when the play started I was supposed to be stood on the free-throw line. What the Hell, this was it, one chance only. Jon Ramey was told to launch the bomb. The plan meant that I was supposed to leap into the air, over the defenders, catch the ball, turn around, and shoot the winning shot. 1.1 seconds. He threw. I leapt. Caught, back to the basket. Turned in the air. Feet touching court after an 180° pirouette. Shot. Then the buzzer. The end of the game. Buckets! It was in. Xavier 70, Wright State 71.

The world exploded. I did a crazy tuck jump into the air, another 180° spin, and sprinted off down the court like some lunatic with my teammates in pursuit. It was pandemonium. The crowd screaming and shouting and above it all the commentator yelling

'This kid's from England! This must be better than scoring the winning goal at Wembley!'

Fans rushed the court and mayhem ruled. Somewhere Coach had sunk to his knees bowing his head: in prayer, in relief, in disbelief. We'd done it. Achieved the impossible. Dotted about were Xavier players; sick, like lost mourners at a funeral, hardly able to believe their fate, that the mighty them had fallen to the merely us.

My teammates were going crazy; Jason Smith had leapt onto the scorers' table, the wildness of his dancing throwing long limbs every which-a-way. Truly, the greatest feeling of my life. And somewhere in that heaving crowd, amidst all those loony Americans, going crazy with joy, all the way from Cheshire, England, sat my mum. By now already on her feet and being dragged onto the court by my classmate Tiffany, overjoyed but fighting every English ounce of herself that told her British people do not invade courts, it's just not proper. I was only conscious through my ecstasy of a fiery joy that she was here to share the experience, and an empty sadness that my dad, Ozzie, the other person who'd worked to make this entire outlandish dream possible, wasn't. The magnitude of what we'd just done was only beginning to sink in. We had beaten a top 25 ranked team, and enabled our NCAA run to continue.

* * * * * * * *

My whole Junior season at Wright State University had been filled with much anticipation. I'd red-shirted[i] my first year and so this was my fourth year on campus; surely now my chance to shine. But with Vitaly Potapenko newly arrived on campus, things were to take yet another unexpected turn. From Ukraine, Vitaly was a 6'10", 285lb genetic giant with NBA written through his middle like some colossal stick of Russian rock. I had a number of decent games myself throughout the season, but with the chance of real NBA stardom, a coup for the college and its reputation, Coach wanted the whole nation to focus on Vitaly. So our entire season was spent pounding the ball inside to V at every possible chance. Even if there were four defenders on his shoulders, which, more often than not, his reputation meant there were.

It was as if Coach had me in handcuffs: unable to let anyone else shine. In pre-season, we'd had a series of six intra-squad scrimmages and, with the teams evenly matched and our Head Coach watching from the bleachers, I was scoring consistently and averaging 20-points per game.

10

There was equality to the scrimmages; we'd move the ball around giving everyone an opportunity to show what he could do, to play his game. Then once the season proper began, with the Head Coach back holding the reins, I fell back into being used predominantly as a role player again, in spite of averaging 35-minutes per game.

It was a hard season; we'd struggled to win half of our games, even with our NBA-bound centre, and finished so poorly in the league that we had to 'play' our way into the end of season conference tournament. Fortunately this year it was to be held at our school, surely an advantage, particularly with the obsessive passion of the Raiders' supporters. So the scene was set; Thursday night we'd open our campaign against Cleveland State, both tied in the conference. We'd play one another leaving the winning team the unenviable task of facing Xavier the next night. Xavier, the Goliath. 14-0 in the conference, and ranked 25th in the whole of America. We'd lost to them twice already but they'd been pretty close games, and I'd always stepped-up, trying to get my props against some of the best guards in the NCAA. When we'd met them at our place I'd had 16-points and 7 boards, and 22-points and 8 boards in the Cincinnati game.

We all felt we'd massively under-achieved during the season and going out onto court were painfully aware that a loss against Cleveland State meant one thing; season done. No NCAA Tournament, no more practice, and no way to salvage anything from our disappointing season. Desperation can ignite passion and talent in a way that nothing else can, and so that night Cleveland State got it. We had mad energy. We were possessed. I was all over the court and had one of my nastiest ever dunks. Dribbling the ball on a fast break, only their point guard stood in front of me. What a mistake! I sized him up, dribbling with my left hand, and took off two-footed on the left hand side of the paint. It started unremarkably, by the casual way I'd dribbled the ball down the court, no one in the gym expected me to dunk it. I jumped over him, with my elbow at rim height, and rammed it on him with my left hand! Ooohhh Teddy P, it was Nasty!

Taking care of CSU meant that our destiny was set. We'd get the chance to face Xavier. No.1 seed versus us, now No.8. We were so excited. Our victory had given everyone a new lease of life. Here we were one step closer to the possibility of going all the way to the Big Dance. Although clear underdogs we had confidence, we had our home crowd, over 8,000 of our fans behind us, and had played them pretty close in our two previous encounters. In addition to this, Wright State (a college which had never enjoyed much national exposure) was to experience a real event in itself, if only for the fact that tonight's game would be broadcast on National TV.

I came out and hit a 3-, then had a tough dribble drive on Pete Sears and after a close first-half I finished with 5-points. The game was close throughout, their other guards Jeff Massey and Michael Hawkins were naughty. Both lightning quick, they caused our guards fits at both ends of the court, leaving me to constantly bring the ball down.

I found it difficult to get involved in the offence during the second-half but our freshman, Antuan Johnson, from Toledo, Ohio, stepped-up big time. With six-minutes remaining the turning point came. With the score pretty much level, maybe there was a chance. And then our world imploded. Vitaly got hit with his 5th and final foul. He was outta there! Total devastation. Our main focus, the pivot of our entire season; gone, forced to watch from the bench. There was no chance of beating mighty Xavier now.

Vitaly walked the length of the court as the refs were setting up for Xavier to shoot two free-throws. Stood in the line-up awaiting the shots, Rob Welch ran up to me shouting *'Pass me the fucking ball, get ya head out ya ass!'* A spoilt guard who'd played his high school career under the coach-ship of his own father, Welch was two years younger than me, an under-classman and a guy I'd never liked. National T.V. or not, I saw red. I ran back up to him grabbing the neck of his jersey, yelling in his face. I knew I was about to do something completely out of character, but the pressure, the night, whatever it was, I was swole'[ii] ! This guy had it coming, no one talks to me like that on the court without something jumping off, I lost all relevance of the occasion; that my mum was there, that this wasn't me, wasn't how I lived my life or how I played my game, that I was being watched by the entire nation. Then the most unlikely of candidates stepped-up to diffuse the situation: Antuan. A real streetwise tough guy, he got in between me and Rob so I couldn't swing on him. There wasn't time to think of the consequences of me battering my own teammate in the middle of such an important game, we had a job to do, I'd forgotten, temporarily, but now it was on, and each one of us was even more fired up, even more inspired.

Although he was clearly our best player, we always seemed to hold our own if not play even better when Vitaly was out. His absence made everything less predictable, as though anything was now possible, and as a result, every other guy would somehow step-up. We traded baskets and the game went right down to the wire. They turned the ball over on a crucial possession and I managed to get the deflection, bruising my thumb in the process. It had been a rough game and prior to this I'd taken an elbow to the throat. By the time there was 1.1 seconds remaining on the clock I was pretty banged-up. And then, The Shot. The glory, and Wright State History.

We calmed down a little in the locker room, we had to, there's not enough energy in a human body to maintain that level of excitement, especially after such a tough fight. Coach was ecstatic. But, as coaches always do, reminded us of what remained, the season wasn't over yet, there were the semis, maybe even the final, it was possible now, anything was. There were other games still to be played that night, so after showering I headed back into the Nutter Centre and was immediately spotted by our fans. A standing ovation ensued: 7,000 on their feet. It was one of the most moving experiences of my life. I felt like I'd finally arrived in the Big Time. Finally got my name out there. Little did I know at the time how far the legend of The Shot would travel. By morning it was across the globe. At 8am I took a call from Europe, Bill Edwards, WSU's former star, now playing pro' in Italy, had just seen The Shot on CNN Sports Centre.

The Shot was voted ESPN 'play of the week' and was compared to the Duke Grant Hill to Christian Laetenner shot a few years earlier. A proud moment and something that gave me increased confidence for the remaining games. We managed to knock-off Detroit in the semis, before falling to Wisconsin Green Bay in the finals. Our exposure continued, the final game was broadcast live on ESPN. Wisconsin Green Bay played outstanding ball that night, and we lost. As sometimes happens, we were simply outplayed by an excellent, well-coached team, who won the automatic bid to the Big Dance.

Basketball can be like this. It can be excitement and glory, tough games, with hard hits and injuries and desperate calls. It can be a crowd of thousands chanting your name and it can be a collective groan as you're fouled out and forced to sit and watch from a position of helplessness. It can be a machine that takes on a life of its own. A truly great team can function as a single entity, working together to combine all their talent into one explosion of victory. But it's also just human. Just individuals. Players who've devoted their lives to sport, who've fought to stand on that court. Some of them born to do it, some of them there having worked and worked and hoped and worked some more. There was a human story behind The Shot; my story.

A month before the game, Jason Smith and I had gone to visit some kids at a hospital in Dayton, where we'd befriended eight-year-old Keith. He loved basketball and was smitten with us visiting him. He was also dying of leukaemia with only months of life remaining. We made follow-up visits to see Keith, and spent 5 hours with him at his birthday party, thrown in his honour by the hospice in which he was cared for. His worsening prognosis meant the party was also a farewell.

In the locker room, just before our much-anticipated clash with Xavier, our pre-game talk had been interrupted by Bob Grant (now Wright State's Head of Athletics) who'd walked in accompanied by Keith. He apologised for the interruption at such a crucial moment but explained that Keith's one last wish was to sit on the bench with his favourite Raiders. Jason and I jumped from our lockers, hugged Keith and lifted him up onto our shoulders. Prior to the game, I'd marker-penned Keith's name onto the side of my boots; I'd already decided that whatever happened I was playing this game for him. He was a true inspiration to me, and The Shot is dedicated to Keith.

Sometimes we're pushed on the court by knowing that glory might be ours. Sometimes we're pushed simply because we love the game and playing (and winning) is all that we know, all we ever want to know. And sometimes what pushes us is other people. Those who've dedicated their lives to us achieving our dreams. My dad, Ozzie, wasn't there to see his boy's ultimate glory, wasn't there to witness that moment which marked the real beginning of his lad's career. But it literally was only death that could've kept him away.

A Story

So how did this lad from England come to be here in Division One of the NCAA, all these miles from an industrial, rugby-obsessed town in the Northwest? In the midst of small-town America, at a college which had previously only ever dreamed of such national recognition. How was that possible?

This is no silver-spoon story, no tale of money and influence and of knowing the right people. It's a story of perseverance, of exceptional talent that would have been nothing without pushing and parental back-up, without being a nice guy, without working hard. A story about being born in the wrong place, which was perversely the right place. Finding the right people, having them find you. Ultimately, it's the story of a remarkable career.

It is possible. If you have a dream and you're willing to work. It is possible.

As a wise man once said to a gangly lad from Widnes:

'If your mind can conceive it, and your heart can believe it, then your body can achieve it.'

Here's how ...

A Boy

Kay was the first person I ever met to whom I was biologically related. I was 23. She was 41. I sat and waited for her in a suburban pub, already out of place just by being there and by not being white. Five years in the States had done nothing for me in terms of how weird coming home would make me feel; in the States I stood out, but for different reasons. I'm not sure if I looked odder then, sat waiting, or after she arrived. 6'6" of black athlete, American twang as I ordered at the bar, sat kind of awkwardly with an older white woman who was clearly nervous and jumping and laughing in that terrified-to-be-here kind of a way. We probably looked like we were on some kind of date, a pretty badly matched one, one that hadn't really taken off, wouldn't really go anywhere.

I knew already, from the small correspondence we'd had, that she'd lived much of her adult life in Scotland, but when Kay spoke to me in the kind of Scottish voice I'd only really ever heard on TV, she threw me off. By now accents were something I negotiated constantly, my stint in the States had given me a US drawl spattered with the odd bit of Manchester, some by now bizarre sounding Northern expressions, and I'd played on teams with people from across the world, always managing to communicate somehow. But Kay looked like me, at least like a white version of me, and so the fact that she didn't sound like me seemed strange, maybe I'd expected her to. Sat against the patterned upholstery of a Northern chain-pub, face to face for the first time with the woman who had, all those years ago, given birth to me and then walked away, I wasn't sure what I'd expected, what I even thought anymore.

She was nervous, more nervous than me I think, and was clearly not prepared for my sense of focus about our meeting; there were two clear things I wanted: to know something about my birth-father and to have the chance to thank her for giving me away. It was impossible for me to muster up any real sense of emotion, in the way that might be expected from meeting for the first time the person who brought you into the world. But I'd never consciously felt the loss of her. I'd never felt the need for a mum, because I already had one. I couldn't mourn for something that, as far as I was concerned, I'd never lost.

With a weird synchronicity, that mum was another Kay. One who on a June day in 1973 had driven the ten-miles to Liverpool in a borrowed Mini and had, along with her husband Dave, collected me from the City Centre. I was passed to her across an adoption agency office in Rodney Street and she made me her son, then and there, just like that. This other Kay, the Scottish one, the one I saw as a mum only in biological terms, I had only gratitude for. How could I reproach her? I didn't know what she'd been through, how the last twenty-three years had turned out for her, anymore than I knew how things had been for her back then, a frightened teenager unable to tell her parents that the baby she hadn't planned was not only on his way, but he was also going to be mixed-race. Had my adoption turned out differently, had my life turned out differently, that resentment or anger might have been there, but for me there was only gratitude. I could only thank her because, had she not have given me away, my story might have been entirely different. My gratitude seemed to throw her off, as though she hadn't expected me to have been so happy.

Maybe I was too pleased, too grateful. People always ask me, aren't you upset that you're mum gave you away? And always find it impossible to believe me when I say I have never for one moment in my life thought why did my mum not keep me, because my adopted mum (my real, real mum) was just my mum. I never felt I wasn't her son and had been made entirely aware (from before I could even understand) that not being born to someone doesn't make them any less your parent, not when they really want to be that, really do love you. It wasn't being adopted that made me feel like I was in the wrong place; it was growing up in Widnes that did that.

Since I could think I'd always known that Widnes was a place in which I completely didn't belong. It's not that I ever felt resentful, just that I knew

- there was something inside me that made me know - I had to leave. I had to get out. A mid-sized town mid-way between the cities of Manchester and Liverpool, Widnes had built any reputation it had on its historical centrality to the chemical industry. Working-class to its core but not a tough place to grow up: no mean streets. Areas of deprivation of the kind you'd find in most towns but no real dramas, no real action. The central pillar of Widnes life however was sport, specifically Rugby, even more specifically Rugby League. If you played Rugby League you belonged. If you played Rugby League to a high-standard, played it with any skill, you reigned. As is probably the case with most Northern working-class towns (at least in the 1970s and '80s) the important thing was to belong. It was fine to want to get on, to build a nice life, but it was more fine to know your place. To not rock the boat: to fit in.

I'd always felt that I was different, as though I was meant to do something special. Maybe it was a defence mechanism, something I'd fostered in order to explain to myself why being different, why standing out, was okay, how it might eventually mean something really positive. It seemed entirely natural; however much my parents might have loved me, really wanted me, there was no denying that whichever street we walked down, whatever shop we went in, the only non-white faces belonged to me and my brother.

You don't process this stuff when you're little, you don't think where am I going, how do I make it possible, you just sort of get on. And that's what I did. I knew I was destined for something special, I just didn't know what that thing was. It didn't matter that I didn't know, just the thought, the belief, was comfort enough, forming and developing in the back of my mind: everything would be okay because I would be going somewhere special, somewhere really different.

My sense of displacement was more geographical than anything else. A psychologist might have a field-day with this, might call it denial, but for me being aware my whole life that I was different was never a huge problem, it was more something that I just accepted like the colour of your eyes, say. I suppose it would be naïve to say it was unrelated to race. I wasn't the first black kid to go to my high school in Widnes; but I was the second. Three-years older than me it was my brother Gideon who'd had to pave the way, and so everything was harder for him. The novelty had worn off a bit by the time I arrived but I still stood out. My home-town is a lot more diverse now and therefore so is my old school, but in the '80s being the one black kid was like a more extreme version of being a ginger kid. I wasn't especially badly behaved but (like all young lads) I liked a bit of mischief whether directly involved or just watching from the sidelines. Unfortunately the colour of my skin made me extra-visible so that if ever a teacher were required to recall which kids had been in the crowd during a fight, or which kids had been seen messing around, I kind of stuck out (just like the ginger kids), and so stayed in their minds. By the time I'd completed junior school one especially harsh teacher had summarized my future for me: I'd amount to nothing.

If I stood out to teachers then I obviously stood out to my classmates. A blessing and a curse, it allowed me to develop a unique popularity (I was funny and kicking-it with the black dude was cool) and simultaneously forced me into proving I could handle myself. No matter how popular you are, there are always some people who don't like difference, who resent other people's popularity, especially if it seems to come naturally to them, and at high school this resulted in a couple of scuffles. Nothing major, never one to really enjoy trouble, I managed to fight just enough to earn the respect to be left alone to be the nice guy. I earned respect through sports too, something which made being me a whole lot easier than it would've been for some shy little kid who couldn't stick up for himself. I was kind of weedy (and would stay that way until the machine of US college ball bulked me up beyond all recognition), but it didn't matter, I could prove myself in other ways. I'd learned early on in junior school that whatever sport I turned my hand or foot or eye to I seemed to manage to perform in better than pretty much every other kid I knew. Hard work and dedication were to prove vital to me as the years progressed but at a young age I was able to just excel and to enjoy the respect and the admiration that sport seemed to bring.

I tried everything. As fads came and went, I'd be in there from the start trying to master and then really conquer whatever it was that had hooked our neighbourhood. First BMX-riding, later roller-skating, all phases that came and went. But while they lasted my focus was always the same: to enjoy myself but, most importantly, to be the best. Even at such an early age average held no fascination for me. Even then I believed you should aim to be the best you could possibly manage to be, whatever that was in. Even if it was BMXing. I developed a respect for achievement, whether via natural talent or through hard slog and dedication, no matter what that achievement was in, sports, playing the piano, being able to draw, anything. My natural physical aptitude (I guess inherited from one of the people I'd never yet met) meant I embraced all kinds of sports, playing Rugby Union and League for school and town teams, cricket, football, athletics (holding a school discus record) and eventually judo. Martial Arts had always fascinated me and at the time pretty much every young whipper-snapper wanted to be Bruce Lee. I loved the dedication of Martial Arts and of boxing, the way both required a focus and a determination to which I could already relate; they wanted to be the best and so did I. I learned pretty early on that being the best at something was a way to win respect from my peers. Maybe I was trying to prove myself, but I've never understood why a person might opt for doing the ordinary if the extraordinary might lie just a little stretch beyond their grasp. Later on, in English basketball at least, coaches would always say go for the safe option: on a fast break get up court and just lay it up. Why would you choose that? If you knew that on the end of your fast break lies the option to slam the ball down, to touch the rim and thrill your crowd with a nasty dunk, why wouldn't you?

Outside of sport it was a different matter. On the court or on the pitch the colour of my skin was irrelevant to my teammates, I was on their side and we'd be winning. What I met was a low-level sort of racism, not an out-and-out confrontation, more a sense that certain people couldn't really handle me being different. Odd occasions stand out to me because of their rarity, like the time a teacher in high school challenged me in front of the

23

whole class: '*What's wrong with you? Apart from the obvious.*' I can hear the hush that followed even now, as the entire class collectively inhaled their shock. I wasn't used to people being so blatant, at least not people on my own patch.

Travelling to other schools to play against them in various sports would be a different matter, as co-captain of the Rugby Union team I was both respected and liked by my teammates who'd regularly erupt alongside me on the pitch when we overheard (as we so often did) the opposition deciding it was time to '*get the Nigger*'. We were a team. We had one another's backs and would regularly end up in some mid-game scuffle. We had a reputation as a tough school and rugby is a tough sport so something was always jumping-off. There was only one time when it got too much. We were away playing a team in Lancashire which included one especially cocky little racist who, in the team line-up at the end of the match (in which the members of each team create a tunnel and clap the other players through as they leave the pitch) I was unable to contain the urge to punch the guy in the face on my way to the changing room. He was ginger, and so I kind of thought he might have known better. It wasn't the kind of thing I did, mainly because it wasn't the kind of thing I had to do. I was friendly and easy-going and a high-profile fight early on in high school had pretty much secured me as (what we used to call then) 'cock of the year'; a weirdly meaningful title which meant that me and the other guy who shared the honour just weren't messed with. There was a difference between him and me though; he was a bully.

I was in the first year of high school, aged eleven, when I'd kind of had enough of the bullying behaviour of a couple of guys who'd come from other primary schools and figured that their status there would automatically transfer. In spite of my weedy frame I had a reputation for toughness at my small primary and so had pretty quickly gotten sick of these guys punking others on the playground. When one day I retaliated by standing up for myself, I was swole' but still sensible enough to utter those immortal words 'After school' which meant that as soon as the bell rang a mob would trudge down the road to the local park to engage in the much anticipated spectacle of one kid 'having another out.' Trouble was as the day wore on my anger had worn off (I've never been one to hold a grudge) and so by the time school was out and I clocked the crowd of what seemed like hundreds waiting for me to arrive, I'd decided it was a bad idea. Certain that we'd get in trouble if seen by school staff, I went to head in the opposite direction. But it was no use, I'd been seen and was expected to see this thing out. The walk down Lockett Road to Victoria Park where the school's imaginary boxing ring was located was like something out of Gladiator. Good versus evil, each represented by its own mob; around ten supporting the bullies on one side of the road and on the other the mass of hundreds behind me.

Even then it seemed a little ridiculous, all this build-up, but it was like a ritual that had to be performed in order for the crowd to be satisfied. Emma Blakemore, a girl three-years older than me and a classmate of Gid's, had taken on the role of trainer and as we stood in our opposite corners, Emma undid my tie and all but Vaselined my eyebrows! All the pomp and the build up was pissing me off, I just wanted it over with, to prove I could handle myself and then be left alone and so I approached the opposing corner as my foe was still undoing his tie with one overwhelming thought in my mind 'Shit that dude's nose is huge. If I hit it dead on it'll split like a melon and I'm gonna throw up backwards.' My first punch was kind of lame, it shook him off guard but my reluctance to crack his big old hooter meant that it sort of hit his cheek and then we were off. I had the upperhand and, after ragging him around some, managed to floor the guy no problem but in the confusion felt him somehow jump up and onto my back. I swung around, knocked him to the floor and saw it wasn't him. His mate, bully-supremo, had stepped in and now two of those jokers were at it. It ended with the pair of them on the floor and, with shouts of '*Kill him!*' ringing off the climbing frame, I held him by the shirt, asked if he'd had enough and calmly walked away. It earned me respect. Next day in school the cheeky rass had the nerve to come up to me and say: '*You only beat me 'cause you hit me when I was still taking off my tie.*' It felt good just to laugh and walk away, never to be bothered again.

25

Outside of school, in other areas of the town where people didn't know me and didn't know I didn't get messed with, I stood out more. They didn't know I was considered hard or could play cricket or tennis or rugby better than all the other kids could. The taunts other rougher kids, usually much older hanging on corners looking for trouble, would shout at me were testament to the power of advertising. They'd yell at me to get back on the marmalade jar, call me the *'jolly brown giant'* and one time followed me along singing *'Here comes the Lilt man!'* doing such a funny impression that it wasn't even intimidating and I just laughed along. Humour was always pretty useful in diffusing a situation if I was out of my depth. Sometimes I was scared, people driving by, gangs of young lads mostly, would shout things at me, but it wasn't that bad, I just stuck around my own area where people knew me, and felt confident that something would come along that would make that difference matter.

Widnes remains a real rugby town, and was even more so in the '70s and '80s, when the local team enjoyed one of its most successful eras. My adoptive parents were both sports fans, my mum loved pretty much any sport and whilst my dad was of course a rugby man, unusually for Widnes he was a Union rather than a League guy. My parents had been together for twelve-years by the time they adopted me and already had two other children who they'd also adopted from birth. The oldest, my sister Kimberley, was five when I arrived and then they had Gid, three years older than me and already a whirlwind of energy. I suppose from the start it was an unusual life, as a family we stood out, because of the varying colours of us brown-skinned kids, but mainly because people didn't get it. They couldn't understand why our parents had chosen to have us; insisting we must all have been biologically related to one another, when any fool could see just by looking that we clearly weren't. They also assumed that the adoptions were inspired by the fact that my mum and dad couldn't have kids biologically of their own so by the time they had my next sister, Kirstie, when I was two, the fact that she was 'home-grown' made people think she must've been some kind of miracle conception. No one could understand that they'd chosen to adopt us just because they wanted to.

Inter-racial adoption seems to be kind of frowned upon now but in the late '60s and early '70s loads of mixed-race kids were adopted and raised by white parents. The difficulties in finding adoptive families for kids like us had long been highlighted and my mum vividly recalls an article she saw in a magazine as a young girl which inspired her to adopt. The pictures in the article showed a basket of new-born puppies and another basket filled with new-born black babies, the headline declared: we've found homes for the puppies. Even though she'd been really young at the time, the article struck something within my mum which she never forgot and once her and Dave felt ready to have children there was no question that they would adopt before having any 'home-growns', biologically theirs.

From an early age it was obvious that Gid and I would be sporty kids. Dad got us involved in the mini-rugby at his club pretty much as soon as we could run and catch and get the idea of it all, and both of us had a frantic energy that needed channelling through some kind of activity. When I was five, dad left home and mini-rugby left with him. We needed something else but it was to be a good few years yet until we'd find it. In the meantime, there were sort of more pressing issues to deal with.

The day I found out dad was leaving home remains frozen really clearly in my mind. I suppose there are just certain moments in life that mean so much they stay with us, whether we're consciously thinking about them or not. It had started innocently enough with Gid and I locked in a battle of marbles using the front hallway as our arena. Both fiercely competitive (a trait that would stand me in good stead for the career I was destined for), it didn't matter whether it was sport or simply a game between brothers, we both wanted to win. So when Gid insisted that his French Gogger triumphed over my Steely I refused to budge. Adamant I was right and unwilling to play on until Gid agreed, he was forced to go to the kitchen to get mum or dad to confirm he was right. Stubbornness has always been a trait of mine, even if the point was something as trivial as the rules of marbles, and so I sat on the stairs to sulk and wait. Ironically, impatience is also something I'm occasionally afflicted by and so, in spite of my lengthy sulk, when Gid didn't return from his mission as I'd expected (probably crowing at having been vindicated), I lost patience and took my skinny butt off to clarify the rules for myself.

Teetering precariously in the kitchen was a pyramid of human bodies looking like some kind of unimpressive circus act. Piled on dad's lap were Gid and my sisters all crying and looking as though the world was about to end. Jeez, it's only marbles I thought, but soon joined in the shambling pile when I was told what was really happening. Dad was moving out. There was probably an explanation, but what's an explanation when you're five and the world has just ended? We were shocked. Mum had done a sterling job at making life seem normal to us whilst her own world was clearly falling apart, the extra-marital relationship dad had begun under the cover of going to his rugby club and had continued for the past few years had become unbearable for her. Refusing to relinquish his club (and therefore his relationship), mum had persevered for the sake of us four kids, but the sudden and unexpected deaths of both her parents within a matter of days of one another had left her with, understandably, no energy to keep on fighting single-handedly. Of course, we knew nothing of this at the time. Mum protected dad from the exposure of the truth until we were all well into our teens. To us, Gran and Granddad had just disappeared, gone to Heaven where we'd never get to see them, and now dad was going too. Okay so his sister's house (his new temporary home) wasn't as far away as Heaven, but it might as well have been.

Looking back now it's almost impossible to imagine how mum coped at that time. She'd been close to both her parents (who'd lived at the other end of our road) and so had we. Then suddenly, aged just 35, she had no one. No parents to lean on, to support her as her marriage fell apart, no husband to comfort her and allow her space to grieve. What she did have was a pair of daughters with varying degrees of understanding (one aged ten, the other three) and a pair of increasingly boisterous sons (aged five and eight) and subsequently no other choice but to simply keep going.

It was some time later when we realized that the visits of Ozzie, a guy we knew from coming to do plumbing work at the house and at houses of various other friends of our parents, were becoming more frequent. We'd all been instantly drawn to him, he was cool with us from the off, 6'3" and a good 280lbs he was a big friendly giant who'd sit at the kitchen table drinking tea and chatting to us all.

Ozzie was like the Incredible Hulk. Always drawn to shows of strength and ability, I was (like any young lad) especially impressed by the tricks we'd insist he perform for us, again and again. Getting him to twist an apple into two halves (something I've never mastered, in spite of hundreds of thousands of dollars worth of the world's best weight-training - seriously, try it - it's impossible!) and tearing an old Yellow Pages into two as though it were a piece of tissue. He never seemed to tire of entertaining us and would stand in the middle of the kitchen a solid oak, arms outstretched like massive branches, and let Gid and I hang from his biceps, prophetically, like we were some fruits he was nurturing. He was funny and friendly and there, and I liked him a lot so when (much further down the line) mum asked us how we'd feel if Ozzie moved in, I remember saying 'Great! That would be great!' and being more excited than I'd ever been before, about anything.

Ozzie being our dad just seemed dead normal. I can't remember if and when I asked whether I could start calling him 'dad'. It might have been when he moved in, it might have been when him and mum got married and we all threw confetti on them in the front room when we got home from school. (This was the early '80s, no one I knew had mums and dads who were divorced, so no one had parents who had weddings, mum and Ozzie took themselves and a pair of witnesses quietly off to the Registry Office and told us all about their wedding in the snow when we came back from school that evening). It might have been when they had Hayley (the first of the two daughters they had together, swelling our happy house to eight when Hannah arrived sixteen-months later). When it was doesn't matter because for as long as I could remember he'd just been dad, he'd been doing all those fatherly things for us and so thinking of him as 'dad', calling him 'dad', was just the most natural thing in the world. Little did I know that it would be his support, his influence, his unerring determination, that would prove pivotal to my achieving things that were beyond my wildest dreams. How could I know it? At this age I'd never even seen a basketball.

A Ball

It wasn't long into his time at high school that my brother Gid's talent for basketball was spotted. As well as being an all-round natural sportsman, he was, even at a young age, really dedicated (much more than I was), and would diligently spend his free time lifting weights and running in addition to all the training that was directly expected by his coach. Even though it might not feel like it, the game has come a long way in England in the last twenty years or so, but this was the mid-'80s, basketball had literally just arrived on our shores and was starting to make a small impact in some areas of the country. Maybe it's to do with that inner-city toughness, or perhaps more because of the large number of black kids looking to identify with something new and kind of 'other'. Either way Manchester paved the way by setting up the area's first ever youth team. About sixty of the most promising kids from the surrounding area were invited to try out and, of the two that were selected from round where we lived, Gid was one.

The Manchester youth set-up will be a familiar sounding scenario to anyone who's ever been involved in English basketball, if only for the weird frustrations of a lack of investment and a sense of having to 'make do'. Training for the team took place in the gym of Chorlton High School. An unremarkable place in an under-invested-in area of Manchester, its entire qualification for selection being that the assistant coach lived across the street and through some connections could manage to gain access to the sports hall (cheaply) on a Friday night. The team's coach, Steve Griffiths, was a teacher at a neighbouring school, whose own gym was so small and pitiful it made Chorlton High's look like some kind of Division One facility. Any English baller will recognise the experience of playing on courts whose basketball markings are almost invisible beneath the criss-crossed lines of badminton courts, netball areas and general scuffing.

31

Chorlton High was no different, that tabernacle was freezing cold, a bit dilapidated, but it was there and it had baskets (it seems kind of fundamental, but I've turned up at venues to coach in recent years, only to find no baskets in their indoor gym at all). Most importantly it had promise. There was a coach, there was a gang of talented, motivated but largely inexperienced players, and it was a start. In a lot of ways, it was the good times, the team was to be sponsored by Manchester United Football Club, was to play under their name and colours, it was, in its own small way, pretty exciting.

As well as being a real honour for Gid, and the other boys selected for this ground-breaking team, playing and training in Manchester, week in week out, was a real commitment. Easily an hour and half round trip in our old Volkswagen minibus, and that was on a good night, when it didn't breakdown or chug the last few miles in need, the next day, of the attentions of some dude dad knew who would always miraculously manage to keep it on the road.

The van breaking down was a constant threat and when one night (some years later) it finally did, I was relieved that at least it had happened on the way home and not the way to practice. As dad pulled over onto the hard-shoulder of the M56, he gave me explicit instructions to just stay put, he'd look for an emergency phone (cell phones still something even James Bond didn't have, not that he'd have driven a battered VDub Campervan in electric orange). I asked him to hurry, my over-active imagination was already setting off and the black fields to the side of us were already containing all sorts of imaginary horrors. There were no lights, but as time passed I realised we were actually quite near to a slip-road exit and figured dad must've headed up there to find help. So I waited. I tried not to think of what might be out there in the dark and I waited some more. And then, after about 45 minutes, I got out of the van and headed up the embankment at the side of the hard-shoulder for a nose around.

Nothing but dark fields as far as the eye could see and, apart from the faceless vehicles whizzing past on the motorway below, not a single sign of life. And then I entered some kind of horror film. An almighty crash, police sirens and a major commotion breaking loose on the roundabout at the top of the slip-road. I tried to focus my eyes and as I did they fell on a pair of huge figures, dressed all in black, who were sprinting towards me. Towards Me. The sirens screamed across the air behind them and all the time they gained on me I fumbled and shook in a vain attempt to get myself locked back inside the van, in safety. As my hands failed my mind went into overdrive. They were running from the police. Running towards me. They'd need a getaway vehicle. The only vehicle seize-able was this one. They'd force their way in. They'd take me hostage. And so I did the only thing a sane and fit young lad would do and ran like hell.

Up the embankment was my only option. If I could get to the top and over down the other side they'd just run past me or stop and try to break into the van (good luck getting it started). I reached the summit and chanced a glance behind, they hadn't run past, they hadn't headed for the van, they'd turned and were now heading up the embankment; straight at me. It was my worst nightmare come true. All those years of fearing that some Widnes scallies[iii] would take exception to my skin colour and give me toes[iv] had been nothing compared to this pair of monsters, all in black, heading right at me in the middle of nowhere. And it was the middle of nowhere, down the other side of the slope was a single fence and then what seemed like miles of pitch-black farmers' fields. So I ran.

You know when you see people being chased in movies and they stumble and fall when you're willing them to get up and run, and you think that would never happen in real life? Well it does and it did. Before I had chance to vault the fence, I fell; so nervous my legs were like a new-born foal's. All was still, the mud beneath me cold and then a single shout rang through the darkness '*Get here you C**t!*' And as I turned to face my certain death standing high above me on the embankment was a sight that answered all my prayers. In the dark it had been impossible to make out, but now it was clear, that pair of monsters were a pair of police officers.

I was so relieved. My legs, now responding to the sense of safety, decided to work again and I stood and walked towards them. 'Oh, you're police, thank God. I thought you were some robbers or something.' It was

33

then they jumped me. Roughing me up, one of them clearly out to kick my arse, and all the time making threats and shouting. In the furore I managed to make out one of them saying: '*You tried to kill one of our officers!*' They were firing questions at me and my innocent answers were getting me into deeper and deeper shit: '*Where you from?*' 'Widnes' '*That's a coincidence, that's where the car was stolen from*'. I was panicking and telling them my story as best I could, I was on my way home from playing ball, 'My boots are in the van, look'. Oh yeah '*You would know that, we saw you just trying to break into that van!*'

They marched me up the slip-road in handcuffs and when we got to the roundabout the scene ahead was something from a nightmare: about ten police vehicles, ambulances, a couple of smashed-up cars, blue and red lights everywhere and loads of angry police. As we approached a C.I.D. guy shouted '*Yeah that's him, he's got the same jacket on.*' And it was then I thought this is it, how everything ends, I was going to get done for something I hadn't done; not only basketball dreams over but life over too.

Turns out the thing I was supposed to have been involved in was pretty major. The police had been chasing a stolen car full of lads. A road-block had been set up to stop them, but when the car had smashed through it, they not only wrecked a load of cars but almost killed an officer in the process. Two of the four lads had given it toes, one of them in my direction, and that's who they now thought I was. In spite of my constant ramblings to prove my innocence, telling them my dad would be back any minute to prove who I was, that my story was true, I was soon in the back of a squad-car on my way to the cells at Wilmslow Police Station, about twenty-miles away.

Although one of the officers who'd cuffed me seemed to be coming round to my story, the other wanted blood and so as we left the roundabout and headed off down a long pitch-black country road I convinced myself I wasn't going to the cells at Wilmslow at all, I was going to die. Hands cuffed behind me still, the 'bad cop' kept turning in his seat throwing little punches towards me and saying stuff like '*You tried to kill my mate, you little bastard.*' The 120 miles per hour drive down winding roads seemed to get it out of his system though and the atmosphere at the station, whilst I was finger-printed and interviewed, was much calmer. After a while a call came through from the scene of the crime. A befuddled Widnesian in possession of a clapped-out VDub was getting in the way of investigations, rambling on about having lost his son and I was returned to him. The slightly slower drive back to the M56 was punctuated this time with profuse apologies rather than threats to injure and maim and as I spilled out of the car and onto my dad I blinked for the first time in hours: the events of that night have become a family legend, we just call it 'Eyes Like Saucers'.

It didn't put me off though. By the time my eyes had returned to something like their normal size and shape and all thoughts of living out the rest of my days with my back to the wall in the 'Wilmslow Hilton' had been demoted to my nightmares and not my every waking moment, we were back to our regular Friday nights. I knew that journey like the back of my hand, as every Friday when Gid would pile into the van with dad, I would too. Travelling the forty-five minute journey without a heater, let alone a radio, was no hardship at all to me, I was happy just to tag along, to sit on the side-line on one of those foot-tall school-gym wooden benches and watch him practice. Too young to join in properly, I'd take every opportunity possible to throw hoops when the court was clear, racing out onto the paint, like some enthusiastic Golden Retriever, the minute the team were sent off to change for home.

It was my earliest experience of the frustration of the helplessness of sitting on the bench, itching to leap up and get involved, and I couldn't manage it for long. As a kid I had a reputation for being a champion mithererv, and it didn't take much pestering to convince dad to talk to the coach about the possibility of me getting involved too. Naturally friendly and gregarious (and notably pretty much the only father there), dad had struck up a friendly banter with Coach and was happy to approach him alongside me with the cheeky suggestion that he might establish an Under 13s team as well. It would be exaggeration to say he might have spotted some kind of potential in me, but he must have felt (as we did) that this could be the start of something exciting; the possibility of a number of youth teams perhaps, in which kids could progress through the ranks and be nurtured into this brand new sport. Whatever he was thinking, he agreed. Under 13s was on.

Sport needs coaches like Steve, people who are just naturally keen and who are committed enough to put a shambles of young lads through their paces in the hope that one day they'll gel into a team, one which might even win something. People who are willing to give their time to do this, on a Friday night after working all week, week in week out, and all for free. Despite any sense of amateurism, of voluntarism, of 'make do', Steve recognised even then that there are few better ways to guarantee young talent not only gets nurtured but comes up through your ranks and not someone else's than creating a series of age-banded teams. That Steve persevered with the U.13s at all was impressive, considering the mix-match of players he ended up with.

There was me of course: naive, innocent, wildly enthusiastic but not yet remarkably tall and definitely in no danger of hitting puberty anytime soon; bony and gangly and without any physical strength. There were a core of strong powerful young lads; Oliver Orr a speedy strong guard who acted in a popular kids' TV show and was a real joker, strong forwards Caff and Nick, and a pair of giants (ever present on any team), Danny Craven and John Brady who both stood at an imposing 6' 10" and had varying degrees of skill. In those days, a school P.E. teacher would see a freakishly tall kid and force him onto the court, whether that kid might be able to catch a ball was pretty inconsequential. We had potential though, that much was clear from the start. An array of talent which made me feel, in spite of my keenness to get on court, that I might have just landed myself out of my depth. The times I felt most like I was sinking, over-shadowed by the sheer talent and force of another player, were when I saw Sean McKie play.

Brought up on one of Manchester's toughest estates, in the notorious area of Moss Side, Sean was (like most of the rest of the team) street-wise and experienced in a way that was a million miles from anything I knew.

These were tough kids. If I thought I'd had it hard, growing up in Widnes with the odd racist taunt, I was kidding myself. If I thought I was experienced and worldly (adopted kid from a broken home) I had no idea: Oz was the only dad at practice because he was pretty much the only dad anywhere. Sean had two things which made him immediately stand out; he was softly spoken and quiet (my mum jokes that he was 30 before she really ever heard him speak) and he was truly uniquely talented, in a way that his moves would make my teenage jaw (still years from having any stubble to cushion the blow) regularly hit the floor in awe. I recently asked Jeff Jones (the Director of English Basketball and at the time one of the stars of Manchester United's men's team) about his re-collections. Jeff's view is simple:

'*In the last 25 years Sean is the best true young point guard to have come through the English basketball system. The best.*'

At the age of fourteen Sean was unbelievable. Still very much a kid, he had the composure, skill and awareness of a pro'. Later on in my career when I would be all over Europe earning money and living that semi-celebrity lifestyle and Sean would be back in Manchester living his quiet life in a series of normal jobs, I would play alongside pros with none of the professional demeanour that Sean possessed in his teens. A cold lesson: talent is not enough. But at the time, Sean McKie was the stand-out star of our team. Like me, he'd spend hours outside of training practicing on his own, but what Sean had was just natural-enviable-unadulterated-pure-God-given-talent. He'd make and see the most impossible passes, and hit the deepest threes, without a thought, with a sort of humble belief that what he was doing was not in any way remarkable, and rarely (infuriatingly) even breaking a sweat.

Out of my depth or not, I still really, really wanted to play. It was early days but basketball was already taking over our lives, at home as much as at weekly practices. Gid and I were always shooting hoops on a cheap yellow basket which we'd fixed on top of a door. We'd practice the motion our hands and arms made when shooting whilst sat at the table waiting for our tea, whether we had a ball or not. We drove mum crazy, as neither of us could manage to walk across the kitchen lino without dribbling a ball alongside us. The house shook to the bounce, bounce, bounce of our obsession. By now, even just months since we'd first picked up a ball, we were both totally hooked. Gid was an excellent shooter and a fiercely impressive defender. For a long, long time he was bigger than me and stronger too. He was also gifted, naturally talented with the benefit of a real one-track mind when it came to his sport. I wanted to be just like him. Even then I was aware that I wouldn't have found basketball in the same way if it hadn't been for him having found it first, I knew that his interest and talent had paved the way for me and I was grateful. But gratitude and appreciation couldn't over-ride my frustration. It killed me that he could beat me, and it fed my determination (grateful or not) that one day it'd be me who was the best.

The records of my first season at Manchester would never set the world alight, and considering that I would be one of the very few players from that team who would eventually make it as a pro', my position in the team at the time seems kind of ironic now. Sean, all 5'6" of him, justifiably dominated, leaving me to play in the position of point. Point is the play-maker, the guy who orchestrates what happens and (like the conductor of the orchestra) moves around invisibly underpinning the team. The hardest position on court. In addition to learning this new position, to feeling my way in the game, I was invariably demoted to the bench, with more experienced, more confident and skilful players ruling on court. In hindsight, it's totally understandable, what any coach who wants to win would do. Of course you play the stronger kids, the ones who'll win you the game. What did I have, other than enthusiasm? That first season I averaged five minutes a game, the stats are so insignificant I can barely recall them, but I can recall for the first time the tiniest seed of a doubt, of questioning whether it was worth it, whether this was the thing for me after all: my first experience of the crushing disappointment that, alongside the most phenomenal highs, characterises sport like nothing else.

Needless to say, the combined talents of Sean and the duel threat of our two enormous players (who towered over most of the other kids we played against) meant that, personal frustrations aside, we won all the local games and leagues. The fact that Sean and I were already becoming firm friends (a friendship that in spite of our very different futures in the game would endure all our lives) meant that I couldn't resent his presence on the team. Outwardly quiet to the point of seeming painfully shy, his sense of humour and personality just made us click, that's not to say I wasn't sharply aware of the need for him to be out of the way in order for me to get any court time and have any chance of developing my own game, rather than spending the next two years playing behind him. I needed a miracle and Sean's talent delivered it: he was being recruited by the Under 17s. Things were taking off for Sean, and deservedly so, he'd soon go on to speed through the ranks: Under 17s, Under 19s, playing on the pro' team alongside the country's finest and Manchester United's great Americans at just sixteen. It takes something special to be able to hold your own at that age, against players of that sort of calibre, especially when you're only tall enough to reach the shorts of most of them.

By now, at the outset of my second season, this basketball obsession was something which had already engulfed our whole family. I was just thirteen and in the time that had passed since the departure of mini-rugby and our adopted dad, dad-Oz had not only embraced us as his own kids but was already shaping up to be one of the biggest motivating factors of my career. It's not unique for dads to become obsessed with the sports their boys love and excel at, the touch-lines of school rugby pitches are lined with men yelling their boys on and the ref' off, but few dads (let alone step-dads) could ever be as committed as Ozzie was to us and to basketball. From day one both he and mum were totally aware that this was going to be our 'thing'. Dad put a full-size hoop up in the garden pretty much straight away, a home-made back-board painted by Gid (a talented artist) and cemented into the ground on a couple of scaffold posts. The yard was transformed into a concrete court, somewhere Gid and I spent every free hour practising, the bounce of rubber against lino replaced by the slap of ball against stone. Mum was glad of the peace, my sisters could now hear the telly and we could practice lay-up after lay-up, free-throw after free-throw, for hour after hour. Dad loved us, that was clear, and he wanted us to do well, but also (even more fortunately) he seemed to love the sport too.

Sean's promotion through the club's ranks meant that looking around the squad at the start of that second season there was only one natural successor to the space that he'd vacated: me. A shortage of point guards meant that this was an opportunity to step-up and see if an increase in court-time could, coupled with my still fanatical enthusiasm, improve my game. As the only possible point on the squad it was vital to the team that Steve would at least attempt to believe in me and allow me the court-time I so desperately craved. He did and his trust (his lack of other options) paid off. My court-time went through the roof and it showed almost immediate results. Steve started to take notice, to see the germ of something in my game that might be worth nurturing. He was interested and this, combined with the free rein at point he allowed me, had me convinced that the position I'd ended up playing in by default was a position I would never now willingly give up.

They say timing is everything; time on the court certainly is: with my average court-time now standing at forty- rather than the previous season's five-minutes per game I improved accordingly. With increased time came a massive stats boost, last year's average of 4-points per game leapt to this season's 17-. I was playing alongside some excellent ballers and, not only that, I was holding my own. I've always been certain that self-belief is one of the most essential elements of success (both within and outside of sport) and this huge confidence boost was a massive factor in my improved performance. After what seemed already to be a lifetime of sitting on the sidelines, of waiting to step-up and take my part, I now felt I'd finally arrived on the Manchester circuit.

By the age of 15 I'd grown both physically and in my game and confidence, but I was still pretty skinny, 6' of boy with everyone around me growing into men. At school I tried to concentrate but had to constantly fight against my increasingly frequent ball-related daydreams and my natural tendency to have a laugh and mess around. In the third and fourth years of high school there was still some space in my weekly schedule to spend time with friends outside of school, we'd roller skate or play golf or cricket or football (for a time still playing for a local Sunday league team, Laportes) but as my school friends grew up and their interests grew towards less innocent activities I inevitably had to choose; to grow that same way or not. As much as I found it embarrassing, depressing even, the fact that puberty still eluded me probably did me some favours in hindsight. I wasn't that interested in girls, I'd started peeping them out but any crush I had was destined to be unrequited. I was a joker, a friendly guy, great for girls to be friends with but no competition for some of my mates, many of whom were already mini-men. I was naturally pretty shy with girls, was mortified by my lack of physical development and was, most significantly, just pre-occupied. As though to rescue me from the teenage hell of unrequited love and constant self-comparison over broken-voices and unshaved chins, a dream started to form somewhere in the back of my mind. A tiny bit of my subconscious dared me to think that basketball might not always have to be just a hobby, might be able to grow from part-time to full-time love. Maybe my backing away from the parties, the Friday nights with a bottle of Cider in the park, the girls, was actually because I was moving forward into an almost unimaginable future.

I don't recall the exact time when we all realised that this new obsession wasn't going to be just some passing phase, not like the roller boots I'd been previously into with my mate Kraily, or the French Horn Gid had arrived home from school with one day, this was the real thing. Whenever it happened, we were fortunate enough that our parents seemed to clock on to the fact pretty much as soon as we did. It was a huge commitment for them, the gym we trained in was more than thirty miles down the motorway and we'd often train on a Friday, early evening, so it was never the quietest or quickest of journeys. As mates from school would beg me to take the night off training to go to a 'pile in' at some classmate's house, in my mind I'd already be in the van with my dad, on our way down the M56, running over in my head some move I'd seen on a US College basketball tape that I was planning to pull out that evening. Soon almost

41

all of our parents' leisure time (not to mention most of their spare cash) was devoted to us. Dad (a plumber running his own one-man business) would get in from work, shower, change and drive us to Manchester, where he'd sit on the bench for two hours as we trained. It would've been impossible without him, even if I'd been brave enough to go there alone, it would've taken me a train and at least two buses and well, that just wouldn't have happened. It was his commitment and my mum's, which got us to practice each week.

It was sacrifice all round. I was sacrificing relationships with kids at school, any opportunity to 'get off' with girls and pretty much all of my free time. But on the court I was flourishing. By now I was playing at Under 17s level at Salford Cadets under the coach-ship of a really inspirational guy, Ged Phillips. Ged showed an immediate faith, a confidence in me and my game, which resulted in good minutes played at National League level. Facing up against some of the country's best teams, we were travelling nationally and playing in cups against the likes of Birmingham and East London. I was fifteen but Ged would give me court-time, selecting me over more seasoned players, and as a result giving me the confidence to really excel. Another coach of mine, Dave West, also had great faith in me.

One of the regular highlights for me at this time would be playing the opener for the men's team at Stretford Sports Centre. They weren't exactly top-class facilities still, but by the time our game would be drawing towards the buzzer the tiny smattering of parents and siblings and by now even girlfriends (although, of course, still none of them mine) would be increasing rapidly with the arrival of the men's away team opponents, the pro's from our club (including the much-admired Americans) and a small number of the pro' team's fans. It was great to have more of a crowd, but the thing that appealed to me most was getting to showcase my ability in front of pro' players. My heroes. To my friends back in Widnes, none of the names of these guys would have meant anything, but to me playing ball with Jeff Jones (an American and one of Manchester's real stars) watching on would be like them scoring a goal in front of Gary Linekar. It

42

was pretty early on that Jeff seemed to notice me, he was friendly and would often chat to my parents at courtside, he was interested in my play and in me, and as one of the pivotal characters in the Manchester basketball scene, his influence would continue to mean a lot to me throughout my career. Mum was pretty taken by him too, alongside the almost life-size poster featuring a shiny and handsome Kevin Penny which covered our kitchen wall, we now had a pair of Yorkshire Terriers, one called Benson, the other JJ (Jeff Jones).

One particularly memorable occasion was when my idol, Will Brown, stopped to speak to me for the first time. It was 1988 and I was a fifteen-year old just about to start to move my play up to the next level. He was a God. A 6' 4" Bostonian point guard who played on the Celtics' summer league team, a fourth round NBA draft pick and a man in possession of the smoothest, silkiest game I have ever seen. I recall the moment that something clicked in my head which made me want to be a baller and nothing else; I was sat in the bleachers at the Spectrum Arena with my mum and dad as FSO Vikings warmed-up and I watched as Will walked nonchalantly across the court calmly dribbling the ball through his legs with each stride and I just sat there all awe-struck and I remember saying to my mum 'If I practice for the next ten years I'll never be able to do that.' I dreamed of being as good as him and when he approached me to comment on our team's lack of enthusiasm for playing any 'D', the fact that his comment was kind of negative didn't bother me at all: he was choosing to talk to me. Our short conversation ended with him saying 'You're gonna be good', an off-the-cuff remark he doesn't remember but which has stayed with me for over twenty-years. I found him so inspirational that I decided to play No.8, just like him. I never allowed myself to imagine then that one day, twenty-years later, I'd sit chatting with Will in a bar as an equal. Even now, with a long career of my own under my belt, it's still an honour for me to talk ball with a man who so inspired me. He laughed as he recalled the pre-season workout which took place during my first summer back from the States when (unknown to me) his pro' team mates were all reluctant to guard me 'You were giving them *fits'* he tells me, and immediately I'm fifteen again. It never sinks in, playing with your idols, gaining their respect. It's something I've never taken for granted.

It seemed, at the time, and looking back, that basketball was full of moments like this for me. That, alongside the training hours, the travelling, the sacrifices, there were these regular moments of unbelievable joy. Of occasions when something seemingly insignificant would happen that would fulfil one of the little dreams that were beginning to be born in me. I was loving it, and began to feel that basketball might just prove to be that elusive thing which would help me to find the place in which I belonged. With the regular trips to Manchester my mind was becoming even further detached from life in Widnes and as a result I was becoming even more convinced that there was another place entirely in which I was meant to be. The shift into Manchester meant that for the first time in my life I was no longer in a minority because of the colour of my skin, it wasn't me and Gid who stood out here, it was the white kids who did that. For the first time ever, I was surrounded by other kids who looked like me: surely my chance to belong.

It didn't take long to realise that belonging in Manny was going to be as difficult as belonging in the white world of Widnes. The square peg had been taken out of the round hole only to find the new hole was triangular. My new teammates welcomed me; they weren't bothered what I was, where I came from. They'd grown up on estates in Manchester in which the majority of people were descended from a West Indian heritage; they felt they belonged so it was beyond their understanding at the time to consider I might not feel that way too. They had a unifying culture which meant they were familiar with the same music as one another, the same food, it was all Country and Western and Sunday roasts in our house, but how were they to know that? It wasn't only the very visible support of my parents and siblings which made me stand-out amongst these kids so accustomed to travelling across the city alone, doing their own thing, it was the way I spoke and one painful moment would bring this home with a cringe-filled strength.

Despite the fact that my new teammates had all been born and raised in Manchester, the majority of their parents had been born elsewhere and so spoke in their own persistently strong accents, meaning that my new friends could couple their Manc' slang with bits of patois in a way that made them seem to me ridiculously cool. I suppose when you're a teenager you spend a lot of time thinking that everyone else is just naturally cool and effortlessly confident. A friend I met at the time, Yorick Williams (now one of England's most talented and feared ballers), would unintentionally highlight this for me years later when, as thirty-somethings, we sat in a West Indian barber's shop and Yorick laughed along with the old guys in there, easily conversing in a way I could barely follow. As we left I asked Yorick what they'd all been talking about.

'I haven't got a clue mate,' he laughed, 'I'm from Rusholme[vi].'

How a person spoke was always massively important to my mum, who instilled in us what she believed to be the proper way to talk. There was no way you'd get away with elongating your words in our house, the Widnes tendency to say 'Noorh' instead of 'No' or 'Dowa' instead of 'Door' was like the equivalent of swearing to my mum and we'd be told in no uncertain terms that to speak that way was unacceptable.

'You sound like a back entry diddler' she'd say and even though none of us had a clue what one of them was, we knew enough to know it was bad. Politeness was also something that our parents were big on. We said please, we said thank you, and we said these always. We asked to leave the table when we'd finished eating (and we didn't leave the table until we'd been given permission to do so). At the time it seemed normal and it's something which now I'm grateful for. Americans (especially American girls) would prove to be suckers for an English accent; they'd like it even more when the Englishman had the manners of a gentleman. But surrounded as I was then by streetwise inner-city kids, it didn't take long for an occasion to arise in which I just sounded (to me at least) like an idiot.

It was the glory days of the Budweiser League and, as a family, we spent much of the time in which Gid and I weren't practicing or playing travelling around the country catching as many pro' matches as we could. One night we'd managed to see an early game in Bury and then drive on into Yorkshire to catch a later match in Calderdale. Calderdale were a strong team with a great point guard; Gary 'Cat' Johnson. The guy could really play and was someone whose game I really admired. After the match came a moment I always looked forward to, the chance to move courtside to catch the players as they came off so they could autograph the game programmes. I kind of knew Cat a bit as he'd worked the annual Leeds summer camp that Gid and I had started to attend and as he approached he smiled and drawled '*Hey, how you doin' young fella?*' I replied 'I'm fine thank you, and how are you?' just as I'd been brought up to do, only to find Cat astounded at the voice that came out of me. He laughed and mocked '*I'm fine thank you, and how are you?*' back at me, as though to him I sounded like a pre-pubescent Prince Charles, and my whole world collapsed.

For Cat it was clearly just funny. He wasn't meaning to be cruel. But to me it was crushing. I was trying to belong. Clearly I wasn't succeeding. He wasn't to know how completely alien from everyone else I felt, any more than I was to know how long that journey towards belonging would eventually take. I didn't know where I came from so how was I supposed to have a clue where I was going? Nowadays I guess (I hope) things are at least a little different. It was completely normal then for people to refer to me as being 'half caste' (rather than mixed-race, or black) and so it was also normal to be in this sort of limbo of not belonging to one race or another. I wasn't ashamed of my mum and dad, I was proud of how much they wanted to support me, of how much time and energy and money they were devoting to helping me to succeed, but as they sat there on the bench game after game they served as a constant reminder of my outsider status, even without me opening my well-spoken mouth. I'd fight back any self-consciousness about this, or at least try to, and remind myself how lucky I was to be getting this kind of backing from home.

As an adult I can marvel at how huge a commitment my parents made to my career, especially as at the time the thought of it eventually becoming a career seemed about as unlikely as it could possibly be. I didn't know what the future held but I knew what the present was costing my parents in terms of time and money and I also knew, even then, how much I appreciated it. Basketball was the most important thing in my world and so the devotion they showed was equally as important to me. If something came up for dad at work, some rare emergency he couldn't turn down, meaning he wouldn't be able to make it home to get me to practice, my whole world would fall apart. Already I was living all week just for one (or, if I was really lucky, two) evenings of practice. It was my life and I'd be absolutely devastated if we couldn't go. Something which miraculously hardly ever happened at all. Somehow dad would always manage to get us there, even if we were a bit late. When, years later, I stood for the first time in the huge arena of my Division One college, with all the opportunities of a life in sport at my feet, and he was back in Widnes dying from cancer, I knew that I was standing where I was standing because of him. We'd talk, back and to on those journeys along the M56, in that cold VW mini-bus with no radio, and I'd tell him that one day I'd be a millionaire, and I'd pay him back for everything he and mum had done for me. He had a dream too, that when we were all grown up, happily doing our own thing, then him and mum would travel around America together in one of those big motor homes. I told him don't worry dad, when I'm a millionaire I'll buy you one of those, I'll pay you back for all these Friday nights sitting in that cold-ass gym, on that wooden school-bench, watching me, willing me on. When I'm in the NBA dad, I'll pay you back.

A Dream

Already, even just a matter of a couple of seasons into the sport, it was clear to me that just playing wasn't going to be enough. Being one of those guys who loved a sport and spent his spare time playing and watching it wasn't what I had in mind. Even in the very earliest stages, at thirteen, still weedy and lanky, no visible muscles to speak of at all, settling down to a life of working all week, playing at weekends, volunteering as a coach once I became too old to play, would never satisfy me. For as long as I could remember I'd been waiting for my 'thing', the opportunity that would help me to escape, to find the place in which I was meant to belong and this was it. I was going to play ball. I was playing in Manchester now, but I wouldn't be forever. I was going to grow too big to be contained by Manchester. I was going to make it a career and in order to do that I was going to need to find some way of getting myself to the States. I was going to be big time and there was no way of fulfilling the ultimate possibilities of this dream, of the NBA, by staying in England, let alone Widnes. My need to escape was now a passion, a hunger I could actually begin to see as a reality. I was going to the States, I just wasn't sure exactly how yet.

Through our playing in Manchester we'd become submerged in a real basketball-based community, one that (though we didn't know it then) would last our lifetime, and it was through that community that we'd heard of the Leeds summer camps which were organised each year by a guy called Dave Smith. For two weeks each summer Dave would take over part of the leafy grounds of the university campus in Leeds and transform it into basketball city. Hoop Heaven for me, for Gid, and for about 150 other basketball-crazed kids from throughout the country. After my first taste of a week's summer camp I was hooked. This was it, the tiniest crack in the door that, should I manage to prise it wide enough, I might just manage to sneak my skinny ass through and end up Stateside.

The camps ran like this: Dave would organise coaches and players from across Britain and, most significantly, America who would work the camps. Kids like us would pay our fee, book our place, get dropped off by our parents on a Sunday morning and would spend every waking hour of the rest of the week (two-weeks if they were really lucky) living ball: all day, every day. From breakfast to bedtime we'd be immersed in a tight programme of events including coaching sessions, informal practices and mini tourneys in which we'd battle team against team for the sheer love of the sport as much as to get noticed. At the time it was really the only event of its kind in the country and it proved to be a real trailblazer. The whole focus of Camp was getting kids involved and nurturing their talent and their love for the sport, level of ability was a secondary issue. Some kids were really young and weedy and as hopeless as they were hopelessly besotted with the sport; others were seventeen, eighteen years old, talented, fast, strong and going places. After our first taste Camp became the focus of our entire year. I lived for it. It was fun and exciting and above all it was a chance to meet people who might be able to support a skinny young lad in his mission to make an impossibly outlandish dream possible.

After my first trip to Camp it was clear (to me at least) a week was not going to be long enough in which to really capitalise on the opportunities that Leeds could offer. I needed two. I started to mither. For mum and dad sending two boys to Camp for even one week (on top of the already substantial petrol bill we racked up travelling to practice and games) was a big deal. There was little extra money and, although by now our eldest sister Kim had left home to move to Gloucestershire to fulfil her dreams of working with horses, there were still five kids at home and only one pretty modest wage to feed them with. But, as ever, if it was important to basketball then the money would be found. That we had such backing was amazing, but was also testament to the seriousness with which Gid and I were taking the sport. It was clear this wasn't any passing phase we'd eventually grow out of, something in us radiated our commitment and we were lucky enough that our parents recognised that and chose to respect our choice. Mum started childminding again (something she'd done off and on to make ends meet since Kirstie was born) and for the first time in my life I had to work too.

Although there were obvious downsides to being the one black face in school (being the one memorable person in a massive crowd of onlookers at the latest scrap in the park, for example), my friendliness helped to make me memorable in positive ways too, and by Spring I'd managed to use my charms and connections with friends' parents to wangle myself not one but two part-time jobs, and a paper round. Of all the jobs the world has to offer paperboy is the one to which I am least suited. I hated it. I not only hated getting up early, I hated being outdoors in bad weather and I hated any physical exertion which took vital energy away from my chosen sport. I think the only time the papers on my round arrived through their doors at the right time was during the weeks in the summer when I was at Camp and my younger sister Kirstie filled in for me. But I kept it up, owing my commitment to two things: my desperation to help fund that extra week at Leeds and the fact that my mum would almost literally drag me from beneath the duvet each morning. The other jobs were easier; glass-collecting during social evenings at the local Tennis Club and helping with the bottling-up in a nightclub owned by my friend Kraily's dad. Indoor jobs, jobs in the warm, ones that required attendance later in the day, much more my style.

Camp brimmed with incentives: the chance to train and play all day and devote myself solely to improving my game, but also more practical incentives, material ones. The biggest accolade (and ultimate prize) available to campers was being crowned MVP. Each year the baller judged to be Most Valuable Player by the team of coaches and support staff would win the prize of going to America to work as a coach at the prestigious camps held at Villanova University and West Point Academy. It seemed like a lottery jackpot to me, completely ignorant of the fact that (whilst the prize was kind of unique) it came with the additional complication of needing to find the funds to fly yourself over to the States in order to claim it. An irrelevant detail, as what the prize really offered, at least to a kid like me hell-bent on finding a way into the States to College to the Draft and then to who knew what, was a chance to make contacts. Real effective basketball contacts that could only help bring a dream like mine that little bit closer to reality.

Thanks to my hunger (which seemed now to be increasing on a daily basis) and my friendly personality I was starting even then to make contacts of my own. I was fourteen and pretty clueless, but I was also abundantly enthusiastic and utterly, utterly obsessed with basketball. I would lap up any bit of knowledge offered and would jump at any chance to pick the brains of the coaches, especially the Americans, some of whom noticed pretty quickly that I already had a tunnel-vision about getting to the States. It sounds precocious, like I might have been a right pain in the arse (or at the very least kind of weird and nerdy), but they didn't seem to mind: possibly just appreciating such a level of enthusiasm, possibly even seeing something of their younger selves in me. There were two guys who especially seemed to understand my passion and see in me some spark of talent; Ricky Pitts and Dean Lockwood, and it would be Dean in particular who would prove to play a pivotal role in getting me across the Atlantic and on the road to my career.

Dean Lockwood was an Assistant Coach at the University of Tennessee and was brought over to Leeds in the summer as the Camp's real star signing. Tennessee was one of America's prestigious Division One Colleges, a school that formed part of the South Eastern Conference, which was home to such players as Shaquille O'Neil, and Dean was a real living breathing walking-around coaching connection to that world. A world infinitely distant from the tiny Yorkshire campus he came to coach at each summer. In his late-twenties, Dean spotted something in me and we struck up an incongruous sort of friendship in which he was an unofficial mentor and I swayed between being agog with awe at his prowess and pummelling him with questions about College ball. The questions began with the general: what was it like, how many students were there; moved through the more fanatical, who was the best player he's coached, what was Shaq like in real life; and soon enough got to the point: how can I get there? It's to my relief now that Dean has such fond memories of me, and doesn't just remember me as a pain in his ass whilst he was trying to work. He's an eloquent guy. These are his thoughts:

'Del was as eager a pupil as we had at our original camps and a kid who absolutely LOVED the game of basketball. At the time the North of England was not a real basketball "hotbed" and it became quickly apparent through the observation of the campers that most of them had not been taught or coached in the fundamentals of the game.

While like so many of his peers, he lacked certain fundamental skills and an understanding of how the various parts of the game fit into the whole, Del was also at once somewhat different. He was more than a kid attending a day camp - he was a true STUDENT. He really LISTENED. He hung on every word coaches spoke to him and really tried to apply what he learned when it came time to execute drill work. Specifically where I was concerned, I clearly recall Del paying close attention to whenever I spoke or whenever I demonstrated a skill. His eyes would be fixed on the particular demonstration and you could almost see the "wheels" in his mind turning and working to process what he was hearing. Almost always, Del would spend extra time, during a break or after a session, working on a skill he had learned and doing so with Seriousness and a focus unlike most other kids there. It took me all of one week to realize that this was a kid who possessed a special love for the game and a desire to grow and develop as a player...

He became what we call "sick" for the game! Questions about how to improve, constant questions, became the norm; whenever I would see Del or work with him I began to expect questions about all aspects of how he could improve his game. The skinny, gangly kid, almost awkward at the game in his early years playing it, quickly became more adept at the game's fundamentals and developed an understanding of how to play. This was to his credit - he did what so many good players do: he simply listened well and applied what he learned. I remember Del not being afraid to try things, to experiment a little or to "put himself out there" at the risk of failure or looking bad in front of others in order to improve himself. So many young players, especially as they hit the early teen years, are very self-conscious *and so afraid of looking bad or being embarrassed in front of their peer group. If Del felt any of this, he didn't show it much; he was always eager and willing to attempt new drills and skills and to test himself. Here again, Del discovered a true cornerstone to player development - being ALWAYS willing to accept new challenges and to test your limits by continually pushing yourself to do a little bit more, be a little bit better. I'm sure there were moments of frustration and discouragement for Del on his path to improvement and self-discovery, but if he felt that he rarely displayed it. By nature Del was a positive kid whose hunger for knowledge, skill and even some of the game's history became insatiable.'*

My goal at Camp was to improve each day. To make the most of the opportunity so that after the week (or the fortnight - those part-time jobs were paying off), I would be able to return to my team and my regular coach and wow them with something new I could do. At least that was my realistic goal, my other goal, the dream one, was to win MVP. To get to West Point and to talk to and meet and impress as many people as possible in the vain hope they might be able to help me find a way into College. Each year I would go to Camp focused on improving but also hoping that I might win, that I might get the chance to go to America. I was 13 when I started going to Camp and had about as much chance of winning MVP as I did of winning Paperboy of the Year. But it didn't matter. I've never been afraid to dream big and the fact that I'd be battling for MVP alongside bigger, stronger, faster guys who were not only naturally talented but were also four or five years older, didn't put me off at all. It was my focus, something to aim for; a window of opportunity which might just be the thing to make my dream of America a reality. The Leeds camps quickly became a marker for me each year, a way to not only measure my progress but also to set myself specific goals. From one year to the next I'd be thinking; ok, so next year I'm going to go to Camp and achieve this. I'd set myself a target year on year and that was the thing that would keep me smiling, because I knew that somehow some opportunity would come up that meant I wouldn't have to stay in Widnes my whole life.

Two significant things collided at Leeds which meant that all my dreams were not only kept alive, but given a sudden unexpected boost in the arm which meant they might actually really start to become a reality. The first was meeting Dean Lockwood. The second was that year's announcement of the Camp's Most Valuable Player, the lucky talented guy who'd wowed everyone with his game and was heading Stateside: it was Gid.

Whilst I was flitting about in any available moment establishing connections and secretly networking for my dream, Gid was just getting on with his game. The natural sporting ability that he'd been just born with, when combined with a level of one-track obsessive commitment, was an explosive mix, one destined to be noticed and now it seemed rewarded. Always a guy with a winning smile, a tiny photo from that day featured in a montage of pictures on the wall of our terraced house for many years, it's almost as though there's a light on inside Gid's mouth, as if the sheer joy of winning that day illuminated him. I couldn't recognise that feeling at the time, but as I grew older and I'd return home from college in the summer vacation, I began to be able to recognise that feeling, to reminisce over the season passed and think of a time in which my face had lit up that way too.

The support of Dean would prove vital to me in the years that followed and also took me by surprise. At Camp we'd got on, he wasn't humouring me and my outlandish dreams, he genuinely seemed to care and to think that I was kind of worth investing in. Dean's influence has stayed with me and remains one of the factors I credit with managing to achieve all that I did. When I first had the idea of attempting to write all this down he was one of the first people I thought to contact. It was some years since we'd spoken but he was still the same Dean. It's easier to ignore how much the past twenty-five years has aged us both over a phone line. Humble as ever, Dean's reluctant to take much credit

'If the time we shared in England and our communications afterward served as an inspiration then it was time well invested and couldn't have been spent any better. To be able to help someone get closer to their dreams is both an honour and a thrill.'

Both talking and walking the walk was something that Dean was totally committed to, even for me, a virtual stranger, a skinny little chancer thousands of miles from Tennessee. When he returned to the States that first summer I was left with only the vain hope that he was as good as his word. I was out of sight and it would've been entirely understandable if I'd also been out of mind.

It was a couple of months after the end of Camp when the first package arrived. A parcel stamped all over with University of Tennessee logos and sitting on the kitchen table when I got in from school, mum grinning right over it. Sharing every step of the dream with me, mum knew how vital any contact from Dean would be, how much it would mean to me, and she shared in my joy as I undid the parcel and out fell the university's new Media Guide and lots of other little bits and bobs from the world of the Vol's[vii]. He'd not forgotten me. We'd exchanged addresses at Camp and I'd hoped he'd keep in touch but hadn't dared to hope that during the next couple of years, our letters would cross back and forth over the Atlantic and every month or so a video tape of a College game would land on the mat for me to watch, and then re-watch, then study, then obsess over and ultimately emulate.

Dean remembers the extent of our communication as well as I do:

'It seems like such a "bygone era" in a way, with the technology of today providing e-mail access and text messages. Back in the late '80s, if people didn't talk by phone it was letter writing...and believe me, that is exactly what Del did! I could count on getting a few letters a year from Del and I enjoyed reading them and responding to them. His letters provided updates on his life and family in northern England, his progress on his game, and usually a few questions. He would occasionally question his ability or if his love for the game and time spent working on it would lead anywhere; I would simply try to be encouraging. These were the letters not unlike any young person in America or anywhere else in the world for that matter - full of hopes, dreams, doubts, uncertainty about the future and an undeniable passion for a game. Del eventually addressed in these letters the notion of attending high school and/or college in the States. At the time, this seemed like an almost unreachable dream to him yet even back then I

could tell that inside of Del burned a glimmer of hope that somehow, some way, this could all come true for him. It was through these trips in England to do camps and clinics, and through these letters exchanged with Del, that I began to pull for this kid...I mean really pull for him. I encouraged him to the best of my ability, tried to provide possible routes or strategies by which he could come to the States and play basketball. As I saw his game grow, I began to realize that this was a kid who, unlike some, was actually "walking his talk." His work output was beginning to match up with the size of his dreams. For those of us who have spent a life in this wonderful game, it is almost impossible to not pull for a kid like that! And so I did. In addition to providing tips and pointers as to how Del could keep improving his game, I also added some thoughts about developing as a competitor, team player and forming great work habits. Del certainly needed little encouragement in these areas, and his responses were just like the wide-eyed eager and skinny young kid whom I had initially encountered at that basketball camp in northern England.

I wanted to somehow convey to Del that his dream WAS possible, that he had an open road ahead of him and that anything could happen for him if he worked hard enough and believed. As I wrote to Del, I was often reminded that it wasn't that long ago that I was a young, skinny kid with huge basketball dreams and any encouragement or positive input I received was like food and water to a starving person. If there was any way, however small, I could help or simply encourage this young guy, I wanted to do it!'

Writing this has motivated me to contact lots of the people from my past who opened doors for me or who encouraged me when what I was trying to achieve seemed so unfathomably difficult, it's an opportunity to take the time to thank people directly, something life rushes us into forgetting to do. It gave Dean and I the opportunity to discuss our joint belief in the importance of being able to 'pay it forward', we both agree, the chance to do that is a very special thing and something we're both committed to. What Dean probably doesn't realize is that I'm not sure how much dedication to paying it forward my life would've included without such a great role model practising what he preached and showing me the way.

Dean has no idea, even now, how much that meant to me. Here was a major player in a big time university taking time to encourage me. The tapes he sent were a lifeline. I'd leg it home from school when it seemed about time one might be due in the hope that something had come that day. If it had it would make my week, my month. Through those College tapes the dream that seemed so impossible was starting to feel closer. My game was improving massively as anytime I wasn't physically practicing I was staring at a grainy film on the small TV in our front room studying the moves of the masters of Duke, North Carolina, Kansas, Wake Forest, Clemson, Virginia, Georgia Tech and Indiana. Night and day I ate, slept and drank basketball with a hunger you wouldn't believe. I wanted to improve so badly. What had started as a way in which I might gain respect, a way to find somewhere to fit in, was taking over my life. I couldn't dictate where I was born, or to whom, or what colour my skin was, but I could totally dictate how naughty a player I would become.

The College players were awesome to me. But it was only a few seasons since I'd been averaging a paltry 4-points, and now I'd arrived at a stage in which pro' players would give me casual props as I left the court and a serious Division One coach had faith in my game: coming that far had seemed unimaginable, but I'd achieved it, being one of those guys on the court of a major US College might just be achievable too. It was at this time that I became aware of Steve Bucknall, one of North Carolina's main men and, remarkably to me at the time, English. A Londoner, Steve was one of only three English ballers in the entire US College set-up. The others, Karl Brown and Neville Austin, were also enjoying major Division One exposure and even though I was in every way worlds away from them, the fact that there was someone paving the way, smoothing a path I might be able to walk myself, was both a thrill and a comfort.

Whatever fate has in store for us, it's always useful to have people walking in front of you, something I was lucky enough to have. Just as Gid had gone before me in high school, Steve Bucknall and Karl Brown trailed an English path through Division One and, even though neither of them knew what a difference this would make to the people who followed behind, I was always grateful for it. The year that Gid won Leeds' MVP I wasn't jealous at all, I saw how much it meant to him and I was also still painfully aware that he wasn't only much better than me, but still bigger and stronger too. I was proud of him and a little bit of me dared to hope that in some way this would also prove a good move for me.

I was right. Whilst in America, one of Gid's fellow Camp counsellors was a coach from an Ohio high school, Jim Riley. He and Gid struck up a friendship and Gid (in a selfless supportive move only a brother could make) told Coach Riley all about this lanky, talented, younger brother of his with a dream so big it had taken over his life. The ball was not only rolling now, it was powering down the court, it might not end in a fierce slam dunk, but it looked like it had the chance of a decent lay-up. Coach Riley was interested. He was more than interested, he was eager. He wanted good players, he was ambitious and had his own dreams of coaching a kid into Division One. But he also, significantly, really liked Gideon and respected that if he said I had a real genuine potential to make it, then I probably did.

On Gid's return everything moved up a gear. The discussions he'd had with Coach Riley had got pretty detailed. Coach didn't see any reason why he couldn't secure me a place on the roll at his high school and Gid refused to see any barrier that might get in the way of transporting me from Widnes, Cheshire, to Uhrichsville, Ohio. My parents were immediately on board. I'd sit for hours at the kitchen table, talking to my mum as she pottered about, just chatting through all the possibilities of my hopes, everything that might happen, and now, for the first time, it really, really might. I kept up with practice and was in the yard whenever possible, running through moves, perfecting shots. I focused on school. The possibility of America and the now very real chance of becoming a high school senior was expertly exploited by my mum and dad who made it plain that, if I didn't get my head down and concentrate on the forthcoming GCSEs, I was going nowhere. Coach Riley had been clear, there wasn't even a chance of a place at Claymont if I didn't get at least four Cs in my exams.

So I worked. Everything was in place; school, practice and fitness. All the stars seemed to have suddenly aligned and I was on my way. My whole family convened in the local park that summer real early one Sunday morning and there, amongst the flower beds and trees, dad's friend (a wedding photographer) pictured us all together as kids for what we thought might be the last time, one little bird was about to fly the nest and everyone else was there to smile to the camera before he was waved off. And then, just when all was set and everything was perfect, everything was off and my world fell apart. I wasn't going to Ohio after all.

A Lost Year

It's almost impossible to describe that moment of realisation which confirmed that the whole thing was off. Being off in reality, in a physical sense, was one thing, accepting it was off was something different. That everything I'd been working towards, focusing on, obsessing over all year was now just not going to happen, understandably, took some time to sink in. It was bad enough that everyone I knew was expecting me to be gone any minute now but this meant so much more to me than simply losing face. I'd been aware all along that other people saw my dream of college ball as being ludicrously far-fetched, something that everyone probably secretly harbours their own version of, and also something that rarely ever actually comes true. And now it looked like they'd be right.

Gid had been working for months, alongside my mum and dad and Coach Riley, to set everything in motion. But the further things had progressed, the more hurdles seemed to be thrown in our way. Coach Riley's enthusiasm, his eagerness to take his part in the dream, had meant that he thought the whole process would be as simple as securing my place on the roll at his school and offering to put me up at his house. His kindness had blinded him, but then some of the problems we encountered concerned issues he couldn't possibly have known about: conflicting curriculums, visas. The longer things went on, the clearer it became that this list would grow and grow. People often talk about the horrors of red tape and here it was, binding my limbs together, tying me to Widnes and choking any remaining life from the dream. And then came the call.

Through sheer bloody perseverance and the kind of commitment that makes you proud, Coach Riley had managed to find a potential way around our problem. The dream of the skinny kid from Widnes, a town that he'd previously never even heard of, had taken over his life too and, discussing his frustrations with friends in Uhrichsville one evening, he'd discovered that the International Rotary Club (who had a Uhrichsville branch) ran an exchange programme which enabled students from all over the world to spend twelve-months experiencing a different culture through living and studying abroad. As committed and enthusiastic as ever, he approached members of Uhrichsville's Rotary Club and, just like that, managed to get them onboard. They were willing to sponsor me as their exchange student, to put the weight of their official backing behind me with a view to welcoming me on the roll at Claymont High at the start of the academic year. All I had to do was get my local Rotary Club on board too.

Through family contacts I managed to get an audience with them. Although he was now much removed from the family, my adopted dad Dave was still part of our lives and we saw him once a week. He had a cousin who was a member of the Widnes Rotary Club and before I knew it I was stood before their lunchtime meeting. Coach Riley had made it clear, this was an academic exchange, developed and supported by Rotary International to ensure that young people experience different cultures through education, not through sport. So standing there before them all in the dining room of a local hotel I glossed over my basketball obsession: sure it was part of my motivation to get Stateside, but not all of it, I lied. Except maybe it wasn't a lie, more an exaggeration. It wasn't just ball, not completely, all those films we sat watching at home, hired for 50p on VHS from the shop down the road, had struck something in me too. 'The Breakfast Club' and 'Pretty in Pink' and 'Sixteen Candles' and all those high schools they featured with the Pep Rallies and the Proms and the kids driving themselves to class, they didn't just entertain me, they inspired me. That's where I wanted to be, having basketball as well just made it better. I convinced them. My main focus would be study and they would back me. We were on.

There was just one small issue. It was an academic exchange and so far all I'd focused on was the academic bit, on what that meant for the official public face of my dream, I'd completely ignored the other requirement: the *exchange*. An exchange of course meant that as I flew off towards my dream coming the other way across the Atlantic would be another me, an

American with a similar desire to live abroad. I felt a bit sorry for them, whoever they were, surely they hadn't actually asked for Widnes specifically? Whatever their motivation, they'd be studying and living here (as I would be in Uhrichsville) and the Rotary Club were expecting my parents to put this kid up.

My mum and dad's previous record of personal sacrifice in support of basketball probably makes their agreement no real surprise. But it was a hard decision, probably the hardest of all the hard decisions (with both financial and time implications) they'd already been forced to make. Although we were lucky enough to live in a large-ish terraced house, it was still a terrace and the size of our family had meant that dad had converted the loft space into a bedroom for me and Gid. We slept up there, the youngest two Hayley and Hannah shared a room, with only Kirstie having a room of her own now that Kim had moved out. Prior to the loft conversion the four girls had shared a room together, but everyone was growing, getting older, needing their own space. Money was similarly tight, and housing and feeding some unknown American entity required a level of blind faith and commitment which (admittedly with trepidation) they agreed to. The only stipulation they made was that (whoever this kid turned out to be) he needed to be a he. Gid would share his space with him: there simply wasn't room for a girl, in our already quite crowded house (currently home to one mum, one dad, Gid, three of my sisters, two dogs and a cat), there'd need to be made space for another. We were definitely on.

Untangling the red tape, now that the Rotary Club where on board, was no problem. There was lots of admin to sort and meetings to attend, forms to complete and lunches at which I'd be required to make presentations and speeches to convince the Widnes branch that, stood there in my donated blazer and Rotary International tie, I would represent them in a way that would make them and the town proud. And then we stalled. Everything was on hold again. Despite my best efforts there would be no way that stages of the programme could be skipped. The application process alone would entail months of approvals and actions, and cutting corners (no matter how desperate a kid was to play ball) was something that the Rotary Club certainly did not approve of. The dream was still there, it was alive, just in a sort of comatose state, which meant that I had to keep on, working, playing, pratising and improving. It would be another year before the place reserved for me at Claymont High could be filled and in the meantime I needed something to do.

Although mum and dad had always been massively supportive of my outlandish dream, they were also realists. I don't ever recall either of them sitting me down for a 'this is all a pipe dream son' type of discussion. They weren't humouring me, hoping that I would grow out of it or get fed up, but they were also never going to support me just lolly-gagging for a whole year, shooting hoops and marking time. They were as committed to the dream as me, as convinced as I was that it was going to come to fruition now, but there was still no chance of me being allowed to spent all day every day focusing just on ball. School was over, I'd done the previously unimaginable and secured the GCSE grades I needed and even if it was only going to be a year my parents were insistent I do something. In hindsight they were right. If the last twenty years have taught me anything it's that you never know when things can end. A slip on court, a bad clash with another player, a car accident, almost anything can pose a risk to your body and health that might mean the end of even the most promising career. All it would take would be a broken ankle and that place at Claymont, on the Mustangs team, would go to someone else. In addition to this, I'd recently learned with bitter regret how easily things could fall through. Something I'd have to get used to; the life of the pro baller is anything but secure.

I was still playing in Manchester of course, shining for the Under 17s and averaging 24-points a game. Mum would sit on the bench with dad, my younger sister Kirstie now old enough to stay at home with the two youngest girls meant that mum was now free to attend as well, and she'd note stats in a little book: rebounds, assists, points, fouls. Keeping an invaluable record that would allow me to study my own performance and focus on anything which needed attention. The sickened feeling in the pit of my stomach which had arrived with the recent (all be them temporary) disappointments remained. It would remain for the whole of the year. How could it not? The thing which had kept me focused for the past five years was now endangered and the sense of being almost literally gutted certainly wasn't going to go away, at least not until I was sure we were back on track, not until that flight was booked and I'd finally said those goodbyes.

Ball aside, I needed something else. School career advisors who'd seen many a kid sit in front of them who was going to be a pop star or a movie star or play football for Liverpool had humoured me for a bit before suggesting a course in Leisure Studies at a college on the other side of Warrington, about ten miles from home. And so I found myself on cold grey mornings catching two trains and then a bus to get to a college I didn't want to go to, to study a course I didn't want to study. The thought of losing a whole year of American basketball, having to go through the motions of this life I didn't want to live, was the toughest experience I'd been through. But I'd tell myself time and again that the dream was still there. I just had to keep on focusing and working, it would still happen. It had to.

Trying to concentrate on the course, a BTEC National Diploma, was almost impossible. I never allowed myself to think of the possibility that the Rotary deal wouldn't happen and so I was studying the first year of a two-year course I knew I'd never complete. A weird feeling which made it difficult to focus; at least on anything other than basketball. But it wasn't all bad. There was a guy from Manchester on the same course who was a baller too, a real tough kid called Andy Heath, a weird paradox of a guy with a skinhead and a temper and a love of a good laugh. We kicked-it together in class and whenever we could we went one-on-one in the college gym. He wasn't too convinced by the American Dream, even if it was looking increasingly certain, some people aren't comfortable when someone else refuses to give up. He was also a year older than me, stronger and a lot tougher, and we had no idea how those daily tussles we had on the court (just mess-abouts to him but essential practice to me) would help toughen me up for the opposition that lay ahead, a few short months and thousands of miles away. Class was okay, I made myself get there, learnt to deal with what seemed like the pointlessness of it all, and managed (as usual) to have a good laugh with classmates. But those cold early morning starts (something I still don't like), and all that crappy public transport, a whole world away from Molly Ringwald and Anthony Michael Hall pulling up outside class in a Chevrolet in the sunshine, really brought the reality home to me of what a life without the dream would be like. I had to get to the States, and quick.

A Journey

In 1962 a young baller by the name of Wade Houston stood poised to set the sport alight. A budding high school senior, all signs indicated that this player would be something special. Hailing from a poor neighbourhood of Alcoa Tennessee, Wade's dreams and career rested (as mine would some thirty years later) on his need for that most generous of things; a scholarship. But for Wade, it was not to be. One simple fact stood between him and any chance of ever being funded through his education and fledgling career by the University of Tennessee: Wade Houston is black. Refused any financial support on the grounds of skin pigmentation, the massive monetary boost which enables so many young players to go places they had previously only dreamed of was denied him. Powerless, Wade vowed to make his life a success. He was eventually picked up by the more forward-thinking University of Louisville, becoming the first ever African-American player in their basketball history. And now I stood, with similar dreams and fewer barriers, in Wade's office. University of Tennessee: the plate on the door read 'Wade Houston: Head Coach'. In 1989 he came back and conquered.

The University of Tennessee dominates the town of Knoxville. Huge on sport and the celebration of sport like so many other Division One colleges are, Tennessee boasted some of the most impressive facilities I'd ever seen. Fresh from Widnes, from playing in freezing cold gyms, from practising on the concrete yard behind our house, from performing in front of crowds consisting of pretty much my mum and dad and no one else, it's no exaggeration to say I was awestruck. To my left the 100,000 seater football stadium and to my right the most impressive basketballing sight I'd ever seen: The Thompson-Boling Arena, 25,000 state-of-the-art seats dedicated solely to the watching of, the worshipping of, College Hoops.

I was naive. I'd never seen anything like it before. I'd imagined it often enough. But I was so used, by now, to dreaming this dream that to accept that I was actually stood here was inconceivable. I half expected to open my eyes, to find myself in the loft at home, emerging into another cold wintery morning only to drag my sorry dreamer's ass off to Padgate College for another day of wishing I was somewhere else. Even a few short hours earlier it'd seemed as if the whole thing was still about to come crashing down around my flat-top.

When I say I was naive, it's really no exaggeration. The distance we lived from Manchester wasn't enormous but it was far enough in terms of English public transport to mean that, if you couldn't drive, it was a total pain to get to some of the obscure suburbs in whose school gyms we'd train; meaning that I'd never travelled to any sporting practice or fixture without having been driven there by my mum or dad. Spoilt, I guess you might call it. Privileged, I prefer: lucky. However it might seem, what it meant in reality was that the flight I was booked on from Manchester to Knoxville (via Pittsburgh) was by far the biggest solitary undertaking I'd ever made. Driven to the airport in that ancient old mini-bus, which had taken me on so many journeys already, the air inside the van crackled. Mum was mortified. There was no way she'd say anything to put me off going, wrapped instead in that mum-blanket of wanting the best for your child, all she offered was encouragement. It would be years before we properly talked about that journey, about how she felt bereft already, just at the thought of me going, how she'd always known I was destined for something different and how grateful she was that I hadn't been willing to settle for something humdrum, something average, whilst there'd been a glimmer of a different life.

In my bag were a clutch of basketball magazines, the only things I ever read, and already well-thumbed to the point that I virtually knew the articles and stats they contained off by heart. I had a Sony Walkman and a couple of tapes and a burning sense of excitement that blinded me to anything else. Well, almost blinded me. I was naive, but I was also well-versed from my experience of America cinema in the dangers that hid just beneath the surface of this land of opportunity. I've always been skilled in

68

scaring the hell out of myself by imagining what might happen and a journey of this magnitude offered so many chances for things to go wrong. The fear of being lost, left all alone in the airport not knowing where to go, of trying to find my way and instead finding myself mugged in the ghetto, all these things only managed to knock the corners from my excitement, dented just a little more by the sense of guilt I felt at my lack of regret. When I thought of what I was leaving behind; the cold mornings, the grey industrial landscape, the classmates who'd been raised to see themselves as superior and me as a 'Nig-Nog', the underfunded limited state that English basketball was locked in, I had to go. It wasn't that I wouldn't miss my family, I would of course, it wasn't that I actively wanted to be away from them, I didn't, it was just that I knew they understood why I had to go and, more than that, that they would always be there, always willing me on from back home.

I was heading for Knoxville. My mentor, and now friend, Dean Lockwood, Assistant Coach at the University of Tennessee, had invited me to spend some transition time with him down in the Deep South; a break before the start of school and my new life in Uhrichsville in which I could acclimatise to the States, helping on a summer camp the university were hosting. It was a great opportunity, the chance to see a little more of the country (in basketball terms at least, which was, after all, the only thing that mattered to me) and to kick-back a little in friendly and supportive company before I travelled on to Ohio and to whatever the year was to hold for me and my burgeoning career. I'd left Manchester that morning with pretty much all the clothes I owned, about $40 in cash and Dean's telephone number.

Landing in Pittsburgh, finally on US soil after all those years of hope, I placed a call to Dean to let him know I'd landed and what time I was expecting to depart and therefore arrive with him. No reply. No worries, I had a couple of hours in Pittsburgh (the kind of airport dead-time which would add up significantly over the coming years) and could call him again. I did. And then I called him again. And again. And every time the same result: a couple of rings, an ominous click and then Dean's cheery

69

voice inviting me to leave a message. I left a message the first time, and the second, and the third. Later Dean would laugh at the way in which, with each message, my voice had gotten squeakier and squeakier. Of course it did. Always a person with a wild imagination, especially regarding ways in which my dream might finally be scuppered, by the time I'd placed that fourth call I was starting to panic. It seems ridiculous now, embarrassing, but I was just turned seventeen, a young seventeen. I'd lived, eaten, breathed, drank basketball for as long as I could remember. I'd never hung around on street corners: I was training. I'd never spent my weekends out drinking: I was training. I'd been nowhere. I knew nothing. What I did know was this: I was in the States, I was thousands of miles from home, from anyone I knew, I had $40 and no way of speaking to the one person who was expecting me to be here. It was pretty clear: I was heading for the ghetto.

I suppose, through all the trials and all the waiting and all the disappointments, there was a part of me which had been waiting all along for the whole thing to collapse. I'd lived all those years so focussed on this one thing that I'd never allowed myself to seriously consider what the alternative might be. There wasn't one. That flight, from Pittsburgh to Knoxville, in reality just a couple of hours, was the length of that whole previous year of waiting. Forced to board without having spoken to Dean, with only the cheery repetitiveness of his answer-phone message for comfort, I was terrified. I should have been enjoying the next leg of my adventure, I should have been giving the air hostesses a cheeky smile, entertaining them with a bit of the old English charm, helping myself to extra peanuts (this was, after all, the land of plenty); instead I spent the whole flight sweating and stewing, the grip on my arm rest ever tightening, the sense of panic in me ever rising.

It took only thirty seconds or so to spot Dean in the arrivals hall at Knoxville, but it felt like forever, that the sea of faces, all blind to my presence, merged before me in a mocking wave of foreignness. Dean laughed. He had, he assured me, been laughing since he'd got home and heard that ever-squeakier voice ringing out across his bachelor pad. It was like a dream. Like it was me walking and talking, seeing and hearing, but as though I was watching myself do all these things from the outside. I was here. Finally on American soil, reeling with happiness and excitement and this enormous relief to be with a familiar face, to not be alone.

Dean was putting me up in his apartment, a modest place that functioned as home for a young guy who was never there. Like me, Dean's life was basketball and so all the hours he wasn't sleeping were spent on campus, where the next day we would be from early in the morning making last-minute preparations for the week's Camp. For anyone visiting America (especially for the first time), it's often the scale of things that shocks the most: the size of the portion of fries you're served, the bucket that your Coke comes in. Dean recalls now my awestruck face when our take-out arrived that first night. A fan of Little Caesar's, Dean knew the deal was order-one-get-one-free, but even that amazed me. We didn't even have a take-out pizza place in Widnes, let alone one that gave stuff away. Dean reckons: '*Little Caesar's made an instant and loyal patron that day!*'

For a seventeen-year-old boy who'd spent every moment of the past few years imagining what the States would be like, it blew my mind. For a boy who'd lived and breathed basketball for all that time, the University of Tennessee blew me away. Set in over 500 acres of leafy campus U.T. is a town in itself. In term time that tabernacle heaves with over 20,000 students. That summer, the only kids on campus were there for Camp or summer school but I could still see it. I could see all the kids arriving for class, sitting out on the grass between lessons, eating lunch and just kicking-it, and for the first time I could see myself as one of them. Well, I was here, wasn't I? I'd completed the first massive step of the impossible, I'd made it to the States, I was enrolled in a school. There was no guarantee of a place in the starting-five of the Claymont Mustangs, but I'd make damn sure I got one, whatever happened. Just like now, as I walked into the Thompson-Boling Arena, I'd make sure I got to a university myself the next year. The next step of the dream was in place. I'd only been on the other side of the Atlantic for twenty-four hours and already it wasn't enough, I was planning what happened next, how I was going to make it.

71

For now, I'd enjoy myself. I'd make the most of Camp because in a few short weeks, I'd be back on the campaign trail, back to my mission.

In a strange sort of way arenas like the Thompson-Boling were familiar to me. Just like when people visit New York for the first time they often get a sense of having been there before. It's nothing spiritual, they have actually seen it all before, a million times on films and TV shows. They've seen it so often it's as familiar to them as their own street. I'd spent so many hours glued to the screen in our front room watching and re-watching the tapes of College ball games Dean had sent that I almost felt I'd been in such places already. To an extent it was the difference in facilities that had prompted my dream in the first place. In England basketball was just one more minority sport in a country dominated by football; even if it took-off big time it would never rival that tradition. But in the States, where everything is bigger, even minority sports can be huge. The University of Tennessee loves its basketball, but it also loves its American football, its baseball, its volleyball, it loves sports and the available money and space allows it to celebrate and enjoy such recreations in the most opulent well-equipped surroundings imaginable.

It wasn't only the locations and the facilities that had become familiar to me through my hours of studying College ball, it was the players. They were my heroes; young men calmly living the dream which engulfed my every waking hour. College basketball is a hot-house for talent. The teams of Division One schools are made up of the future stars of the NBA, scouting high school players is big-business, signing the most promising talent is an obsession for Head Coaches, nurturing that talent through four years of play (bringing them and their team glory along the way) is crowned by that final achievement of seeing your player through the draft to the NBA, and the tapes I'd watched had featured young versions of Shaq, Jim Jackson, Bobby Hurley, Conrad McRae, Chris Jackson and a host of others who would go on to be the greatest players of their time. One such player was Allan Houston. Al would go on to a massive pro career. After graduating from Tennessee as their highest-ever scorer he'd be selected in the 1993 draft 11th overall by the Detroit Pistons, he'd become a gold medal winning Olympian, be twice an NBA All Star and one of the Knicks' legendary players: but for now he'd just be stood in front of me, literally stood in front of me in his dad's office on my first day away from Widnes. The thought that we'd become friends was as incongruous to Dean as it was to me. He recalls: '*One of my mentors during my college years was fond of saying that "water seeks and finds its own level." I believe this occurred with Del and Allan - they were kindred spirits of sorts through the game we all loved.*'

Neither of us knew any of this, of course. Neither of us had any clue what the future held for us. Just as neither of us knew that the bond, which began in Wade's office that day, would be as strong as ever twenty years later. That one day Al would fly me to New York so that we could clink our glasses together in a suite over-looking Times Square prior to setting off for his retirement party: that we'd always feature in one another's lives. How could I have known? I could barely even speak. I'd watched the 1989 McDonalds High School All-American game on tape hundreds of times back home, and here was one of its stars standing in front of me as though he were just another kid, just like me. Dean introduced us and I was grateful that the Camp was due to start and we needed to go. I needed a little time to get over the shock, the excitement, the last thing I wanted was to make a fool of myself, standing there all slack-jawed, lolly-gagging at what my life had suddenly become.

It wasn't until mid-afternoon that our paths crossed again, our involvement in Camp over for that day, Dean had gone to his office to tie-up some work and left me to have a look around on my own. Allan called me over; he was sitting in the bleachers chilling with his cousin GJ, watching some cheerleaders and dance teams practice on court. We chatted for a while, they wanted to know who I was, what I was doing here, but more than that, they seemed to just want to hear me talk. It was something I'd get used to. The accent I'd thought was a bit embarrassing, not cool at all, and the politeness and the phrasing that had made me stand out from my more streetwise teammates back home, would be a miniature fortune to me here, and pretty soon Al and GJ were cracking up. Al was intrigued by my accent and found it weirdly entertaining that a black kid would talk this way. It was clear from the start: we'd get on.

After a while Al asked *'Man, who you staying with?'* and when I told him his Assistant Coach he immediately said *'Nah man, you gotta come stay with me!'* And that was it. After a single night and one meal with Dean I thanked him for his hospitality and went to stay with Allan Houston. Skinny Del from Widnes, the dreamer who told everyone he was going to the States, that he was going to make it as a baller, kicked it the whole week with a kid from the Big Time.

Spending time with Al and his friends was like being a celebrity, my accent and sayings attracting attention and hilarity from them all. It felt surreal, like being in a sitcom, like the Houston's were the Huxtables and in this episode a long-lost cousin from England arrives and Al (in the role of Theo) showed him how they kicked-it Stateside. He took me to play golf, we took Lynn and Patty (Al's sisters -Vanessa and Rudy?) and razzed all over that tabernacle like Lewis Hamilton in our golf carts.

As the week went on I realised that, in spite of our hugely different upbringings, Al had the same strange sense of humour as me. Man, he cracked me up. Going places with him was already funny as he was kind of famous in Knoxville and people would seem awestruck just to see him. It was made funnier by one of Al's favourite jokes, which went like this: we'd pull up at say McDonalds and whilst placing his order Al would intersperse his words with all sorts of crazy sounds. Remember Bobcat Goldthwaite from Police Academy 5? Just like him. Al would be like, *'Can I have a arrrgghhhh...uuhhhhh...eeeeehhhhhhhh... Big Mac please, and some aarrrrrrrrhhhhh...eeeeeeehhhh...meeooooow fries with that, please?'* I would be rolling with laughter, falling off the passenger seat, and the server, already a little awestruck that they were getting Allan Houston's order, just wouldn't know what to do: had he gone mad? And, if he had, what would that mean for the Vols next season? The funniest thing about Al was something I'd never really managed to master: the way he could do things like this and keep a completely straight face. He'd do it everywhere, even at the airport when he dropped me off for my flight: *'Excuse me, what time does.... ooooooohhh...eeekkk...aaarrrgg.... plane arrive in...burrrpppp... eeehhhh Pittsburgh, please?'*

Although it was basketball that had been at the centre of my dream to leave Widnes, to get to the States, it wasn't the only force driving me. Adopted people often talk of the difficulty they feel in belonging. Finding a sense of their own place is hard enough, it's made even more of a challenge when skin colour is an issue. Prior to coming to America my life had been a bit of a racial paradox. At home, with mum and dad and my brother and sisters, the colour of my skin just wasn't an issue. We felt like a family because we were a family. Kim, Gid and I knew, from before we could even understand, that we were adopted. There was never any great day of revelation, of sitting down to talk about it, because it had always been something we all talked about, like it was normal, because for us it was. We'd sit round the kitchen table at meal-times and one of us would ask 'What was my name before you got me?' or 'Tell me again, where I was born'. It was totally normal to have once had a different name to the one we had now, to have been born in some other place we never even remembered being in. It might have been easier because there were three of us, us eldest kids all shared this hiccup in life when the path we'd begun on was abruptly halted only for another completely different one to appear. We were all the same, in our entirely different ways, it was Kirstie (the 'home grown' kid) who was the odd one out. Outside of home it was a different story. I don't know whether I was conscious at the time of the way in which we stood out, at least not when I was very young. And it wasn't that people were actually abusive (not often anyway), it was more this unspoken thing, this vibe of difference that, as I grew up, I could begin to relate to colour.

I had found other black kids to be friends with through basketball, and had also found to my confusion that they weren't like me either, maybe America would be different. Through my basketball friends, Sean McKie, Yorick Williams and others, I'd spent time in areas that, if not predominantly black, were at least predominantly non-white, but when Allan took me to meet his extended family in Alcoa, I'd never been anywhere like that. In our whole time there I never once saw a white face. Even the postman was black. I told Al how weird it was for me, but how could someone understand when they hadn't known what it was like to stand out in the way I had?

My week in Knoxville flew by, it was everything I wanted it to be. More even. I hadn't expected in my wildest of daydreams that I'd go from one-on-one in Padgate College gym with Andy Heath, to one-on-one here with Allan Houston and (one especially memorable day) a bare-foot Alvin Harper, a standout wide receiver and high jumper who went on to star in the NFL with the Dallas Cowboys. I lost by the way. Like I say, he was a high jumper. Playing alongside and against those guys was a real test for me, a chance to finally see whether I could hold my own or whether I'd just fall flat on my flat-top. It was something Dean was interested to see, as well: '*I couldn't resist an occasional urge to peek into the gym and watch Del play in those games. I simply wanted to see how he would fare. As I saw him hold his own, and even progress and improve some during that week, I couldn't help but really think that this kid certainly could play college basketball somewhere and even had a shot to become a NCAA Division I scholarship player*'. I left Knoxville on a real high, although gutted I had to go, I was acutely aware of the need to start my own journey properly. Dean remembers his thoughts as vividly as I do mine: '*As Del left Tennessee, I remember thinking...and believing....that this kid was going to do well and I was willing to help him however possible. This once skinny, wide-eyed, almost awkward young boy was transitioning into a young man with definite possibilities as an athlete and I was proud of him and excited for his road that was ahead.*'

I was walking away from the University of Tennessee, from new friends and the best week I'd ever had, but at least I was staying in the States, embarking on the next stage of my dream. It wasn't like I was going back to Widnes.

Except I was. Sort of.

A Senior

Uhrichsville, Ohio, is interlinked with the neighbouring village of Denison and together the two places make up the area known locally as the Twin Cities. Uhrichsville, by far the larger of the 'cities', has a total area of just under three square miles and a population of 5,500. We only had to begin our drive from the airport for me to realise this wasn't just a plane ride from Knoxville, this was a world away. Of course I'd been spoilt, I was aware I was heading away from a major Division One school, with an Athletic Department whose facilities would rival those of most top-flight Premiership Football Clubs, to go to something completely different, and I could deal with that. What I was shocked by was how rural the landscape we were heading through was, how remote it seemed and, when we finally arrived, how very, very quiet Uhrichsville was. I'd been met from my flight by Jim Carrothers and Coach Riley. It was great to finally meet them both, especially after the journey Coach and I had already shared together from different sides of the Atlantic, and he was everything I'd come to expect he'd be; friendly, welcoming, enthusiastic and as eager as I was to get the season underway. The contrast that lay before me would fire that enthusiasm further still. I'd seen the Big Time now, and I knew more than ever that it was what I wanted. It had been an exhausting week, full days and late nights and our initial greeting was followed by the 100-mile drive from Pittsburgh airport, most of which I spent fast asleep. Although when I woke up I felt it might have been a bit rude, it was sort of a compliment to Jim, my host 'dad' who was driving me to Uhrichsville as Coach went onwards to his family vacation, as I already felt comfortable with him, felt part of this new 'family'.

It was clear from my first look around Uhrichsville that the centre of my world would be the park. It would have to be, there wasn't really anything else there. The park contained a small baseball field, a small outdoor pool and a basketball court where all Claymont High's former and current stars hung out. 84' by 50' of space that would be the focus of every free hour. In dropping by there that first day I'd already met some of the Mustangs who were spending their summer shooting hoops and keeping in shape. Most of them knew I was coming, one of the real positives of arriving in a place like the Twin Cities was that introductions weren't really required. Everyone knew who I was, I was a stranger, and you don't get many of them in Uhrichsville. The guys on the team might have been expecting an English kid in class in the Fall, but none of them knew I was a baller, that I'd come here to complete a necessary step on the road to my master plan of success, or that I'd spent the previous week hooping against one of the NBA's future best-ever shooting guards. I kept that to myself, I was already causing a bit of a stir simply by being there.

It was easy enough to imagine how they might have felt about my arrival. High school (particularly the latter years) is a time in which we all know our place, whether we like it or not. And the last thing anyone wants is for a stranger to arrive and push us off our spot. It's more than this in America though; high school sport may be a massive step down from college sport, but it's still an enormous leap ahead from English high school sport. I was (perhaps not that surprisingly) captain of the basketball team at my old school, Fairfield High, and we never played a single game in which we were watched by anyone other than the teaching staff who coached us. No one's parents came, certainly no local sports fans came, and it was unimaginable that they would. For a start, where would they sit? If you reached over the side-line to catch a pass you were in danger of banging into the wall. In the States it's entirely different. High school sport is big time, in Uhrichsville, it's as big time as anything gets. I'd already heard about the size of crowd which crammed itself into 'The Pit' (Claymont High's gym) and, although tiny in comparison to what I would enjoy just a year later in college, it was a world away from anything I'd experienced before. Ball was a business here, okay a small business, but still kids were on the basketball team at Claymont as a step towards a lucrative career, just like I planned to be. The last thing they wanted was some foreigner coming in and stealing a piece of that away. As I arrived one guy's father had such a problem with the potential threat I posed he'd already transferred his son to a rival school; a move that would actually come back to haunt us later in the season.

It's not conceited to acknowledge that I was a threat to them. I was good and, more than that, I was getting better by the hour. So that first day when I went one-on-one against some of my future teammates on the park court, we were rivals as much as anything, eager to check-out one another's skills, to see what the competition for the starting-five would be like come Fall. Except this wasn't England, was it? We wouldn't just roll up in the school gym one day after class and have a throw-about. You wouldn't win a place on an American high school basketball team by just being willing to turn up at 3 o'clock with a pair of trainers like you did back home. This was the miniature big time, and there was nothing miniature about pre-season.

I'd only been in Uhrichsville for a few weeks when pre-season training began. I'd settled in well with the host family that the Rotary Club had placed me with, who were welcoming and treated me like a son. The Carrothers family, Jim and his wife Jeannie and their two kids Rebecca and Matt (a Claymont junior and freshman respectively). Jim was a Rotarian who had offered to accommodate me free of charge. It was immensely generous. My parents were doing something similar back home in Widnes, but they were getting the added bonus of seeing their son achieve his dream as a pay-back, the Carrothers were just doing this out of generosity of spirit, something I've always admired and appreciated. I got on well with the kids and we had a laugh together from the off. The other great bonus of my host family was Jeannie's cooking, her French Toast and cookies I'd quickly become addicted to. I was going to need the calories, pre-season was beyond anything I'd ever imagined.

I'd already met a number of the guys who were most into ball in the park, and in such a small town word of my arrival got around so quickly that by the time school started most people knew who I was and that ball was my thing. As pre-season began the impact of Jeannie's amazing cooking and the late physique-boost puberty would finally deliver still hadn't started to kick-in, and I was still so skinny I had to pretty much run around in the shower just to get wet. Back in England training had consisted of a total of two hours per week, was spent doing drills and practising plays, and culminated in a bit of scrimmaging before home. Man, was this a different ball game! Each afternoon following the end of class we were to report directly to Coach Riley. Sometimes it would be straight down to the track where a gruelling programme of countless 200m, 400m or 800m sprints had been lined up. Other times we'd convene in the school gym. I was relieved the first time that happened, I've never been a fan of outdoor training, even in the sunshine of late-summer Ohio, but any relief rapidly disappeared, jolted from me by the hours of jump-rope sessions (I learned pretty quickly not to call it skipping) we were expected to endure. I'd never experienced anything like it. I'd always trained, but my training had focused more on perfecting my shot, on completing lay-up after lay-up until I knew the motion required of my every muscle as well as I knew breathing. But it didn't take a genius to work out that a bit more hard-core strength training might have had a positive impact on my physique. I was fit and had stamina, I could play forty minutes on court no problem, but my body was weak, it was frail, and after a week or two of pre-season it was also shocked. Whatever practice consisted of, sprinting, skipping, it was always topped off by a final hour in the weight-room. Any photo from back then can be exhibited as evidence that I had never lifted weights. It was alien to me and I stood in awe as my teammates casually threw up 100kg. It was like some episode of Mr Bean, all these burly American dudes excelling as I struggled and felt sick to my stomach as I wrestled with just 60kgs, puny arms fragile as un-cooked spaghetti beneath the weight's threat.

Three hours a night, five nights a week was nothing to these guys. It was overwhelming to me and every time I'd think about the enormous gulf between what had gone before and what was happening now, all I could do was smile. It was exhausting, but this was what I'd always wanted, the chance to take it all seriously, to really devote myself to achieving my ultimate potential. Still the thought lingered: if this was high school what the rass[viii] would Big Time College Ball be like? As I left England I was nudging 6'3" and was around 165lbs, and through the few short weeks I'd been in Uhrichsville my frame grew as quickly as my reputation. It was as though inches would be added to me overnight and within a matter of weeks I'd sprouted to 6'5". The Twin Cities' grapevine had gone into overdrive with my arrival and by the time school started the games we played in the park were attracting quite a crowd, not least of all because with the added height came a new skill. Dunking!

Uhrichsville is a pleasant place, it's safe and homely and people look out for one another (whether you want them to or not), but it's also pretty isolated from the outside world. When people asked where I came from there was no point in saying Widnes (of course, who would have heard of Widnes, any more than any Widnesian would have heard of Uhrichsville?). But there wasn't even much point in saying Manchester. England was London and that was it. I'm not being judgemental, there are parochial people everywhere, it was just that some residents of the Twin Cities, like a lot of people in small-town America, had barely ever been beyond the state-line. Uhrichsville lies directly between the cities of Pittsburgh and Columbus, 100 miles from each, cities that were the limit of many people's travels. The surrounding countryside is just that, a rural landscape dominated by agriculture. Farms run by white families who bred their sons tall but not necessarily light on their size thirteens. Powered by my new twin vices of good pancakes and Kool-aid, I found I could launch my new frame higher than ever before. Perhaps now I'd be able to start performing some of the nastier moves I'd studied so long on those college tapes.

There was a real buzz around town about me being there. It was probably good training to have grown up in a place where I stood out, as things here weren't about to be any different. It had never even crossed my mind that the American place I'd wind up in would be anything at all like Widnes, but in many ways Uhrichsville was. Apart from anything else, as its official demographic stat's attest, the population of the Twin Cities is 97.58% white. I was in a white town, living with a white family and I was playing ball on a predominantly white team, the only other black Mustangs being Ryan Simpson and another newcomer by the name of Steve Sherrell. 6'3" with an unbelievable 220lb build, Steve quickly became my boy, both on court and off. Steve had silky passes and post moves, a warrior attitude and an outstanding ability to rebound. He stood out on court for his skills as well as for his colour and for the fact that the guy had Hops! He was the only player on the team who could consistently dunk, except for me. I was improving everyday and relishing my new found ability to slam the ball down into the basket, and mine and Steve's dunks were such a novelty to the Mustangs' fans that every time either of us performed one of our signature moves the crowd of 'The Pit' would go hysterical; thrilled with the pair of 'brothers from a different mother' (at least in the Hops department) they'd acquired themselves.

Although a predominantly white highly conservative town, and also a place with some intense underlying prejudices I was yet to encounter, the people of the Twin Cities were crazy about basketball. It was at least a two and a half hour drive to any place where anything like a top-class team might be playing and making such a journey for a ball game was just unimaginable. Shut off in their town, Uhrichsville's basketball fans didn't give up, simply resorting to watching their sport on TV, instead they threw every ounce of their passion behind their local high school team; us, the Claymont Mustangs. The difference between the high school set-ups in America and England is laughable. Two years before this my English high school team was managed by a Rugby coach and played its games in front of no one. At Claymont, in addition to running on the athletics track every other day and daily sessions in the team's own weight-room, we also had 10 hours of weekly practice, matching team boots and track suits, radio interviews, live TV coverage, college scouts, cheerleaders, pep rallies, school bands oompa-ing us onto court and the small matter of 1,000 basketball-crazy, Mustang-possessed fans. A team I was playing on, starting on (a high school team at that) had fans. One thousand of the rowdy tough-necks[ix]!

The level of training involved in pre-season reflects the seriousness with which high school ball is treated in the States. Coach Riley explained that there were official rules set down by the Ohio High School Athletic Association which determined what could and couldn't be included in any conditioning program prior to the season's start. Conditioning is permitted but any coaching of the fundamentals or teaching of strategies was strictly forbidden. I was already looking forward to reaching this change in training, the weightlifting, conditioning, footwork, and running program that took up the eight weeks prior to the official start of practice, in early November, was taking its toll. I was getting much stronger physically and this of course had a positive mental impact on me, but my poor body was crying out for the more familiar patterns of the type of training I'd been used to. It was having an effect though, as Coach Riley recalls: *'I could see Delme getting bigger and stronger in a few short months. He loved the practices. He thrived on it. He loved being a part of the team. He loved the drills and the atmosphere and continued to improve throughout the season. With the regularity of practice and games, his skill-level kept elevating. I could see that he was a very gifted athlete with exceptional insight into the game of basketball. He was a 6'6" guard, but could play forward or even inside with his back to the basket. But it was becoming more and more clear that he was best with the ball in his hands, creating shots for his teammates. He kept getting better and better.'*

Although no coaching is permitted in pre-season, schools tend to conduct a programme of what's known as 'Open Gyms', games in which the players of a team organise themselves into opposing sides and play games. Any involvement by coaching staff in this exhibition games is strictly forbidden, but coaches are of course there, eagerly watching the embryo of their future season, hawk-eyed as a new year's worth of talent parades around the court and competes alongside and against those already established. By the time we got to 'Open Gyms' Coach Riley was already excited about my game. After he'd collected me from Pittsburgh those few weeks before he'd then set off on his family's summer vacation, he told me some years later that he arrived back from his holiday to find a friend of his (and huge Mustangs' fan) Ronnie Scott sat waiting for him on his front porch. Ronnie had been unable to wait any longer to tell Coach about the fits I'd been causing everyone in the park, about how exciting the forthcoming season might just be. '*Jim, wait until you see him play,*' he'd said, bizarrely Coach still hadn't, '*he's got a lot of raw talent.*' Raw was a good way to describe me, raw but tall, tall and although still pretty thin, bulking-up rapidly.

As well as offering the chance for our own coach to see how we were progressing and to begin to get a sense of how we might gel as a team, 'Open Gyms' are an opportunity for college scouts to attend schools on the lookout for potential freshmen. I was desperate for 'Open Gyms' to start, for the chance to get out there on court to show off some of my new moves and to try out the new body that I was developing, like letting a new car rip on an open road. When I heard there'd be scouts there, it was on! Coach had understandably had some concerns about my frame when we first met, my limbs were like long lengths of string dangling from my torso, but he could see as well as anyone else that my size and shape were changing rapidly. He could also see that alongside the enthusiasm there was natural talent and now he could see my commitment, he'd been unsure when I first arrived as to how I'd adapt to the punishing schedule of pre-season conditioning, and had also had reservations about how I'd cope with training once it began, as it was a world away from anything I'd experienced in England. But he'd had faith and I was proving his faith was justified, he was excited, so excited that he got on the phone to ensure that at our first 'Open Gym' there was quite a crowd of scouts lining the bleachers.

Talent is, of course, essential for anyone who's going to make it to the top of any profession and sport is no different. But talent is nothing without hard work and utter, utter dedication to pushing yourself to the limit. And neither of these things is anything without luck, the breaks and, perhaps most important of all, someone to believe in you. I'd had this already at home and now I had someone else who believed in me, who shared the dream, I had Coach Riley who at this really early stage, even before the season had started, had been on the phone each night to college coaches convincing them they should drive out to Uhrichsville, down to the middle of nowhere, to check out his new player. Coach Riley had been coaching high school ball for many, many years. He'd always dreamed of seeing a player through his team to a Division One college and a professional career and was now prepared to put that reputation on the line. If he had that much faith, then we were on, weren't we?

Dotted about the crowds of those first 'Open Gyms' were Bobby Huggins, from the University of Cincinnati; Tommy Massimino, Assistant at Villanova University; Marty Marbach, Canisius College; Eldon Miller from Northern Iowa; and Bill Brown, Assistant at Ohio University. This was major. Cincinnati was a very big player in Division One. Villanova were also huge, still riding high after their 1982 National Championships victory over Patrick Ewing's Georgetown Hoyas. They were big time and more than that they were there to see me. They chatted with Coach during and after the games and, although I didn't know this at the time, they all concluded that Coach Riley was right. I was very raw, but also very talented and certainly a prospect they'd be watching eagerly as the season progressed. Coach Eldon Miller, from Northern Iowa, had driven six hours to come to see me play that day and probably summed my situation up most accurately: '*If this kid was 15 lbs heavier, every major Division One school in the country would be after him!*' It was a comment Coach Riley was wise to pass on to me. The last thing I needed now was to let all this excitement, all this attention, go to my head. I needed to keep grounded, I was going to a Division One College, I'd already decided that, and I wasn't about to win a scholarship to one by resting back on the little success I felt I'd already achieved.

I'm not sure why I wasn't nervous playing for the start of my reputation (or the loss of it before it had even begun) in front of all those Big Time scouts, but I wasn't. I was conscious of not wanting to show-off and was subsequently a little too unselfish (something that's often held me back) as we played pick-up. The fact that some of my teammates were a little jealous of the attention the new guy was getting from Coach had started to creep into my consciousness. No one had directly said anything to me and I was getting on well with the majority of the team who'd seemed relieved that, as well as being able to play, I was also able to have a laugh. Nonetheless, I was aware of the way in which I was stepping on people's toes just by being there. It's a positive thing in life to be empathic to others, but this was the start of my discovery that there's little place for empathy on the high school court, less room for it in college ball and in the world of the pros something that most of them wouldn't even be able to spell. I couldn't help being a nice guy but I also reminded myself I was here for a purpose and to complete that purpose I'd need to stay focused on my goal.

Staying focused off court was no problem. After my initial shock at the quietness of my new hometown I quickly came to appreciate the lack of other distractions. There was nothing to do in the evenings in Uhrichsville and so when it was light enough and the weather was good I'd spend all my spare time on the court in the park. When winter arrived any time I had free I'd spend with the new friends I'd made over at one another's houses. Spare time was limited. School was busy and places in the line-up of the Mustangs were reserved only for those who were achieving what was expected of them in class as well as on court. Training and conditioning was extensive and the lifestyle here just so different from what I'd experienced back in Widnes. By now all my old school friends were in their second year of college, their social time revolving around weekend partying. Here the drinking age was 21, still three and a half years away, and so opportunities to be distracted were slim. They were slimmer still when it came to girls.

If I'd been something of a novelty back home, in the Twin Cities I was an unassuming celebrity. I was new and different and that counted for something, I was English and spoke 'properly' and that counted for more, I had milk in my tea and three sugars and I drank it warm. I was also a baller, not any old everyday baller, one who was about to set 'The Pit' alight. I'd always been friendly and enjoyed a laugh, always made up silly phrases and sayings, or borrowed them from Harry Enfield or Victoria Wood (a huge favourite in our house growing up), which I'd keep as a catchphrase for a few months until something wittier came along. At home it was funny, but here it seemed to be hilarious. Girls especially seemed to enjoy the banter of the old English charm and I'd noticed a couple of times that guys in my class seemed to be irritated by it. I put it down to jealousy and, empathic as ever, figured I'd be pretty swole' too if some foreigner came along and muscled his way into everything. Crunch-time was coming, we were heading for the first game of the season and it was time to prove that the buzz and the hype that surrounded me was justified, that or confine myself to having been just a lanky English let-down, after all.

All those hours spent at home, with me and Kirstie watching '80s American films on grainy VHS, had taught me to expect much from the build-up to high school sports games. They'd taught me to expect it, but I could never have been prepared for the level of hype that surrounded the first match of the season. It was mental. The entire town was buzzing with expectation. Our Principal led the entire school in the pep rally, a sort of carnival of hype of the likes I'd never, ever seen, firing-up the fans as much as the team as if we were Mel Gibson and the lads striding out onto some Braveheart battlefield. It didn't stop there, the opening game seemed to be all that anyone around school was talking about. Signs and posters festooned every inch of that tabernacle, the marching band were ready, the cheerleaders had been perfecting their moves all summer long, and we, the Claymont Mustangs, had something to prove.

It was nerve-wracking but we were confident we had a good team; our 'Open Gyms' had given a taste of what the squad might be capable of and there wasn't a guy on our starting-five who stood at under 6'2"; big for a small Division Two school like Claymont. At centre was Larry Browning, 6'7" (they breed them big in the country) who was smart and an excellent mid-range shooter who always faced the basket. On the wing was our captain Andy Meister, an out-and-out warrior who never backed down, but who was also very experienced at varsity level. Even from the casual scrimmages in the park in the summer it had become clear to me that Andy's feistiness meant that we'd probably clash before the season was through, the guy had a lot of skills, but to be blunt, he was a gun. Not always a negative, as the season progressed he hit many big time shots for the Mustangs and it's never a bad thing to have a guy like that on your team. Rounding out the starters, besides Steve and I, was Ryan Patterson, a guy with the season's hardest role as he had to learn and start at the point; not his natural position, but we had no one better at this level. He had his ups and downs, but he was also a fiery competitor with a lot of balls, and he never gave up when times were tough. He'd prove how vital he was to the Mustangs pretty soon in a now legendary clash with Steubenville in two games time.

I left the locker room on a high. Pumped up with nervous energy and the thrill of sitting in front of a locker engraved 'Herriman 32' whilst waiting to be called onto court. Coach Riley had laughed at my undisguised glee when he'd handed out our gear at the start of the season, but none of it was getting old, the guys around me had no idea what ball was like in England, we barely even had matching warm-up tops, let alone engraved lockers. We'd already experienced something of the intensity of 'The Pit' in our exhibition games, which had attracted a crowd of around 700, by far the largest I'd ever played in front of, and the noise they made was, even in friendly matches, pretty intense. For this they'd be pumped, they'd been hyped to hell and back by the atmosphere around town and had almost took the roof off the place in pre-season when I'd tentatively thrown down a couple of my soon to be signature dunks. I had Hops now and boy was I going to use them. Before the game kids who'd been at the 'Open Gyms' would come up to me in the halls and say '*throw it down*', '*throw one down*'. Who was I to disappoint?

I knew I had done all the conditioning necessary and that the hard work would pay off. I also knew that all I really had to do to make the crowd go wild was 'throw one down'. It was a circus, complete with dancing girls and chanting crowds and at its centre, Coach Riley, the ringmaster who, circus aside, wanted to win. A more gentle, lovely man you'd rarely meet off the court; on the sidelines it was a different matter. So we're at the jump ball, and after all that hype just one tip of the finger gets the 1990-'91 season underway. Steve Sherrell won the tip. The ball came to me. I took two dribbles. And Boom...Tomahawked it down! 'The Pit' erupted. Prayers answered. Instead of falling on my face and not living up to the small legend which had preceded my run out onto court, I finished the game with 20-points, 10 rebounds, and most importantly, our team finished with a victory. In the morning the front page of the local paper showed me hovering above the ring mid-dunk, my Kid n' Play flat-top almost reaching the top of the back-board: the headline was me. Not just Delme Herriman, but Del 'Thunder Jam' Herriman. I not only had a reputation, I had a media nickname!

We opened our campaign with two straight wins and felt on good form as we approached our first real challenge of the season, a game which lives still in Claymont history as one of the team's most memorable encounters. We were to host the Steubenville Big Red, a much feared team who had, along with the Mustangs, made it to the previous season's regional finals. Man, that team had players; most notably a great point guard called Bubba Donelly, who (in spite of the dodgy name) had an uncanny ability to pull the 3-balls from anywhere, and Gary Steele who was a monster inside. If hype had crackled around the corridors of Claymont for the first game of the season, then expectations for this match were in danger of setting the halls alight. The Mustangs' fans were real genuine basketball fans, they didn't just want to see their team win, they wanted to take part in an epic battle, fulfil their role as sixth man in the craziest most vocal way imaginable, and then see their team win. Claymont had a reputation as a capable team, but we also had a reputation for the noisiest gym in all of Ohio. 'The Pit' had a capacity of 1,000 but they were 1,000 of the most insanely rowdy fans I've ever experienced and the acoustics of the gym seem to somehow amplify their every yell, turning the whole building into some kind of gladiatorial arena.

If ever we were on for a battle, it would be against Steubenville. In the two games we had at the opening of the season it had become apparent to me that I was improving all the time, especially in terms of my Hops, and I found myself exploiting every available opportunity to try out ever more impressive moves. The Mustangs' fans loved it. It was a total war out there.

I played the whole game and both teams pressed. It was tough but we were having none of it, there was no way the biggest game of the season to date was going to go down like this so we put on the full-court press and managed a couple of cheeky steals, and before we knew it I was on the end of a one bounce and sweet pass from Andy Meister. I took off two-footed quite far out and slammed it down two-handed on top of a couple of Steubenville guys: it gave us the lead.

'The Pit' went through the roof; I'd honestly never heard anything so loud in all of my life. Nor had anyone else, the broadcaster who'd been announcing games at Claymont for thirty years said it was the loudest he'd ever heard 'The Pit' go. To give some context to the importance of a team like the Mustangs in a place like the Twin Cities, this game is still being talked about now. Coach Riley recently sent me an article from the local paper in which my host 'dad' Jim Carrothers (the Mustangs' long-time clock operator) was asked about his most enduring memories from 'The Pit'. Jim cites this clash against Steubenville as one of the most exciting and memorable he'd witnessed. I'll let him take up the story here: 'As everyone knows, 'The Pit' was an exceedingly loud place to play and the stands were always packed during that era, with sold-out signs on the doors. The noise was as loud as I ever heard it in 'The Pit', when a missed shot went down into a crowd of Steubenville and Claymont players Del Herriman grabbed the rebound and made a two-handed dunk. The noise then reached a level, which I had never before and have never again experienced. It was a noise that you couldn't hear, but you could actually feel and it hurt your ears.'

Steubenville were fiery and skilful and apart from that it was the days before the 45-second clock and before we knew it we were 9-points down going into the fourth quarter. Back then a quarter was only eight-minutes long and teams such as Steubenville who were (in spite of their impressive players) actually a lot smaller than us would spend that eight minutes keeping hold of the ball without daring to shoot at all: for the entire quarter; a ridiculous rule which led to frustrations for both the players and the fans. Nonetheless Coach was impressed. After the game he'd spoken to

90

the University of Akron Coach who'd attended to scout both teams. I could start at the two guard spot on his college team tomorrow: a massive compliment and we'd only just showered the sweat from game three.

After all those years living for a dream I was now actually living in it. It felt like some magical experience that I never wanted to end. Coach Riley was genuinely shocked by the progress I was making, but that I was here at all was down to him, he'd really gone out on a limb for me. He hadn't known what to expect when I arrived, he didn't really even know whether I could play. He knew I was a point guard and that I'd been averaging 24-points per game for Manchester Under 17s at a National level, but this was England. What that even meant was unclear, he had no concept of the level of competition and therefore no idea whether I was going to make it or not. I was coming into a team which Andy Meister describes as being categorised by *'little self-doubt, that was our mark. For good or bad, we felt we had our little world by the balls.'* And Coach Riley was understandably not the only one with reservations about me, as Andy puts it *'We didn't know whether Del would be cool, and thought whatever happens now we're stuck with this cat and Coach Riley is more or less obligated to use him as a player on our team. What if he sucks? But once Del arrived here in the States his own enthusiasm for being a part of our little community eased any apprehensions'.* The joke was that the point guard, the 'cat', Coach Riley had taken a bit of a punt on didn't only have enthusiasm, he now had a new body. By the time winter came I was 6'6" and had added a much-needed stone of weight to my previously feeble frame. It was more than pounds though, with all the plyo-metrics, weights and overall conditioning I'd suddenly become very quick and athletic, something I definitely hadn't been back in England. When I left I was just starting to scrape in a few dunks but all ballers dream of just coming down and being able to do crazy slams, in traffic, on the break, on some unsuspecting guy's head. Until now all these dreams had been in my imagination, but now I was starting to amaze myself. Things on court were shaping up very nicely indeed; things off court were a little less rosy.

Although the Carrothers family had been extremely welcoming to me and I'd settled in with them well, living as a part of a completely different family was always going to be tough. The exchange programme was clear; you were housed and fed and cared for by the host family's generosity and in return you did what was expected of you, which usually involved abiding by the same rules that the other kids in the house lived by. All this was fine by me, I was so grateful to even be in Uhrichsville after all the ups and downs surrounding my departure, I wasn't going to even think about getting into any trouble. Even if I had been that kind of kid, there was far too much at stake to risk by messing about. I slotted in to the family and focused on school and of course on basketball. An integral part of the family's life was their Sunday morning worship and I was, of course, expected to accompany them to church each week, just as Rebecca and Matt did. I wasn't a stranger to religion, the primary school I'd attended in Widnes was affiliated to the neighbouring Church of England and we'd attended services regularly. But as I'd got older and moved to a secular high school, I only went into church for weddings and christenings and I hadn't missed it at all. It's not that I stopped believing, quite the opposite in fact, I've always believed in God, but believing in God and engaging in organised religion are, for me, completely different things. I don't believe you find God under a stone (a church roof), my belief is that He is in the next person you may meet or in the song on the radio that makes you smile just when you need it most. Most of all I don't like other people's ideals being forced on me, religion included, and this was how it came to feel.

I'd pretty much kept my thoughts to myself and gone along with the family under secret duress, to keep the peace, but also to not offend them. They were being exceptionally kind to me and the last thing I wanted was upset them or appear unappreciative of all their support. But it was coming to a head. After a couple of months, the family decided to start attending a Sunday school which involved an hour and a half of study prior to the start of their regular church session, and this was way too much for me. At a similar time, one of my teammates, Ryan Patterson, had suggested I could stay with him at his place. Ryan lived with his mum, Lorrie, and although the food might not be as good, the atmosphere at their house was entirely different, more relaxed, with Ryan and I pretty much free to make our own rules. This was much more like home for me (aside from the cooking), we'd been brought up to be respectful and to obey the rules of the house, but by the time we hit late teens we were also entrusted to make our own decisions based on the fact that we'd proved ourselves to be trustworthy. I thanked the Carrothers for their kindness and moved in with Ryan and Lorrie.

The Rotary International Student Exchange Programme had a requirement that students would live with more than one family during their trip, so it was never the intention that I would stay with the Carrothers right through to the summer and they understood my desire to room with a teammate, exactly what I'd be doing next season if I was lucky enough to gain a scholarship. They weren't offended by my decision and there were no hard feelings between us. But a problem was beginning to surface for me in Uhrichsville, one that I hadn't been at all prepared for: prejudice. Life on court was nothing short of crazy and even in the early stages of the season I was developing a reputation as some kind of Mustangs' hero. But when the smoke cleared after the game and I was left with the reality of school life, life in the Twin Cities, it was a different matter. The people of the town were more than happy to have me on their team, the majority of them wouldn't have dreamt of saying anything that might be deemed as blatantly racist and treated me in a kind and friendly way, but the deeper entrenched I became in school life, I was devastated to discover an unwritten (but nevertheless steadfast) rule regarding us black guys. Do what you want, we'll invite you into our homes, feed you at our barbecues, smile at you in the street, cheer for you on court, but whatever you do, don't date our white daughters.

I had spent my entire life growing up in Widnes's predominantly white community and so of course I was attracted to white girls; white girls were the only girls I knew. There were a couple I especially liked at Claymont and, being the novelty I was, the feeling seemed to be mutual. One girl in particular used to wear my gold chain (complete with #32 pendant) whilst

I was on court, a sure sign of teenage commitment, but there was no way anything was going to progress even as far as a date to a diner for a Coke. We sat and talked about it one day and she enlightened me about the 'rule'. She did it very kindly but almost as if I were a child and she was having to patiently explain something as simple as walking, as obvious as breathing. White girls could be friends with black guys, close friends, so close they could mind their prized bling for them as they sweated on court scoring points for their school, they could do that no problem. If it went as far as an actual date then, well, then there would be trouble, so much trouble that the girl risked being disowned by her friends and parents. It was as if Rosa Parks had stayed at the back of the bus. For a week or two I thought maybe it was an excuse. But being on the wrong end of an 'it's not you it's me' would have been much easier to deal with than this. I asked my friend Steve Sherrell (the only other black guy I was close to at school) who sort of laughed it off; not because it was funny, but because it was obvious. Racism had reared its ugly, ugly head. It was about to start breathing flames.

Steve and I were pretty tight and in school he was the main guy I hung-out with. He was in the year below me, but was one of the toughest kids at Claymont, where he (like me) stood out in the white, wrestler-dominated halls. It was good to have Steve on the team, aside from his formidable skills on court, it was always a relief to feel I had an ally when we travelled to some of the schools that were even more rural than ours, where the term Redneck wasn't an insult as much as a badge of honour. He was also there to give me the lowdown on what life was really like away from the spotlight of the basketball court. One day, as school was beginning, I went to my locker and noticed someone had scribbled something on it. In pencil, as if aware of its power and the need for it to be wiped away easily enough, the graffiti read '*Nigger go Home*'! I was absolutely mortified. Before this I'd been walking around school with a big smile on my face, so, so happy to be there. Things were changing.

The power of the word Nigger has changed over the last twenty years or so in some respects, and has been reclaimed by young black men who have stripped it of some of its explosive force and violence by deciding to own it themselves. To me, in 1990, it was as shocking as a word got. No one, literally no one, said it within my ear-shot at Fairfield High. Once in class some little thug dared to call me 'Nig-Nog'; a laughable derivative but, even so, the horrified hush which swept the classroom was as though he'd just pulled out a gun. And now I was stood in front of my American high school locker, a yard of metal I'd always imagined owning, and some little racist had used his HB to, with a couple of small strokes, defile my entire dream. Next to me were some friends who stood and looked and didn't know what to say. Their embarrassment crippled them. The friends I'd made in Uhrichsville saw me as different from the American blacks, my skin a bit lighter, my home 3,000 miles away, my accent cute. But this was a wake-up call. It didn't matter how well I played, how many points I scored, how quaint my language was; to some people I was still just a Nigger. For the first time in my life I could see how racial divides are made and galvanised. The natural reaction to an experience like this, to an attack, is to choose sides. I left my friends standing there with their awkwardness and ran and told my boy Steve. Someone had written on his locker too.

I walked through the halls that day like a stranger for the first time. Since I'd arrived everyone had been so welcoming, outwardly at least, and I'd felt as though Claymont was where I belonged, at least for now. I walked that day with an uncomfortable gait and an edge of suspicion that left me eye-balling everyone I passed, as if trying to pick out the culprit. Returning to my locker at the end of the school day I found a note stuck between the grates of the door, it opened with ironic affection: 'Dear Niggers,' and was followed by an exhaustive list of the black students at Claymont High (all nine of us), 'You will all be dead before school is out!'

Although the Twin Cities was largely a welcoming place, it was also a place in which gossip spread like a fire through a parched field and I'd picked up much unconfirmed talk about active Ku Klux Klan members residing around the district. I didn't doubt it; the largely agricultural and isolated county surrounding Uhrichsville was in many ways very backward, untouched by the last thirty years of progress in many things, not excluding civil rights. My emotions were running wild now. Always one to feel the drama of a situation readily enough, the note had sent chills down my spine. Okay so it could have been a couple of dirt balls' idea of a sick joke, it could equally have been a real threat posted by the son of a real live KKK member, pissed beyond all sense at the attention this black kid was getting himself. I searched out my boy Steve. He would know something. By now he was mad. Steve had heard (on the old Uhrichsville rumour-mill) that it was two guys from his year who were the culprits.

We were called into the Principal's office. Some anonymous student (representing Uhrichsville's decent majority) had told him of the day's events and he called us in to assure us that this was an unacceptable situation which he intended to deal with sternly. We left the office only vaguely reassured. I was relieved he'd reacted that way and seemed willing to take a stance against racism in the school but the day had done something to me, and to Steve. We were swole', and as we re-entered the hall we bumped straight into the guys Steve had heard were responsible. Before it even registered, Steve had one of them by the throat, choking him up against the wall. His accomplice stood and watched, doing nothing. They were terrified, bricking it as Steve threatened everything to get him to confess or reveal the identity of the author of those disgusting notes. Nothing. Just denials and begging and eventually Steve let him go. What was the use?

It was the first and last incident of blatant aggressive racism I experienced within the walls of Claymont High. The guilty were never caught but there were no more letters and the graffiti, once cleaned off my locker, never reappeared. It was over, but it had taken a toll on me. A part of the dream had been tarnished. I was leaving Widnes to find somewhere to belong, in the land of the free, in a country in which I believed such prejudice was a thing of the past. This experience at Claymont made me long more than ever for college. To get to a bigger place, somewhere more cosmopolitan where perhaps people's horizons would be a little wider, their minds a little more open. I vowed then, that if I got to university, I would only ever date black girls. A knee-jerk teenage pledge which I really meant, and kept. For a while at least.

I didn't realise at the time that anyone had felt the reflection of this on the court but Andy Meister recalls being conscious of it: '*I always felt that Del and Steve grew tighter and created a distance between themselves and the rest of the team.*' He says '*It may have been that they were both new and had a racial common-ground, but it was always something that I thought occurred as the season went on*'. I guess he has a point, one that was kind of inevitable considering how we felt about what we'd experienced, but it's sad to think that this forced segregation '*was one of a few factors that kept us from being the team we could have been*'. Andy's recollections also made me smile though. After all those years of striving to escape Widnes, it's kind of funny now to think I ended up in a town so similar to the one I'd been so desperate to escape. Andy says: '*Del really shared a lot of himself in the short time he was in the Twin Cities. His personality was a fresh addition to the routine that comes along with small towns. Not everyone leaves that little shit-hole, so seeing someone come in with a plan to get out really reinforced my vision of going to play college ball somewhere. Del never appeared to be down, and carried himself with a bounce. That's a gift and it can be infectious.*'

Life settled back into to its new-found routine after 'lockergate' and things on court couldn't have been going better for me and the team. We ran through our league, going 8-0 and achieved our ultimate aim of being crowned East Central Ohio League champions; sealing the title with a victory over Cambridge High, Geno Ford's team. Geno was a great player, a scoring machine of a point guard, who went on to star at Ohio University with Gary Trent, before ending up playing a season in the BBL[x] for Leicester Riders. It was a great win for the Mustangs and another great performance on a personal level; I finished the game with 20-points and managed to seal us the win with two final free-throws. The season had flown by in a blink and now all that remained for us was to focus on the play-offs with the ultimate aim of getting to the State tournament in Columbus. I'd been struggling to score near the end of the season and so

Coach Riley took the decision to change me from the two to the four spot. Outside to inside. It was tough at first because in spite of the massive physical developments which had taken place I was still kind of frail, but I was now 6'6", quick and athletic, with a useful knack of scoring round the hoop with either hand. Coach had been right about the move, the change worked almost immediately and buckets started coming a lot easier.

In addition to my physical and skills development, I was also learning a lot about myself as a player and a person. I had always had a frustrating habit of saving (or leaving) the best until last. With hindsight it's happened a lot over my long career and was something that seemed to galvanise at this early stage, here in high school. It's not the most helpful habit, saving the best of yourself until your back's up against the wall, it's far more productive and healthy to try to play each game as though it's the last chance you're ever going to get to play. Productive and healthy, but bloody hard. We travelled away to Dover for our last regular game of the season. It was all coming to an end far more quickly than I liked, I'd had much attention through the season from various coaches but still hadn't been offered anything like a contract for the year ahead. I needed to focus on Dover, you never knew when you might suddenly come to the attention of the one guy who wants to sign you more than anyone else. Dover had a big crowd, pretty much twice the spectators we attracted and the game was televised live, something that had only happened to us maybe four or five times throughout the season. One of the thrills of the broadcast games was the crowning of an MVP, not only a great honour, but one which was accompanied by an amount of exposure, increasingly vital to me by this stage. I went 10-10 from the field, dropped 25-points and walked from the court as the game's MVP. Having beaten Dover comfortably on their home court (something I've always loved doing), I managed to gain myself the ultimate amount of props. Saving the best 'til last, you see.

Although the season was winding down our hopes were winding up and all I could think about was going to the State Tourney. This would be big time, Claymont had gone to the regionals in the previous season and although the Mustangs had suffered the torment of losing by a single point, they'd also enjoyed the thrill of playing for a crowd of around 5,000 fans. The exposure that came with the State Tourney was major and was also something I desperately needed. College coaches can track players through high school over a number of years and often spot new talent through the series of games played through summer vacations. Having arrived here late in the summer from what now seemed like another planet, I had none of this history of exposure and was trying not to let myself focus on how this might be my very last chance to get signed by a college. I wanted to play Big Time Division One ball, I needed a full-ride scholarship in order to do this, and for any of this to be at all possible, we had to get to the regional finals.

It was a simple enough format. One and done: you lose, you're out of there and back home, season over. We opened our campaign against a team called Tri-Valley away at Zanesville High School. We were nervous, but had reason to be confident having trained hard and gone 20-4 through the season, but so much depended on this that it was inevitable we'd begin to feel the pressure, not least of all because of the previous season's disappointment. The game against Tri-Valley was amongst the strangest I've ever played, it seemed as if anything that could possibly go wrong did, and more. There were a series of the most ridiculous calls by the ref'. Andy Meister missed a bunch of lay-ups which any other day would have been unthinkable for him not to have sunk. Steve got into serious foul trouble, and Ryan Patterson was fouled-out in the fourth. Tri-Valley hit the big shots, held the ball away from us and played in slow motion. We were a team who liked to run but Tri-Valley were having none of it; we ended up losing by 4-points.

And that was it. High school career finished with 17-points in the final game but an overall loss. I was totally gutted my dream season was over. And in spite of all the highs I'd experienced I was not only disappointed but terrified. Was I going to end up in Widnes again? My mind was a blur, I knew deep-down that I hadn't produced enough, hadn't been seen enough in the games against the better schools at the higher lever. Most importantly, I knew I hadn't been spotted in any way that really mattered by the big college scouts. It was my first real experience of that end of season lull, of stepping off the crazy wheel of the season and into nothing, not knowing what was going to happen next year, or even if I'd ever really get to play again at all. It would be a feeling I'd need to get used to. As most professional players know, there's a lot of time spent not knowing where you're going to next, if you're going anywhere at all. The only high of the next few weeks was a trip I took to Ohio State to watch the State finals from the bleachers. There were some great teams at the finals and a number of players who would go on to star at Big Time Division One. Most notably a guy called Tony Miller (who I'd go on to play with seven years later as a pro in Holland) and a team by the name of Dayton Chaminade Julienne which included three incredible players who would soon be setting Big Time College ball alight: Chris McGuire, Eric Wills and Darnell Hoskins (two of whom I'd become closely acquainted with myself before I knew it).

The tournament at Ohio State was amazing, but I was lost. I wasn't sure where my basketball career was heading now, or even if I was to have one at all, and the size and scale of the tournament taunted me. There must have been 10,000 spectators there and I was gutted that the Mustangs had lost the chance to perform together one last time on a stage such as this. I'd heard through the grapevine that there were several guys being offered full-rides to big schools and I was terrified that I'd missed the boat. There was no way I could apply to a college of my own accord, be accepted, show up and hope that my skills might win me a place on their team. At that time in England studying at university was free, all parents had to find was the money to secure their kid's accommodation and they were away. In the States, it was a different world. Tuition fees alone ran into tens of thousands of dollars and even a fraction of that would have been leagues beyond anything my mum and dad could have afforded. For me it was the full-ride or nothing and I had one chance left to prove myself.

The Eastern Ohio All-Star game loomed, I needed to be selected and then I needed to shine. This season's game was to the played at 'The Pit', meaning that if I got on a team the Mustangs' fans would have one last chance to see Del 'Thunder Jam' Herriman in all his crowd-pleasing dunking glory. Luckily I was selected for the West All Stars. I'd finished the season averaging 13.7-points and 6.4 boards a game, not bad considering my limited shot attempts, and by the time the game rolled around most of us were already feeling a little out of shape. I felt mashed and decided that all I wanted to do was to go out there and have fun. This would be my last opportunity to play to the home crowd who had buoyed us all season, who had whooped and cheered every cheeky move, and had given me one of the greatest experiences of my life. I owed it to them, and I owed it to me, to try to shine. I gave myself a good talking to; these were all the best ballers from all the best teams I'd played against all season; I needed to go out there and shoot the ball. I knew that the rules for All Star games meant every player got equal minutes and so time on court would be limited and there were plenty of guns from other teams who I was now playing alongside. I got myself into the right frame of mind and felt no pressure at all. There wasn't much chance that the crowd would contain any big scouts, mainly because, aside from me, our league didn't contain any Division One prospects and at this late stage it was almost unthinkable that anyone would trek all the way down to Uhrichsville, the unofficial capital of the middle of nowhere, just on the off chance they'd completely missed someone during the season. I played an all around game and led my team in scoring; I hit a couple of 3-s and wowed the crowd in the half-time dunk contest. If there was anyone out there watching, anyone with any clout at all, it might have been a good game to have seen me in.

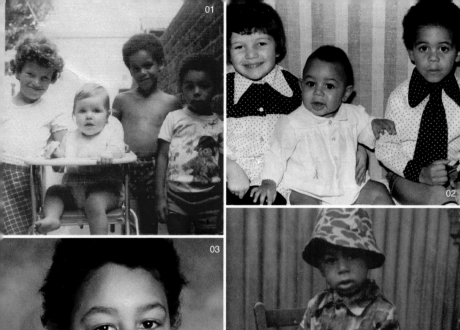

01

02

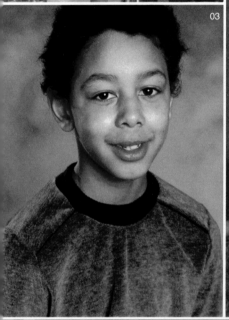

03

04

05

06

07

08

09

10

13

14

15

22

23

24

A Full Ride

It's strange to think that we go about our lives obsessing over small details and worrying about things that turn out in the end to not matter at all, and that all the time we do this other forces are exerting their power on other people, some we don't even know yet, that will ultimately affect us in the most fundamental ways. As I was spending the last few weeks of the basketball year shifting between being so, so grateful for the amazing season I'd had and fretting myself to death over having not been offered any hint of the scholarship I so desperately craved, three-thousand miles away a persistent cough was starting to worry my step-dad Oz, and closer to Uhrichsville a guy I'd never heard of was mulling over whether to make the four-hour trip down to the All Star game at Claymont.

Jim Brown's coaching career at Wright State University in Dayton, Ohio spanned twenty-seven years, time in which he'd scouted and recruited over 120 basketball players onto the college's Division Two and subsequent Division One programme. When he took the decision to drive all the way down to Uhrichsville to take a look at a player who might just fit into the final slot of WSU's 1991-'92 programme, his career high had been a victory in the NCAA Division Two National Championship in 1983 which had propelled the school into Division One, into the Big Time. He'd been reluctant to attend, it was a long drive, but the chance that the guy playing in that night's All Star game might just be the missing player WSU needed was enough to convince Coach Brown to make the trip. You don't forge a successful twenty-seven year career by not going the extra mile. By the time warm-up for the game had finished Coach Brown was already regretting his decision. The player he'd been tipped-off about wasn't what he was looking for at all, seeming slow, un-athletic and a long way from being worthy of a full-ride to the Wright State Raiders.

Geography can so often play an unsuspecting part in fate and the remoteness of the Twin Cities meant that the stars shone down on 'The Pit' that night. Coach Brown had driven four hours for this disappointment, he wasn't about to drive another four hours straight back home, not before a break anyway and so he settled down to watch the first half of the game before setting off on his long journey. A first half which confirmed Coach Brown's initial thoughts; the player simply wasn't good enough for the programme Wright State offered and tomorrow morning he'd need to go back to the drawing board in order to fill that remaining slot. Half-time promised a dunk contest, always good entertainment, and so Coach Brown decided he'd stay to watch before heading back off home, empty handed.

It was a revelation. *'One player caught my attention immediately,'* Coach Brown recalls, *'he was about 6'6", kind of skinny, but very athletic'*. The player had escaped much notice during the first half of the game but had caught Coach Brown's attention now. Twenty-odd years of experience was testament to his talent-spotting ability, but then if this kid had already played an entire half without being noticed, maybe he was one of those unfortunate players who could jump and wow the crowd with his crazy Harlem Globetrotter moves, but couldn't cut it at all once he was actually out on court in the game for real. Either way, Coach Brown was intrigued; he was staying for the second half.

'With each play I became more and more impressed with this young man's game.' He remembers checking out the All Star programme and noticing that the player had only averaged a little over 13-points per game that season. Perhaps he was just some okay kid simply playing the game of his life, but he made a couple of shots, a couple of great passes, and seemed, in Coach Brown's vast experience, to be the best player on the floor. He was intrigued and eager to find out more, if this kid could play like this then why hadn't he come to the attention of WSU scouts before? He asked a couple of students in the crowd whether they knew if the player's coach was attending tonight's game. They pointed Jim Riley out and as soon as the full-time hooter sounded, Coach Brown was on the floor asking questions about the young revelation he'd just seen. *'Jim told me the player's name was Delme Herriman and that he was a Rotary Exchange*

student attending Claymont High School. He said that Delme had only been in the US a short time, but was a great young man, liked by all the students and had adjusted to the American High School game well.' Coach Brown asked to be introduced.

By the time I was approached after the end of the game, Coach Riley had pretty much filled Coach Brown in about where I was at. He'd been assured that a return to England was the last thing I wanted and that it wasn't only my dream to play US college ball, it was the motivating reason for me being in America. Coach Brown seemed really cool, immediately telling me all about his university, Wright State, and the basketball programme they offered. It wasn't a college I was particularly familiar with, but I had heard of it. In homeroom one day, perhaps a month or two before, a friend of mine who was on the cheerleading squad had joked *'Why don't you come to WSU, with me?'* and I recalled my now ironic reply: 'Do they even have a basketball team?' They certainly did. They not only had one, they had one that I was now being recruited onto.

The decision to take up a full-ride, if one were offered, was a no-brainer for me. It almost didn't matter what the college offering it was like, what their programme was like, how their team were doing. If they had a team at all and played in Division One, I'd have gone. But Coach Riley said there were other schools expressing their interest, and whilst Wright State was an excellent opportunity for me, I didn't need to be too hasty. I agreed to go and visit WSU but, in all honesty the place could have been like Colditz and I probably would've signed on the dotted line, as long as it was Colditz with hoops.

Under NCAA rules, a player looking to be recruited is permitted five official visits to interested schools and before our court-side conversation ended that night Coach Brown had invited me down to Dayton for my first. An official visit is essentially a recruitment strategy, a chance for the school concerned to do all they can to get you to sign. I'd heard rumours of the underhanded tactics some schools employed; offering fat cheques to recruit's families and even cars. On the flight to Dayton I wondered what I might do if something like this happened. It's unethical, of course, but I wasn't about to start complaining.

I needn't have worried, bribes were unforthcoming, but I was nonetheless treated like royalty throughout my weekend stay. It was another world entirely. Coach Brown met me at the airport and barely paused for breath as he filled me in regarding Wright State's basketball history. After dominating in Division Two the Raiders had won their Division's NCAA National Championship in 1983 and had been improving steadily since their promotion into Division One. Their facilities had been improving alongside them and, just a couple of seasons before, the Raiders had moved from their old physical education building (which had seated around 2,000 spectators) into the huge and hugely impressive Ervin J. Nutter Centre, first stop on my tour of Wright State.

Having introduced me to the rest of the coaching staff, Coach Brown led me to the lift and then along the concourse level with an assurance that there was something I really must see. At an opening along the concourse he gestured me to step forward, his pride was visible: '*Take a look at that*' he said. His pride was justified; beneath us was the most breath-taking sight I'd ever seen. From our level, the executive boxes, 10,800 seats tiered down to the wooden court where a huge emblem of the team's mascot Rowdy Raider was emblazoned. I was in love, not with Rowdy, alright yeah with Rowdy, with the ridiculously named Nutter Centre, with the thought that this could be my home court for the foreseeable future. I was beaming. Coach Brown asked '*How would you like to play here?*' It was a question that needed no answer at all.

As we headed back down to Earth, Coach Brown managed to excite me further still with his talk of the Raiders' star player, Bill Edwards. Bill, a 6'8" junior played at the three or four spot and was the team's greatest prospect, so great he was already being touted as a future star of the NBA. My ears pricked up, I was still harbouring that ultimate dream of making it to the NBA myself and such an outlandish ambition would have much more of a chance if I could spend the next couple of seasons playing in front of the NBA scouts who would be in the crowd looking to recruit Bill. Coach Brown's ultimate plan, he told me, was to train me up as Bill's replacement when he graduated in two years' time. We played similarly, he said, although Bill was more of an inside player as he was a lot bigger than me at the time.

I was too blinded by all the talk, by the facilities, by the casual dropping of 'NBA' into the conversation to think much about what it would mean to begin my college career in Bill's shadow. After all, what a shadow to be under! But I needn't have been concerned. As if pre-empting me, Coach Brown explained that the staff had already thought of 'Red-Shirting' me for my first season. An undergraduate degree programme at an American university is generally a four-year course, this meant that half of my playing years would essentially be spent on the bench waiting for Bill's farewell as he launched towards stardom. Except, that is, if I agreed to red-shirt, a ruling which allows a player a five-year time frame in which to complete four years of eligibility. They didn't want to waste me, lolling on the bench as they played their star instead, so if I sat out my first year, just practising with the team and going to class, I could use that extra year to get accustomed to the college game and, most importantly, get stronger in the weight-room. The next year I would then return, still as only a freshman, but with the enormous benefit of a year's worth of intense college practice and experience under my Raiders' jersey. A few minutes before, I could hardly believe I was being recruited by a Big Time Division One school, and now it was just getting better and better. They not only wanted to recruit me for a full-ride, it was the fullest a ride could get with all tuition fees, rent, food and books provided for not only four whole years, but five!

I just couldn't fathom that this was happening to me, getting to practice and play in this brand new 11,000-seat arena every day for the next five years of my life. I'd come from a world where the first basketball skill to master was to work out which of the eight different sets of lines on the court were meant for your sport, where folded-up trampolines and crash mats lined the halls we played in, where any towel used to wipe up the sweat after a fall would be rotten with dust as soon as it touched the court. And now this: Heaven.

Colleges assign a current player to act as host for any future team prospect visiting campus and mine, Mike Nahar, a 6'11" light-skinned dude from Holland, was as welcoming as anyone could be. I'd remember his relaxed style and his infectious enthusiasm during the years ahead in which I'd act as host to many potential Wright State recruits. Mike and I got on instantly and he showed me around campus, introducing me to all the current players, and wound up taking me to the pub. A nice European touch I especially appreciated. Without getting up to anything too wild, I had a great time and gave Coach Brown a verbal agreement before I left that I would come to Wright State that Fall and become a Raider.

I was buzzing as I flew back to Uhrichsville. I could see a whole other world opening up before my eyes. I'd have to stop thinking of it all as my dream; it was becoming my reality. Coach Riley was pleased it had gone so well for me in Dayton and told me that I still had four other visits I could take if they came up. He recommended I make some less official visits to some of the other schools in Ohio before I made a final decision. And then I called home to tell my mum and dad that Wright State had offered me a full-ride. There were tears all round and the shared amazement that everything had fallen into place just as we'd always dreamed it would. All the things I'd dared to hope for from a college, Wright State were offering: to play in a massive stadium, check; to get NBA exposure through scouts, check; to live in a nice environment with the added chance of major court-time, check and check. Head Coach Ralph Underhill made the official offer; he faxed a copy of the contract to Coach Riley's office, which we then faxed to the Post Office in Widnes for my mum to pick up. Coach and I took a moment. It had been quite a journey and none of it would've been possible without him. In his thirty-year career I was the only player he coached into Division One. We'd helped one another to fulfil our dreams. It was a privilege to be coached by him and a privilege to sit in his office as I signed my scholarship contract with him looking over my shoulder like a proud surrogate father. In the end I'd been offered four scholarships in all, the other three by the University of Akron, Canisius College, and Niagara University, but there was no doubt in my mind that my future lay in Dayton.

So now I could relax, about the future and about the end of school. I kept playing in the park with Steve, Ryan Patterson and Andy Meister as much as possible to keep in shape and focused on enjoying the last few months of my life as an American high school senior. It was fun, almost just like the movies. I was recruited onto the athletics team, and represented Claymont again in the 110m high hurdles and in the high jump. Practice was tough, a different type of tough from basketball, but the sun shone and my friends, Cindy Heavilin and Angela Harding, kept me entertained. Graduation was approaching fast and as it did I could feel a sadness come over me. This had been the best year of my life and it was rapidly coming to an end. With the close of the school year came that other icon of American high school, the Prom. I was dreading it: I didn't drink, I didn't dance, and worst of all, I didn't have a date.

Who was attending with who seemed to be all that anyone at Claymont could talk about. My bitter experiences from earlier in the year told me that there was no way any of the girls I was interested in would dare to stand next to a black guy in that all important Prom-night portrait. So it was open season for Claymont's two black girls because they knew I was an easy target. One girl hounded me the whole month leading up to the prom, like some Uhrichsville hunter after its prey. I didn't want to go with her, she was a nice person but I wasn't attracted to her and barely even knew her, but the worst thing of all was the reaction of the other girls in my classes, especially the ones I was most interested in, who'd smile sweetly and suggest *'Why don't you go the prom with such and such, you'd make a lovely couple?'* I got vexed one day at the unfairness of it all and said the unsayable, the thing that they really meant: 'Why, because we're both black?'

Graduation day came and with it one of those tragedies that no one foresees. Early in the morning on our last day as seniors, the day before graduation, my classmate and good friend Becky McConnell was killed in a car crash as she drove her mum to work. Becky was a really sweet girl and her loss would have been felt at any time, it was even more poignant to have lost her on this of all days. The whole senior class was devastated and as each of us trudged up onto the stage to receive our high school diploma we gave a silent glance towards the seat in which Becky should have sat. Her cap and gown draped over her chair as though she'd been there and had simply vanished. It was my first adult experience of the death of someone close to me and I had no way of knowing that another one, this time of a person as close to me as it was possible to get, was looming silently in the near future.

We'd planned all along that whatever the year brought I'd return home in the summer vacation. There had been a number of times, especially late in the season, when I thought I might be returning home to England for good. Visiting home now would be just that, a visit. Was it even technically home anymore now that I'd committed myself to living in Dayton for the next five years? A couple of nights back in the loft with Gid assured me that it was, that it always would be. I'd been excited about my return to England and felt like a warrior triumphant after his victory. The spoils of war a video I'd made on a borrowed recorder before I left; to show Uhrichsville and my friends to everyone back home, but also to freeze it in my mind. It had been a phenomenal year, but it had been so short and now with all the adventures that lay ahead I wasn't sure I'd remember it in the way I wanted to at all.

I was greeted by every member of the family as I stepped out into Manchester's arrivals hall and every one of them almost fainted when they saw me. The returning soldier looked very different from the boy who'd departed. Three-inches taller than when I left (six if you count the flat-top) and a good stone in weight heavier, the boy was now a man and, dressed top-to-toe in my donated Tennessee gear and matching boots, I was quite the Americanised man. It felt incredible to be home, there were times throughout my year at Claymont when homesickness was so intense it was a physical pain and to be finally home was the best feeling ever. To know I was going back made it so, I'd missed everyone intensely but there was no way I wanted to return for good. I'd seen the Big Time, I was a small part of it myself now, and no amount of homesickness would make me give that up. I could barely wait to tell them of my experiences, but more than that, I couldn't wait at all to get to Manchester to see my old teammates and wow them with my new skills. As I sat under the eaves in the loft in Widnes, I allowed myself a quiet moment of reflection. My year had been successful beyond my wildest imaginings: mission accomplished. Part of it at least.

A Redshirt (and a son)

Sport is a world of highs and lows. It allows you the opportunity to be adored, to experience the thrill of crowds of people willing you on, making you feel like a hero, but it also leaves you exposed, believing that the things that happen on court are the things that matter most. When ball is your life it's difficult to keep perspective and so maybe the odd kick in the teeth from God is something we need, just to keep us human. The season I'd spent in Uhrichsville, absorbing basketball and skills through my every pore had been a hard time for everyone back at home. I'd known that dad had been sick; that a cough he'd acquired in the New Year had lingered and lingered, eventually proving impossible to shift. He'd been back and to from the Doctor and had eventually been sent for a series of tests towards the summer. How much mum and dad feared that cough I don't know. If my mum had been starting to worry that it might have been something sinister that's exactly the kind of thing she would have protected me from, for as long as she could at least. Trans-Atlantic phone calls were expensive and so rare, I wanted to tell her all about the season, all about Wright State and the last thing she wanted was to me make me worried and frightened. After all, I was 3,000 miles away, what could I have done to help?

A few weeks after I arrived home dad had a hospital appointment to find out the results of the latest round of tests which had so far not proved anything conclusively. He didn't seem unduly worried as he and mum left, just assuring us that as soon as they returned home we'd be heading off to Leeds. My mum and dad were to drop me and Gid off at the summer's Leeds Camp, where we were both to spend a fortnight working as camp counsellors. I was excited, much of the last couple of weeks I'd spent hooping in Manchester, catching up with Sean, Yorick, Trevor Campbell and my old friend and mentor Jeff Jones. It had been great to reconnect with them all and being invited to work the Leeds Camp (as opposed to just attending) was like achieving some rite of passage, as though I'd graduated from dreamer to achiever. Leeds offered another added bonus this year too, as Coach Riley was coming over to visit England with his family and was also going to work the Camp with us. It meant a lot to me to have him there, to show him where I came from, the place the dream we now shared had initially begun. As had happened so many times before Camp had consumed me and so, sat with bags ready in the kitchen, my mum and dad coming through the door surrounded by this air of anguish was a slap in the face.

Seeing your dad cry for the first time is one of those experiences that no one ever really talks about but everyone silently acknowledges as a sign that you're now an adult. There had of course been times over the years that I'd forgotten my mum and dad were people in their own right, selfishly thinking of them as the support staff of 'Team Del'; but seeing their faces as they walked through that door made me certain I'd never again take either of them for granted. The sight of dad, so huge and always so strong, clearly now devastated was mortifying; it was as if someone was eating my insides like a plate of noodles. They told us to sit down and I prepared for God to deliver that kick.

The cough that had afflicted dad had been worse than I knew, sometimes so severe that a bout of it would leave him so starved of oxygen that he'd completely pass out. The obstruction that had been found inside his lung was a cancerous tumour, positioned so close to dad's heart that an operation (which had been talked of) was simply impossible. Everything was simply impossible. A course of chemotherapy and a subsequent series of blasts of radiotherapy were prescribed. That's good then, I thought through my horror, there's something can be done. They could be done, mum said, but they would only ever be treatments which might prolong dad's life, not solutions and certainly not cures. There were no cures. The man who'd entered our home and our lives, turning everything upside down, just eleven years before would be leaving us. How long? There were no guarantees but the cells that made up dad's tumour were what his consultant referred to as 'gallopers'. They took no prisoners, invaded your body, did their worst and did it with lightning speed. Who knew how long really? A few months, perhaps.

Life as it was would continue as normal, at least as normally as it was possible to continue now that everything had shifted on its axis, and so after sitting and talking and crying together as a family we did what we always did, took solace in the normality of ball. That night in my dorm room at Camp, once mum and dad had left for the drive back home and Gid had gone to his own room, I broke down. As if the gravity of what we now knew had ambled behind us along the M62 and had finally caught up with me. My dad, the person who had shared my outlandish basketball dream for all these years, was going to die! All those miles of motorway; all those hours of sitting in gyms watching practice; all those nights of rushing home, shower and in the van; they'd all come to nothing. I might still make it, but did it even matter anymore now that he wouldn't be there to see it?

As anyone who's ever been forced to face the devastating spectre of terminal illness will know, you're left with no choice but to just get on with it as best you can, and so we did. Life got back into its old rhythm and, whilst none of us forgot for a second what was happening, what was gnawing away beneath the skin of dad's chest, we lived as close to normality as we could. The cancer stood in the corner of the room, like some ugly bit of inherited furniture we knew we were forced to keep, and we tried as much as possible to just not look at it. The summer went by quickly, and as Fall and my return to the States approached I began to feel the pressure. There was no question of me not enrolling at Wright State that September, it was unsaid and it was definite. We'd started this dream together, mum, dad and I and there was no way I wasn't going to finish it, even if only two of us might be left to witness its finale.

This season was going to be for real. This season was NCAA Division One. My game had to be ready. The dream had taken on a new form now that I was what I'd always wanted to be; a college baller. The summer's devastating news had morphed it even more, from something I'd previously been passionate about into something that mattered in a life and death sort of a way. There was nothing which could be done to save dad, nothing short of a miracle anyway, and the very least I could do for him was ensure that the dream which had been such a big part of his life transcended his death and stood as some sort of life-affirming eulogy to him. I dedicate my career to dad, and so I also dedicate this book to him. Right now I needed to make sure that once I landed back in the States, once I arrived on campus, arrived on court, I would make him proud.

****

I'd never lived on my own before, not that I was going to be living strictly on my own now, but I'd never lived in a way which meant I had to fend for myself. I hated cooking and so had avoided the need to ever learn how to do it, and I had no idea what to buy to feed myself in a way that wouldn't leave me either back to the old days of being able to count my ribs through my skin, or into a whole new world of having to lumber my ass up court like Barry White in a Raiders' jersey. I was used to American food by now, after a year of living in Ohio, but it had always been placed in front of me by Jeannie Carrothers or by the waitress in a diner. I hadn't had to think about it. If they'd have existed in the States, I'd have lived off my favourite food, Findus Crispy Pancakes, even if I couldn't manage to cook them as well as my mum did. It was going to be an interesting year.

There were four freshmen signed to the Raiders that season. Alongside me were two of the stars of the previous year's high school State Final game, Eric Wills and Chris McGuire, who'd both played for Dayton Chaminade Julienne, and a guy called Jon Ramey from Indiana. As Eric and Chris were old friends and teammates it was obvious they would room together, leaving Jon and I in the second of the two apartments we'd been allocated; the first sign of luxury: they were far from being Cribs-style gaffs, but they were a world away from the shared dorms the other students lived in. Jon and I got along great from the start and before his mum left (having dropped her boy and his belongings off in the big wide world), she took us grocery shopping so that, at least for the first week or

116

so, we'd eat something with some nutritional value. We waved her off and college life began.

Campus in the first week of a new school year would be something I'd come to recognize. Brand new freshmen from all walks of life moving their childhood belongings into their soon-to-be adult rooms, hugging families goodbye with choked-back tears; the buzz of excitement as the whole place takes on a new life; wily upperclassmen, sat back, chilling, confident and comfortable as they scope out the new female talent. Before I'd know it, I'd be one of them, but for now I just drank it all in, determined to savour every second of what it was I'd always wanted.

I'd been beside myself with gratitude since Coach Brown's suggestion that I redshirt my first year, but meeting the rest of the Raiders, the upperclassmen, made my gratitude reach new heights. Damn, I thought, they weren't only way better than me, they were also grown men. I was no longer the breakable little whipper-snapper who'd arrived at Claymont, but I looked it next to these guys. Would I even be able to hack it in practice? How would I cope playing in front of 10,000 screaming fans? Would I even make it that far before I drowned in self-doubt? The first team scrimmage down at the McLin Gym was an eye-opener; the upperclassmen came out on court like wolves smelling fresh blood. First scrimmage is a rite of passage for freshmen and is a time relished by the established players; if they thought a guy couldn't ball then he was a waste of a scholarship, and believe me they weren't too shy to let the coaches know that.

I was eager to see how good the other guys on the team were and to show what I could do. I always liked a challenge and instead of feeling intimidated I brought my A-game. Bill Edwards, Renaldo O'Neal, Sean Hammonds, Mike Haley and Mark Woods, were the players who impressed me off the bat. My fellow freshmen could ball too. It's important to solidify your place on a team from the off and to gain the respect of other players, in college ball (just like in the pro' world) first impressions count and players need to bring-it in their first encounter or accept that they probably won't ever get the chance to bring-it again. These were major ballers. Mark Woods, our starting point guard, would go on to lead the entire Nation in steals and assists for the majority of the '93 season. He was one of the team's elite, one of the nations best point guards, one of the toughest guys I've ever played with, and Wright States' all-time leader in steals and assists. After I grabbed a strong rebound off the top off the square and exploded down the left sideline, shaking all the oncoming defenders and then finger-rolling it over two 6'8" guys with my left hand, I heard him shout: *'Damn! He got game!'* It's as natural for an upperclassman to try to punk a freshman as it is for a freshman to want to get his props; this was as good a start as I could have hoped for.

Being allowed to redshirt my first year was the cherry on top of the icing on the cake I'd never dared hope someone would bake for me. It not only meant that I could spend the entire season practising and training without the added pressure of having to perform on court, it also meant that I could spread my classes out over an additional year and so could be spared some of the academic pressures as well. Places on college ball teams are precious, getting one is like finding Willie Wonka's Golden Ticket, losing one because you can't keep your grades up is like discovering at the gates of the factory that you're allergic to chocolate. Being a redshirt meant that I could focus on improving, on developing both physically and in terms of my skills, it meant a whole season to get used to how unbelievably tough Division One ball was before being thrown in there to cope myself. Except that's precisely what I wanted. My passion and obsession weren't dented at all by the sensibleness (the flattery) of the decision to redshirt me, I was as fired-up as ever, more even, and so having a great practice midweek, playing well enough to be a starter, and then not being able to take to the court once the weekend came was about as close to torture as I'd ever experience. It was one thing to spend time off court because you couldn't hack it, something else to know you could but wouldn't get the chance to, at least not this season.

This was how the whole year would pass; practicing every day, still dedicating my every-waking second to ball, and then putting on my casual clothes come game night. I hated it and it embarrassed me. People I knew vaguely from class would always come up to me: *'How come you're not playing?'* My complicated explanation would leave them blank and as they walked away I couldn't shake off the feeling that they probably just thought I was crap, not good enough to make the squad, when in reality the opposite was true. Wright State were investing in me, paying for a whole extra year of my education, just so I wouldn't waste a season of my eligibility sat on the bench behind Bill Edwards. The only potential drawback to redshirting is the chance that a serious injury later in college would put you out for a whole season you'd never be able to get back (having already used up that season buffer). I would advise any young player (if given the chance) to redshirt their first year at college, even if it does leave your classmates thinking you're some mouthy knob, whose silky skills don't live up to his smooth banter. They'd see.

After playing my season at Claymont thinking every pass, every shot, every second on the clock counted (because it did) it was great to spend a year with the pressure taken from my narrow shoulders. The transition from high school to college basketball is really tough, with players often experiencing a roller coaster of thrills and slumps as the pressure of performing on the big stage whilst attempting to live up to that high-school-star potential takes its toll. To get onto a Division One team a player needs to be outstanding, which in turn means that (for the previous season at the very least) he must have set his high school court alight, must have been amongst the best players in his State. There were additional pressures for players such as Chris and Eric, who'd played their high school ball in the same place as their college ball, and subsequently found the eyes of the whole city beading their every move. Unfortunately for both of them, those scrutinized moves were pretty much confined to shuffling along the bench. Getting the clock in your freshman season is really difficult, big stakes are attached to every game. Coaches' jobs are on the line as they are financially incentivized to win. Allowing freshmen court-time nurtures their talent, but risks results. If a freshman's on a team with a lot of upperclassmen on the roster, then he'll spend a lot of time picking splinters from his bum.

I wasn't used to things being so quiet for me on court, this was the first season in five years I hadn't played competitively and I missed it. I tried to focus on school and on training and took calls from home as much as was possible to get updates on dad's condition. By the New Year of 1992 he'd already surpassed the doctor's predictions of the amount of time he was likely to live and so I dared to hope that I might get to see him in the summer after all, if he could just hold on that long. I was adjusting well to campus life and for the first time was part of a real social scene. We ballers practised, studied, ate and lived together; we also hung out with one another and, many of the guys whenever possible partied. Word Wednesday was a regular party held on Wright State's campus that had a reputation beyond school. It was a black party and attracted many guys from neighbouring colleges who would come along to check out our WSU honeys. Lots of the players went but not me, as a freshman (and a redshirt) I felt an additional responsibility to behave and so didn't party or drink at all that first year. Although redshirting took some pressures away, being the recipient of such an enormous financial investment (literally hundreds of thousands of dollars over the five years, and every penny of it someone else's cash) made me feel the need to be more focused than some of the other players, who felt a different kind of freedom from mine. Not attending wasn't an issue and one particular night I'd be extremely grateful that I'd decided to keep my well-behaved ass at home.

Our apartment block, Forest Lane, was situated on campus and we lived on the top floor at the front. Our doors all led off a small landing and were, more often than not, left open so that we could wander in and out of one another's places. One Thursday, around 1am, Bill was nodding-off on his sofa with his front door open when he heard a commotion coming up the stairs. Freaked out and disorientated Bill's natural reaction (thankfully) was to run and he sprinted across the landing into Renaldo O'Neal's apartment. The commotion was a bunch of guys; eight of them in total all armed with baseball bats. They took advantage of Bill's open door and trashed the place. It turned out that, at the previous night's party, one of our upperclassmen had called a girl a 'bitch'. It wasn't a wise move, she was the girlfriend of a known guy from Dayton's hood who hadn't taken it well and (knowing the culprit was a baller and where us ballers lived) decided to pay us a little visit with a couple of car-loads of his friends. After their bat-wielding antics they'd had a couple of attempts at kicking in some (now closed) doors before finally heading off back to the hood.

In the morning when I heard the news I was terrified. They'd entered our apartments from the back and not found the guy they were looking for, so by the time the day was out I'd convinced myself they'd be back and would this time of course come round the front, where I was. I couldn't sleep for the next few nights, instead lying in bed thinking of car-loads of guys driving around our campus looking for some of our senior ball players. Nothing happened for a few days and I was beginning to let myself hope that the whole thing was going to die down and disappear. I was still as skilled as ever at imagining scenarios with which to scare the crap out of myself and now, for the first time in my life, there was actually some justification for it.

The following Saturday, in broad daylight, just as the dust was settling, the pissed-off boyfriend finally managed to confront one of our biggest players and punched him in the face. When I heard this I was shocked; that it had happened at all, but more so that our guy had just taken it and not retaliated. Why hadn't he just battered him? The answer, I was assured, had been the pissed-off boyfriend's gun. This shit was getting too real for me. Our guys, the ones from out of town, were calling all the people they knew from back home for protection. I was afraid; who did I have for protection? All the streetwise dudes I knew were 3,000 miles away in Manchester and, as much as some of them liked a scuffle or two, travelling that far for a kick-off was beyond even them. I was also afraid because any one of us could've been targeted just for being part of the team, even if, like me, we were innocent of all girlfriend-offending charges. Eventually everything calmed, an older brother of one of our players managed to resolve the situation without shots being fired and the whole kerfuffle was quashed. Thank God. It could have gotten real ugly, and aside from that I didn't want to spend my time wishing I was back at home, wasting this opportunity I'd been given by getting involved in something that (before the availability of live firearms) would have been just a petty squabble.

By the time the end of the school year rolled around our little brush with the boys from the hood was all but forgotten. We didn't want to totally forget it, now that any real threat had passed and all was calm it was turning into quite an anecdote, and I knew by the time I hooked up with my boys in Manny that summer, I'd be able to impress them and have them laughing with tales of it all. The year had been a great introduction to college life and to life in the Big Time. It had also galvanised the change that had begun in me at Claymont. Life at WSU was more free from racial tensions but was just as segregated, albeit in a different way, and as the year had progressed I'd found myself increasingly identifying with the black culture on campus. I'd only really notice it in my proper (my second) freshman year when my brother Gid came to visit. At a party a couple of the guys referred to a black dude we knew as an 'Oreo' (black on the outside, white on the inside) and when Gid saw me laughing along, he called me a knob and said that I'd changed. I couldn't argue, I had changed. He thought I was laughing at him, but I didn't see him in that way. Growing up in Widnes there'd been no black culture for us to have identified with. I'd changed because I felt I'd found something to belong to, but it hadn't changed my respect for him.

As the year had progressed I'd watched my teammates grow on court and it left me more pumped-up than ever to explode into my 'freshman' year all skills blazing. Chris and Eric had both developed throughout the season in spite of inevitable court-time frustrations. They'd impressed me since the first time I'd seen them both play back in high school and by now we were all good friends. On the court Chris was a cat-quick point guard with mad skills, off the court he was a joker who was liked by everyone. He reminded me a lot of the star of the sitcom *Martin*, comedian Martin Lawrence. Eric was an excellent defender, really strong, and could move his feet laterally as well as anyone I'd seen play. He had a pure 3-point stroke, and was a great shooter, but sometimes struggled getting to the rack and finishing. Eric kind of adopted me; he was a local boy and took it upon himself to take me under his Dayton wing. Through our freshman year we'd often visit his parents' house for some much-craved home cooking, we'd go to watch his old high school play, hit the malls, and just generally kick-it together. Too young to be hitting the bars and clubs, we found our fun elsewhere and for the first time I managed to properly combine training and a social life.

I'd always manage to squeeze in some time down in Knoxville with Al whenever I could and by now no place and nobody was safe from the little pranks we'd spend our time entertaining ourselves with. One time we went to a mall so that I could buy some dress shoes; being at the mall with Al was always funny. By now he was like some kind of God in that tabernacle and, knowing him so well now, it would make me laugh that any person serving us would want to please him so much. It seemed strange: he was just a person to me. Anyway, this day we thought it might be funny to see how far we could push it and that poor shoe-shop guy had run back and forth showing us every possible pair of shoes imaginable. '*How do you like these, sir?*' he asked, pulling out these ugly thick-soled boots. 'No thanks,' I said 'I'm not planning on hiking today...meooooow!' We were laughing uncontrollably surrounded by a fortress of shoe boxes which seemed to seal us off from the rest of the shop. It was a little mean, but our japes were always more mischievous than malicious.

It was great to be surrounded by young guys like Al or Eric who were in the same boat and shared both our free-time and loads of laughs. At WSU I'd found a really tight group friendship with the other guys on the team and when I'd look back over my year, the absence of any game time at all meant that my abiding memories were of fun times like these; of messing about with Al, of cruising round in 'yellow princes' car; a dude we knew called Tony driving a bunch of us all packed in tight. He had a thing for those 'Vanilla Tree' air fresheners and had so many adorning his car that you could smell it coming up the road. The chemical scent was enough to make you dizzy and every time I smell one, I'm there, cruising the streets of Dayton all young and carefree.

A Freshman (finally)

My second year at Wright State (sophomore year in that I'd been a student for twelve months already, but freshman in terms of playing) was a year of enormous contrasts. Although aware of the intense excitement of returning to college and now finally getting the chance to go out on court with the team, I left England under a cloud. The goodbyes we'd made were almost unbearable. Somehow, in typical defiance of all medical expectation, my dad had already survived for months beyond anything that had been initially thought possible. But it had been a gruelling year for him, a long course of draining chemotherapy had been followed by enormous blasts of radiation to shrink the original tumour and the treatments had taken their toll. Although physically he hadn't changed too much (he would eventually die still weighing in excess of 280lbs), anyone who knew him could see he was gravely ill. A grey tinge never left his skin and even standing for a few minutes would leave him so strained his breathing would become a physical presence in the room, something with an existence all of its own. I'd left the previous summer in fear that I would never get to see him alive again, and he'd proved me wrong. As much as I wished it, I knew there was no way that could happen for a second time, and so the goodbyes we said now were sure to be the last moments we'd share.

How can you say goodbye properly to the man who raised you for thirteen years? What are those words? Stood on a cold dark street in Liverpool city centre, waiting for the bus which would take me down to Heathrow for my return flight to the States, none of it made any sense to me. I feel the pain of it every time I think of that goodbye. I must have found those words, what they were is now long forgotten but the mark they left will always remain. The paradox of the moment added to the complete unjustness of the whole thing. No one wants to be faced with this kind of trauma and, poised as I was on the brink of the culmination of everything I'd ever wished for, the whole thing was reduced to some futile nightmare. Dad would never have forgiven me had I abandoned this once-in-a-lifetime window that we'd worked for so long to prise open, but the cruelty of the timing and the choice I was forced to make has always haunted me. It always will. We agreed that I would go back, that I'd make the dream a reality in every single way I could, but the fact that I was off in the States, all those miles away, having a great time, whilst my family was back home watching my dad suffering and dying every day, is a spectre hanging over the birth of my career. In some cruel way, life made a man of me that year.

Once back in Dayton, I'd have to force such thoughts into a different form. Instead of beating myself up, distracting me from the thing that I'd vowed to do for him, I turned thoughts of my dad into a driving force. I'd always been doing this for him and my mum as well as for myself, only now that whole sentiment had so much more power, an energy that collided head on as I arrived back on campus with the electrical buzz of anticipation that was already surrounding our Midnight Madness. In the crazy world of American college ball, every single atom of movement is something to be celebrated, an opportunity for commemoration and excitement, and so something even as seemingly insignificant as the first day of practice is jumped upon and mauled into an excuse for a party.

Through my years of following college ball via the tapes that Dean had shipped over to me, I'd got to know the sport inside out; its intricacies, its idiosyncrasies and above all it characters. None of whom, for me at least, came bigger than Dick Vitale. A former coach, Dick Vitale progressed from New Jersey high school basketball legend, to Head Coach and Athletic Director at the University of Detroit and on to coaching the Detroit Pistons through the 1978-'79 season and into the season of '79-'80. Abruptly sacked as coach twelve games in, a friend offered him work at the fledgling cable network ESPN to fill time until another coaching opportunity appeared. Over thirty seasons later, he's still there. Initially reluctant but encouraged by his wife who urged him to *go on TV and have some fun*, he turned out to be the kind of natural broadcaster who transcends the commentary box to become a legend in his own right: the voice of college basketball. I loved him. Listening to his commentary was a dream for a kid like me, always one for a quippy one-liner and anything I might borrow to adopt as my own catchphrase: Dick Vitale has made a career from these.

Totally over the top, some of the crazy sayings he coined are now part of the fabric of basketball. To Dick Vitale a promising freshman is a *'diaper dandy'*; a game which is full of *'trifectas'* (3-pointers), played by *'P.T.P.ers'* (prime-time players) and ends in a *'Maalox Masher'* (a close finish) would be *'Awesome baby, yeah, yeah, yeah!'* Managing to communicate his utter love for the game through his words, back home in our front room I'd be laughing myself sick at some of Dick Vitale's commentaries. He describes a really exciting play as a *'super scintillating slam jam bam!'* and the kind of slam dunk that used to make the crowd in 'The Pit' lose the plot, as a *'dipsy-doo, dunkeroo, diddle-dop, slam-jam-bam pudding pop baby!'* Although embedded in college ball, he also commentated on NBA games and has become such a national treasure that he's also featured in cameo roles in a number of films and TV shows. In the world of Big Time, Dick Vitale is worshipped and somehow Wright State had managed to get him to host our Midnight Madness.

The celebrations that go along with the first day of practice in college ball go some way towards explaining just how big time the Big Time is. At the stroke of midnight, the Raiders would take to the court and undertake our first training session of the season, accompanied by the school band and cheered along by not only our cheerleaders but a massive crowd of fans all so eager for the season to start that they were prepared to come to the Nutter Centre in the middle of the night just to watch us have a bit of a game. There was much anticipation for our 1992-'93 season and to have the legendary voice of college ball there to rev our fans up even further was so phenomenal it was almost surreal. Every player was acutely aware that if Dick Vitale mentioned your name on air then you truly had a shot at making the pros, and here he was, in our gym, coming through our loud-speakers, commenting on our intra-squad scrimmage. Awesome

Baby!

Much of the hype surrounding the forthcoming season centred on the fact that it was Bill Edwards' senior year, his last year as a Raider, and all predictions stated that the season's finale would be his recruitment into the NBA. A pre-season favourite for conference player of the year, and a projected late first-round NBA pick, Bill was all business. He'd finished the previous season with an average of around 21-points per game and had returned to college with the expressed intention of upping that average to 25-. Bill was one of the main reasons I came to WSU. To be around a player of NBA calibre was valuable experience in itself and to have coaches say that I resembled him was an honour. I watched his every move on the court closely trying to pick up new things. Long and thin, he was nonetheless really strong and dominated every practice. I've a vivid memory of the moment I realized how far I still had to go. It was seeing Bill bench press 315 lbs. In college he was one of my idols, he was great at rebounding, had an uncanny scorer's touch, and a definite scorer's mentality; he could shoot the 3-, not just stationary, but could cross you up, then hit one in your mouth from deep. Pretty impressive for someone standing 6'8".

Getting the opportunity to play alongside someone you idolize is pretty special. Performing in the same forum as players you've always looked up to allows you to focus on the progress you're making. As well as Bill I was also at the time a massive fan of Ron Harper, Sean Elliot, Scottie Pippen and a player called Anfernee 'Penny' Hardaway. Penny was unbelievable, lauded for his versatility, he'd started his career at high school with a per game points average of 36.6! At the time I was a freshman at Wright State he was about to be drafted by the Orlando Magic and would enjoy a career of highs and lows plagued as he was by career-threatening injuries. The following summer, I'd find myself playing against him. At the time he was dating a WSU girl and hearing that he was coming to visit a group of us arranged a pick-up game with all the best ballers from our school and around Dayton. I got the 'nod' and was privileged to play with a future NBA All Star. He was serious, giving even my boy Bill a hard time on court. He was 6'7", had devastating quickness and Hops, and was a true point guard. I wanted to be just like him. I played really well that day, and almost burst with pride when he gave me some props. Little did I know then that years later, when I became the first English guy ever to play in Italy's Serie A, I'd earn myself the nickname 'The English Penny Hardaway'.

Back on court us Raiders started the '92-'93 season in style. Bill, true to his word, was working to achieve his points-average and in one early game he left the court, ten minutes still remaining on the clock, with the 45-points he'd dropped under his belt. It was great to play alongside him that season, he was a true leader and I looked up to him a lot but it was a tough relationship. Maybe he'd heard all the talk of me stepping into his vacated shoes and needed to make sure I was up to the job. Whatever it was, he was always on me to toughen-up, cussing me out, telling me I was weak. Years later, when I asked Bill for his memories of this time what he said floored me: *'The coaches had been raving about Del's skills as a player and I remember he had a wiry frame with a quick first step and leaping ability. I'd been the leading scorer on the team the previous two years but as I watched from the sidelines, I thought "Wow this kid is good! I'm going to have to step up my game if I want to stay the Man on this team."'* I had no idea that Bill had been thinking these things at all and when he told me *'Your talent level helped push me to be a better player and compete in practice to be better'*, it kind of shocked me. Bill could have a mean attitude sometimes, but then maybe that's what you need in the world of ball. Maybe a little more of that meanness would have taken me to different places, had I had it in me. He wasn't mean all the time though. My arrival had been tough for him too as some of the elder Raiders statesmen would use my presence to wind him up, saying he had competition now. Sometimes Bill managed to laugh it off and many times I'd leave practice to shouts of Bill putting on his 'English' voice: *'Oh he's off at four again, off to take tea and biscuits with the Queen!'*

Whatever I thought he was thinking at the time, Bill stood around 5th in the national table for scoring and was about to lead the Raiders to the conference finals. Facing the University of Illinois at Chicago (UIC) at home, we needed just one last victory to gain an automatic bid to the 'Big Dance', the NCAA Tournament which pitted the final 64 teams in the nation, the cream of the crop, against one another for the season's ultimate crown. UIC had some amazing players, and their point guard Kenny Williams specifically enjoyed an outstanding game that night, but their efforts were in vain: Bill doggedly put us on his shoulders and dropped 38-points!

The game was crazy, and our victory sent the home crowd wild, storming the court as the buzzer sounded and leaving such a scene of elated mayhem that Chris McGuire had to be taken away on a stretcher. Our program had enjoyed only seven years in Division One, and now here we stood ranked among the top 64 teams in the entire nation! It had been a good first season for me all round and to top it like this was amazing. Even though I was officially a freshman, I'd enjoyed more court-time than I'd dared hope and only had one game in which I didn't get on court at all (the first of the season against the No:1 ranked Kentucky Wildcats, at Rupp Arena). We'd come full circle by the end of the season; my final freshman game was against the new No:1 seeds, Indiana Hoosiers. I was now enjoying 33 minutes of court-time; a statistical measure of progress and of the increasing strength of my position in the team. As so often happens, my success was (in part) due to the misfortune of another player. It's a basketball theme, there's only room for five out there and each man on court is watched from the bench by his teammate who might only get on court if there's a reason for him to get off. In the third game of our season the most disgusting sight I'd ever seen on court occurred, with Sean Hammonds and his kneecap (so dislocated it was forced around his leg to the reverse of where God intended) being stretchered out of the season. A world of highs and lows, his devastation was part of my opportunity and as sorry (and as sick) as I felt, I needed to step-up. I did. Starting in ten games (five early on, and then the last five of the season and into tournament play), we ended up with 20 wins and 10 losses and stood an impressive third in the nation in scoring, at 93-points per game.

The 'Big Dance' loomed and an air of excitement buzzed around campus. A week before the start of the tournament the match-ups would be announced live on ESPN. It was a massive deal for the Raiders and seeing who we would be facing was both exciting and terrifying, something that might mean the difference between glory and devastation. It was arranged that the team would go together to the Holiday Inn on Sunday afternoon for a team meal. A big screen would be put up there so that all the players and staff, some fans and the TV crews would get to see the draw live. It was a monumental day for Wright State, something the team as a whole had been working towards since some of its current players had barely been starting elementary school. We were really excited. And then, that morning, the phone in our apartment woke me up and God delivered his blow.

My dad died on Sunday morning, 14th March 1993, just as the sun was breaking through the spring clouds. It's a testament to his strength and to the strength of my mum and the rest of the family that he was able to live out his illness at home. The day before he'd seemed remarkably bright, after a difficult few weeks he'd got up and spent some time downstairs. He'd gone to bed that night tired, but then he'd had eighteen months of tired. Tired is what fighting cancer makes you. In the morning he'd barely woke. His breathing had an ominous rattle and at around 11am he'd breathed his last. In his own bed, with people who loved him. The phone call that woke me came a little later. Mum giving me the chance of a little more sleep before the knowledge of the day struck. It was expected and simple and just how life is, *'he's gone'* mum said and he finally was. When my roommate that season (our starting centre Mike Nahar) came into the room, laughing and joking like usual, he found me crying. He tried to console me as best he could, but what was there to say? This was my dad, the man who had been such a part of my dream, the dream I was finally here living, one that he would no longer now be part of.

Being alone, without my family, was probably the hardest thing. Back in Widnes everyone was together, Kim being driven up from Gloucestershire where she lived, Hannah's friend who'd been round playing in the garden gently sent home, relatives and friends arriving and endless, endless cups of tea being made. I was apart. Miles from anyone, and due in a couple of hours at the Holiday Inn, to celebrate the draw of the biggest tournament in our team's history. A year of contrasts. I walked through the day in a daze, what else could I do? When we got to the hotel I asked Coach Brown to step aside. He'd always been a massive support to me and by now we were good friends so it was him I wanted to tell first. He hugged me and, as discretely as possible, told the coaching staff and team members that I'd just lost my dad. It put a real damper on everyone's mood. It was ironic timing, we were facing something that a few hours before had seemed as important as life and death and now suddenly life had reminded us that nothing is as big as death, not even the 'Big Dance'.

A few of the guys said some kind words to me and we watched together as the Raiders were drawn against Bobby Knight's Indiana Hoosiers, No.1 seed and (at that time) the greatest college ball team in the land. It was a double-blow: not only being drawn to face such an imposing team, but also a team who played only two hours' drive from Dayton. We'd been hoping for some amazing trip out to play in the sunshine of Florida or California, but the upside would be how many of our fans would now be able to travel to the game and offer their support which, in all honesty, we were going to need. The extent of the tournament only truly struck me once we'd stepped off our coach at Indiana's Hoosier Dome. An indoor football stadium, the Dome was the biggest space I'd ever stood in, even with half of the 100,000-seat capacity cordoned off by black curtains for the tournament, the size of it was damn near rude. Each of the eight teams in our region had been allocated a one-hour practice time in the Dome. Second to last spot, right before Indiana's, was ours. The place and the atmosphere was amazing, and the informal warm-up and shoot around we had was watched by a bank of press (who took up the Dome's first 15 or so rows) and around 20,000 college basketball fans. For the first time in my short career, even practice made me nervous.

As we strolled off court we were replaced by the Indiana team, whose presence made the crowd go absolutely crazy (even before they'd shot a ball) and who immediately lay down on court in a configuration of bodies which spelled out the word 'THANKYOU' to the elated crowd above. I had never seen anything like it before. I'd had two years in the Big Time and now here I was in the crazy world of full-on razzamatazz and mayhem which had, just a few years earlier, been the thing that fired me up to become part of it all. I was a permanent starter by now, and in the long walk from the tunnel to the court I tried to focus on getting my nerves together. All I could think about was dad. To fly me home for the funeral would have meant money we simply didn't have. It would be found somehow if that's what we'd decided, but mum had made it clear to me from that first phone call; given the choice, dad would have wanted me here, to face the biggest game of my life, not at home standing in a crematorium where he no longer was anyway. I knew she was right: this was the biggest stage imaginable; I was (finally) a freshman, starting against the best college basketball team in all of America in front of 43,000 fans, being beamed live across the world to an audience of millions. I forced his memory into every muscle of my body, heard his words in every cell of my being, taped a black strip across my jersey and sprinted and sweated all over the hardwood just for him.

Am I setting you up for a Hollywood ending? Sorry, Indiana was an outstanding team. They were immensely strong and included the 1993 NCAA Player of the Year, Calbert Cheaney. Bill Edwards felt a lot of pressure. NBA scouts packed the bleachers[xi] and Bill forced a lot of shots, shooting several air balls, and performing way off his best. He had carried us the entire season and it was heart breaking for him to go out on such a sour note, tarnishing his NBA hopes just at the moment it mattered the most. To use an old Manchester term, we ended up getting battered; by 40-points. My own time on court left me with just 6-points (and a fond memory of a nasty dunk in traffic, just to soothe the pain). Our dream had been obliterated, and with it, reality set back in. The season was over. It was back to class, and to the summer lull that preceded the whole crazy carnival starting over once again next season. Somehow Gid had managed to scrape together some cash. There was to be a small ceremony in a week's time, a family-only thing that would see the burial of dad's ashes in a plot in Widnes cemetery. I'd be able to fly home briefly to attend and then fly back to finish the last few weeks of school before the summer vacation began. We didn't tell mum, thinking that the surprise would give her some much needed pleasure and when I walked into the kitchen that day, she looked as though she was seeing a ghost.

A Sophomore

It was early in my sophomore season that the enormity of life in the Big Time hit me for real. I was laid up in my apartment watching TV when the sports news came on, and there I was. A show-reel of some of my highlights to date was followed by the grave announcement that I'd be out of ball entirely for the next two weeks due to a separated shoulder. It was news to me. I knew I was hurt of course, I'd been icing my shoulder since that afternoon's practice when our walk-on guy[xii], Sterling Collins, had pump-faked as I went up to block his shot and I'd landed on my head and shoulder. It was sick; I'd been really high up, had come back down to the hardwood with a thud and was now laid up, for a fortnight apparently. I couldn't help a cheeky smile through the pain though, not only was I about to experience the best sports medicine that money (or, in my case, a scholarship) could buy, it seemed I was also now big time enough for my absence to feature on the sports news. Not the way I wanted recognition, but it was recognition nonetheless.

That it was Sterling who made me land on my head seemed to spark something else off. At 28 years old he was a 'walk-on' which meant that he hadn't earned a scholarship, but was nonetheless part of the Raiders' team and therefore practised alongside us each day. His age made him stand out. In some ways it was odd to have a guy so much older than the rest of us on the team, but his maturity was priceless, a team of young guys, hungry and desperate and in-experienced, often benefits from a little grounding: we called him 'Pops'. In addition to having experienced something us college guys had yet to even think too much about, the real world, Pops was also a Lieutenant in the U.S. Air Force and along with the full weight of his body, it was his role in the forces that now struck me and sparked-off an idea.

The summer had been difficult. The first time I'd spent more than a couple of days back in England without my dad being around. Dad had left a huge gap in everyone's lives and his death seemed to prompt a summer of conversation and introspection which in turn prompted me to do something I'd been thinking about, off and on, for some time: trace my biological mother. I spoke to my mum about it and she was immediately encouraging. She'd always made it clear to us adopted kids that should we ever want to expand the limited knowledge we had about our parentage then she'd be right behind us. So what did I know? Well, at the time very little. When I'd been collected at the agency office in Liverpool I'd been handed over by staff. The woman who'd given birth to me had decided to leave me in temporary foster care for the five weeks it would take to sort out the paperwork which would officially make me Kay and Dave's son, and so I was delivered into their care with nothing but a blanket and a letter written by my biological mother. In it she'd detailed the barest minimum, her age and a little of her background, and had included some information about my biological father. He was black, he was in the Air Force, and the few dates that they'd shared had come to nothing (except the production of me, of course) and so he was completely unaware of my existence. And that was it.

Getting in touch with my biological mum was actually really easy. The lady who'd arranged my adoption had left details of how to contact her in the future, which were miraculously still valid all these years later, and she was able to give me an address for my maternal grandmother. Aware that I was only in England for a matter of weeks, I wasted no time in writing and she immediately responded, including her telephone number and an invitation to call. That call was surreal, I said 'Hello this is baby Leon' and she sounded so thrilled to hear my voice, the voice of baby Leon, 20 years old with a deep American twang, that I was really touched. She was really interested to hear that Leon Courten had grown into Delme Herriman, who now lived in the States, and couldn't wait to call her daughter to tell her that, after twenty years, baby Leon was making contact. I was due back in the States, so I left my details and my grandma assured me Kay would be in touch.

Wright State University is on the doorstep of one of the biggest Air Force bases in the whole of the United States: Wright Patterson. I started to think it might be fate. Since I'd arrived at WSU the unlikely thought that any one of the guys based at Wright Patterson might be my dad had been gradually developing. I didn't know whether my biological dad was still in the Air Force now, I didn't even know whether he was English or American, but what I did know was that this burning desire to be in the States had so far shaped my life, and I wondered if perhaps there was some kind of other destiny underpinning that. A letter came from my biological mother, Air Force Lieutenant Sterling Collins landed me on my head and I put the potential of two and two together and allowed myself to think; what if? The intrigue about my biological dad had been getting stronger since I'd been about 13, it sort of coincided with the birth of my love of basketball and maybe the two were interlinked: meeting all those guys in Manchester whose dads had the same coloured faces as them, it wasn't conscious but it was possible. Now I began to think that maybe Sterling, with his Air Force links, could help me trace my dad. But if that was going to happen then I needed a little more info to go on.

Maybe Kay and I were never destined for the tearful mother-son reunion, maybe my interest in my dad overrode any real interest in her and maybe that stung her a bit, I don't know. It was good to get her letter, to hear a bit more about her, but it had always been my father I was most interested in hearing about, so I responded to her letter immediately but with a barrage of questions about who my dad was and about where he might now be. All I could do now was wait.

It didn't take too long for my first major injury to heal. Thanks to the unbelievable level of care and treatment that college ballers get, the predicted two weeks was all it was and I was back to practice and looking forward to the season ahead. I was still just a sophomore but my role on the team now differed greatly from the previous season. Two of the Raiders' best players had moved on (Bill to the CBA) and the main task for the season ahead, in addition to winning games, would be rebuilding the team in its new form. Mike Nahar, centre, 6'11" in his socks, was our go-to guy now and things would need to be re-shaped. Mike was a great mate of mine; I'd instantly liked him from when he'd been my guide on my WSU recruiting visit. We got along great and had some significant things in common: growing up in Europe; being of mixed-heritage; both having sat thousands of miles away dreaming of one day playing college ball overseas; not having our families in the country and having to negotiate a new culture alongside a new sport (there was, at that time at least, a major gulf between European and American ball). Mike had been a WSU project. For his first two years of college he'd been really skinny and weak (something else I could relate to) and hadn't taken too seriously to the sport. He was an excellent student, but boy was he wild when he drank. Mike loved to party and when he'd get this crazy look in his eyes, we'd get a little scared and know all too well he was about to pull some crazy prank. Mike had also been a red-shirt and during his non-playing year he'd decided to get more serious about ball. He started to live in the weight-room and it quickly paid off. His upper-body was now huge, his attitude to ball was now set and, if we could get our new structure together, his central role might see us achieve big things in the season ahead. It's funny the images that stay with you: after all the hours of drama we shared on court, and the two years we roomed together (him fulfilling the role of surrogate big brother), my most prominent memories of Mike are of him driving the first car he bought at WSU. He'd paid $800 for an old Caddy, so retro its tunes came on an 8-track. That damn thing must have been 30' long and he sailed it up to the front of our apartment block like he was negotiating the canals of Amsterdam.

There was little time to focus on re-configuring the team; we'd have to do that on the hop. Our season began in San Juan, Puerto Rico, at a tournament that featured Marquette; one of the most big time of Big Time teams with Tony Miller as point guard (a player who just a few years later would become a great teammate and friend of mine). It was the opening to a season of highs and lows. Mike had some big games and was one of the nation's leaders in field-goal percentage. Alongside Mike was Sean Hammonds, a 6'5" rebounding powerhouse who'd missed out on last season's 'Big Dance' due to that mashed-up knee. They were great players, driven by either having something to prove or something to make up for, but still we struggled. Jon and Eric had fallen out of favour with Head Coach and we'd lost Chris McGuire completely following his wise transfer from WSU to Miami of Ohio. With the other losses we'd suffered as senior players had graduated, the team we were left with was miles from the one we'd achieved so much with in the previous season. Both our guards, Rob Welch and Rick Martinez, were freshmen and were required to play a lot of minutes. Little Rick, a Mexican from California, had come with a rep'. He played in the smallest division of high schools and was lauded as an amazing shooter; he held a record for most 3-s in one game (if memory serves, 13!) and had racked up 26 assists in another. He was a great player but, to me, the best parts of his game were his handles and his passing. He also had some really tough defence, and a tough attitude to go alongside. He had a naughty crossover and fed me with many nice dimes over the years but (as this season would prove) he never really seemed to find his range and constantly struggled with his previously legendary shooting. As time passed I'd identify with some of Rick's frustrations. He got homesick a lot which didn't help his game and a part of me could feel where he was coming from.

The season passed unremarkably. The stability a team needs in order for its players to perform to their potential just wasn't there and we finished disappointingly with wins in only about half of our games. It wasn't only the turmoil in the team that affected us, it was the imbalance between the skills and talent of the players we'd lost and those we'd gained. Our new recruits just weren't good enough, not in comparison to the calibre of players who'd seen us into the 'Big Dance'. There'd be further changes to come, too. As the season wound down my roomie Nahar was looking for a job overseas. Without much of a shot at the NBA Mike signed a contract to play in Europe for the Portuguese team Benfica and so when the new season rolled around, he'd be gone too. It was an exciting time for him and in spite of knowing how much I'd miss my good mate, it was great to see him starting out on his pro career. It was clear that next season would bring more upheaval, but I had no idea then that I'd be trading one European giant for another and that the 7' hole left by the Dutchman would be filled by 310lbs of Ukrainian training machine.

In spite of the dramas on court, off-court life at Wright State was pretty good. I had a stable girlfriend, Tiffany Miller, who was a real rock throughout most of my college career. She was a year older than me and was settled at WSU, which in turn helped to settle me. I'd go back home with her sometimes and so her family became a sort of surrogate family to me. It was great having a home to go to (even if it wasn't my own) at the festive times of the year. No one wants to be the only guy on campus over Christmas and thanks to Tiffany and her family I always had somewhere to go to for good food and good company when Thanksgiving rolled around.

By now I felt really Americanised, it was no longer a novelty to scran-down on pancakes at the Golden Nugget' Pancake House in Huber Heights, it was normal. I'd never really identified myself as belonging in Widnes but it had still been home. By now leaving at the end of the summer was already easier. Dayton was home now, I had found somewhere I felt I was meant to be. By the time I was entering my sophomore year I had started to mainly identify myself with the black culture within Wright State, something that was reflected by the friends I mixed with and the parties I went to. I fitted in, almost. I had lots of white friends at WSU, too, but it was my acceptance into black culture which meant something different to me. It didn't matter that I was foreign; I was cool, from England, black and could ball and so I was accepted. But, acceptance or not, the question remained, where was I really from? Who was I really? I wasn't like my black friends back in Manny, I didn't have a Jamaican parent, nor was I like my new American partners, who tended to have parents who were both black and identified themselves as descendants from the atrocious days of Slavery. I didn't know where my culture was from and the even though the questions I'd put to Kay had finally been answered, her response hadn't helped at all.

My biological father, she wrote, had been based at RAF (Royal Air

Force) Stafford, in the Midlands of England between the years of 1972-'75. He and Kay had dated briefly, with their short relationship mainly consisting of evenings at RAF Cosford's weekly dance. After a really short time my dad confessed he not only had a wife but also two small children and ended his relationship with Kay. Soon after, discovering she was pregnant and fearing the reaction of her parents should they discover her pregnancy (and that the child she was carrying was mixed-race), Kay went to live in Yorkshire with her sister and I was born in the town of Harrogate. That was it. At the time I thought it was a lead, something to go on, a point at which to start. I was intrigued to know now that somewhere in the world I had at least a couple of other siblings I'd never met, but was also frustrated. The only piece of him Kay had managed to give to me was his name: Cass Williams.

It's not that I needed a father, what I needed was that click inside that I was sure would come if I could just get to know who I was. Cass. Was that short for something? Cassius, maybe? Caswell? Was it a nickname? Was Williams just a cover, after all, if he was some kind of player, hiding a wife and kids, what's to say that was even his real name? Was he Jamaican, American, of African origin? Was he in England? Might he be here in the States? Was he a sports fan, a baller, a guy at home watching an English kid beginning to get his props in the NCAA, not knowing the kid was his son? I was no nearer to knowing, but I was nearer to the realization that, regardless of where this dream I was now living eventually took me, I would never feel whole, never settle, until I knew where I came from. It's sixteen years since that letter and, in spite of a huge amount of searching, of contacting people who also served at RAF Stafford in the mid-'70s, his name is still about all I know. Recently I finally received a photo of him, sent to me by one of the amazing ex-service men and women who've been helping me in my search. The photo's black and white and features the guy we think is Cass on the back row of his basketball team! And it turns out his real name was Cass McCurdy!

As sophomore year came to a close, the summer promised something a little bit different this time. The past few years had been a pretty steady pattern of finishing school, returning to England, catching up with friends in Manchester and playing for the National Team. This year was going to be a bit different. I needed to stay a bit longer on campus to attend classes at summer school, an awful prospect, summer on campus is no fun at all with all the vibe having been packed up and shipped back across the States with the other students who dispersed across the country until September rolled around. This summer mightn't be so bad, though. I'd just turned 21 and had passed through the joke of a driver's test which would have constituted about lessons one and two of learning to drive back in England, and was looking forward to my boy Sean McKie heading out to see me for the first time. The ink barely dry on my license, I couldn't wait to get out on the road to take Sean for a spin and show him a few sights, so we hopped into a rental car and set off to visit my boy Allan Houston, way down in Knoxville, Tennessee. After all, it was only 5-hours away.

I'd managed to fit in visits to Al whenever possible over the last couple of years and the friendship we'd forged over ball and daft sayings in my first week Stateside had grown with us. It was great to finally get to take one of my boys from back home down there with me and, after a week or so of laughing, playing ball and kicking-it with Allan, we rounded off our stay with a particularly memorable night at a black club. It was on the wild side of town, but just off the University of Tennessee Campus and so nothing to worry about. Beneath several fly-overs and located in an ominous dead-end, the place gave my over-active imagination a strange feeling. It was weird and it made me nervous. But I put it down to my naivety. After all I'd never been to a black club in the hood before and so I said nothing. Al knew where we were going and I trusted him. Sean was unperturbed. He's from Moss Side, he was used to this kind of place.

Once inside I felt no better. And after an hour or so of strained tension we heard 'pop', 'pop', 'pop' and everybody ran towards this tiny space behind the stage at the back of the club. People were screaming and smoke filled the air. It was pandemonium. Everyone panicking and shouting about shooting in the club and once we made it outside, it was no better. Trying to drive away from that tabernacle was just ridiculous, the one-way

142

out meant that a jumble of cars were all jammed together jostling to get out of the dead-end. It wasn't my idea of a good night. But we managed to get out of there fast at the first sign of trouble and it left us with a good tale to tell. Sean wasn't bothered; like I say, he's from Moss Side.

Although it only happened a couple of times, such brushes with danger left me feeling innocent and foreign and were the only times I ever doubted whether I belonged in the States. The most shocking occasion was once when Sean and I were in a truck belonging to a guy from U.T. who I knew but wasn't close friends with. We were parked up and a guy close by was drunk and yelling. He started bothering us and I remember saying to the driver, 'Man, he's acting crazy!' '*He isn't going to get too crazy*' he replied and then, as if to reassure me, reached under his seat and flashed me his gun.

My chin hit the floor. I was so shocked. I had never even seen a gun up close before, and had no idea that this guy we used to kick-it with and have a laugh with in Knoxville owned one, let alone thought it was a good idea to drive round with it under his seat. Back in Widnes I'd wanted life to be like a movie and when it was on court or on campus I loved it; when it was like this, something from a whole different type of film altogether, I'd wish I was back in England being heckled at for not being white. I'd only wish it for a minute though.

A Junior

Whilst I was languishing the summer away kicking it in Manny, getting my props with the National Team and stocking up on Findus Crispy Pancakes, over on the other side of Europe a drama in which I'd play an unlikely future role was unfolding like some kind of James Bond sub-plot. Coach Brown had been given a tip-off about a young Ukrainian player who had more than a little promise and a burning desire (not dissimilar to my own) to get to the States and take a crack at the NBA. You don't have a career like the one Jim Brown's enjoyed without going that extra mile, whether that involves driving four hours down into the sticks of Ohio to follow up the whiff of potential or telephoning a complete stranger in Eastern Europe when you don't even speak the language. The first time he called Kiev, Vitaly Potopenko's mother, understandably enough, hung up on him. Coach waited a few days, maybe hoping that just willing it to be true might make him suddenly able to converse with whomever picked up the call. It wasn't to be: an increasingly baffled Mrs Potopenko hung up again. Tenacity is a much underappreciated trait in a Division One coach but it's absolutely vital if you're going to achieve anything at all and after a third unsuccessful call (by this time Mrs P might've been forgiven for thinking something dodgy was afoot), Coach decided to try a different tactic in order to get to speak to the increasingly mysterious (and still extremely promising) Vitaly.

Employing the might of the academic world in which he existed, Coach decided to enquire whether there was a Russian speaker in WSU's language department. Unbelievably there wasn't, but there might be at the University of Dayton. Within a couple of days she'd cracked it. She sat in Coach Brown's office, dialled, spoke calmly (and most importantly Russian-ly) to V's mum explaining that the weird hint of American stalking she'd been getting was actually a Big Time Division One US

College calling to woo her boy, and she put V straight on the line. The powerhouse of Ukrainian training machine who would arrive on campus in a few short months would prove worth the persistence, and the commitment of Coach Brown would stand once again as testament to both his tenacity and to his skills as a scout. But I'm jumping ahead, it was one thing starting to recruit V with talk of what WSU might be able to offer him, it would be a whole other ball game entirely trying to get the kid out of the Ukraine.

Ball works differently in Europe than it does in the States, and so does life. Especially in the Ukraine. As soon as Vitaly's current club got word that an American college were scouting round looking to recruit their star player, they were on the phone. WSU already had a lawyer on board, a friend of Coach Brown's who travelled back and forth to Russia on business and had agreed to help with V's recruitment, but it soon became clear that the type of negotiation that V's coach was interested in wasn't the type that conventional lawyers could help with at all. The Ukrainian club were swole, and wasted no time in calling Coach with their demand: WSU could have V, that was no problem, but to get him would cost a one-off payment: $50,000 cash. Coach, ever the gentleman, tried to laugh it off, explaining that was simply something which Wright State were neither able nor willing to do. They were offering V the opportunity to advance his career in the ultimate way possible, that was the deal, and they certainly wouldn't be engaging in any kind of white slave trade buy-out of the kid. With all the drama of a Ukrainian soap opera, Vitaly's coach slammed down the phone with a shout of *'You'll never get my player!'* He had the upperhand; he drove straight round to V's house and he confiscated the guy's passport.

It's difficult to imagine this type of Mafioso basketball world, but it certainly exists. Ball brings money (more money in some countries than in others, but money nonetheless) and where the potential to make money exists, so does the potential to abuse power and exploit people. It's laughable to think of Dave West or any other of my English coaches wanting to stand in the way of any chance I had of getting to the States and making it big, let alone him driving round to our gaff to steal my travel documents in order to keep me. The geography of where we're born matters, in a strange way it mattered to me and, for the moment at least, it really mattered to Vitaly Potapenko.

Although my story lacked any of the drama, the subterfuge, the mobster threat of V's, we shared that level of love for basketball and commitment to fulfilling our dreams which meant that whatever stood in either of our way, we'd overcome. And he did. On one of his trips to Ukraine, Coach Brown's lawyer friend managed to secretly secure Vitaly a new passport, tie-up the paper work and leave the country without anyone but V's immediate family and the Raiders' coaching staff knowing anything about it. All V had to do was wait. He couldn't tell anyone of his plans. Any teammates who'd heard about the college looking to recruit him were assured it was all over, he'd declined their offer and was, he promised, not going anywhere. When the time was right, V's parents drove him out to the airport. Paranoid they'd be spotted, and terrified of the consequences if V was caught trying to sneak out of Kiev, they left him huddled in the back of their car as they checked-in his baggage for a flight ultimately bound for Dayton, Ohio. When the last available chance to board came, Vitaly rushed from the car, into the airport and boarded his flight with seconds to spare. He'd made it. By the time V called home from the campus of Wright State to let his parents know he'd arrived safely, they'd already had a visit from his Ukrainian coach and the threats had begun.

Unaware of the spy-drama that had unfolded over the summer, I'd come back to school with a real buzz. I'd been anticipating my Junior year since I'd arrived at Wright State; I knew it was going to be a challenge because that's exactly what sport is, one challenge after another, one level reached only to be striving to supersede your achievements the minute you've mastered them. But I had a real sense that this year was going to be my big moment. It was time to step-up, be the man and show what I could do, to try to follow in Bill's footsteps and show that all that faith in me was justified. It was a fair enough assumption; I was the main returning starter and with no new recruits expected, it would be my season. When I walked into the gym on our first day of pre-season training, I knew immediately that things weren't going to be as straightforward as I'd assumed. Coach was working out one of the biggest kids I'd ever seen and, size aside, I could tell from first glance that he had something special: that indefinable thing you can only call 'it', Vitaly had it. The swagger, the mannerisms and the composure of someone who, in spite of being a 19-year-old kid, immediately identified him as a player who'd go places. Under Coach Brown's watch, Vitaly was playing two-on-two with a couple of other guys and as he spotted me, Coach beckoned me and another player to join the game. After the briefest introduction we got to play and I thought 'wow'. V decided to guard me, trying to deny me the ball all the way beyond the 3-point line! This guy was something else, 6' 10", 310lbs and trying to deny someone as quick as me the ball 25' from the hoop! It was going to be an interesting season.

Although his arrival had clearly tipped everything on its head for me and my expectations for the season, I took to V right away. He was cool, laid-back and fun loving with an ego the exact opposite of his enormous frame and talent. Rumour abounded right away that he'd been recruited as an NBA prospect and, before the reality of having to get him the ball on every possession sank in, it was exciting to think that we'd have renewed interest from NBA scouts, seeing them at the games like we'd done when they'd been looking at Bill. Soon enough the pressure would kick-in for everyone, not least of all for V himself, but for now I kind of took him under my wing. I knew all too well what it was like to arrive at a Division One college when you'd only ever dreamt of how it might be, I also knew how it was to have to acclimatise to a new culture at the same time. For V it would prove even more extreme; that dude barely spoke any English at all.

That Vitaly's few words of English included *'gym'*, and *'weight-room'* was completely indicative of the type of guy he was. The only things V wanted to do was play ball and lift weights. I had never been around a player more dedicated than Vitaly, and I'd been around some pretty impressive guys. By now Bill Edwards and Mike Nahar were carving out names for themselves across Europe and my old friend Allan Houston had been drafted 11th overall by the NBA's Detroit Pistons. But even these goliaths of ball had nothing on Vitaly when it came to utter one-tracked determination and focus. The guy was a machine. Coach Brown recalls how V stands out for him amongst the hundreds of massively talented guys he coached throughout his career, it's simple to sum up: *'I don't think I have ever coached a player who worked any harder than Vitaly'*. Even in pre-season his dedication and enthusiasm put the rest of our guys to shame. He'd work out three times a day and every single time I walked into the gym or into the weight-room, there he'd be. This one time, close to the start of the season with his American English rapidly improving, he asked if he could borrow me for a minute. I went over thinking he just wanted me to spot him for a while but he said no, that wasn't it at all. When I worked out what he wanted me for, I couldn't believe what I was hearing. Vitaly wanted to escalate the level of his workout. He already used to run up and down the steps of the 11,000-seater Nutter Centre as part of his regime and he felt it needed stepping-up. It would be more of a challenge for him if he could do that with me on his back! Ever obliging to a teammate, and always interested in a laugh, I agreed. We only made it half way up, mind. Like some 500lb lanky arachnid, he set off with the weight of us both like a man possessed, and when I realised how serious he was, I also realised there was no way I could risk my entire career on the chance that this crazy Ukrainian might drop me down hundreds of stairs. Although it would have secured me some kind of a legend, 'most undignified end to a career' wasn't the kind of accolade I was hoping for.

By now I had gotten used to practising in an 11,000-seat empty arena, and being stretched-out before every practice by one of the five student trainers who made up part of the enormous staff which looked after us like precious treasure. Such treatment was the norm here and throughout my fourteen-year pro' career I can honestly say I never had it better. Even practices were great. They'd already been very intense and now with our new Ukraine-Train amongst us, it was even better. There were a number of big boys on the Raiders' squad, specifically Thaddeus Burton who, despite being very young, was 6'9" and 270 lbs of man-child who loved nothing more than to mix it up. But even he couldn't come close to handling Vitaly and there were many times in practice that those boys were inches from coming to blows, turning the paint into some kind of wrestling arena. Vitaly's attitude was entirely no-nonsense. I'd experienced the attitudes of a number of Eastern European players already through my international experiences with England's National Team. They had a reputation for being completely obsessed and focused, but V was on another level. His mid-range game was ridiculous. I swear that guy never missed. If he got it on the block, it was curtains. I remember getting switched-off onto him in the post a few times, it must have taken me about five seconds to try and fight around him for position in the post. He was unbelievable and he brought with him another dimension to practice and to our team which turned everything upside down, on court and off.

Us Raiders had experienced something in the way of hype already with our recent excursion to the 'Big Dance' and the interest that had surrounded our former star Bill. But already this was something else. There was so much publicity and media attention around us; so many whispers and rumours and a real electric buzz about this kid from Ukraine and his NBA potential. And in all this, at the centre of the storm where it's quietest and most calm, stood Vitaly. V was just a kid and, to be honest, all he wanted to do was work hard and play. Yes he wanted to make the NBA (who didn't?), it was his dream, but all the pressure and the exposure sat uncomfortably with him. He had never played College ball before, nor had he ever been the centre of attention. Not like he was at WSU. And there were times (even early into our season) that the scrutiny and the intensity got the better of him. In order to perform to the level that Vitaly performed, treating even every weight session like some kind of Olympic shot at proving the limitless of your capacity, you're required to be completely singular in your thinking and it wouldn't always pay off for him. I asked Coach Brown for his memories of V and, in addition to his enormous praise regarding his dedication and the way he'd managed to adjust his style of play to fit into the American game, Coach reminisced *'you know, he could be very stubborn and sometimes Vitaly would just do it his way regardless of what any coach might say.'* It's one of the balancing acts of achieving greatness. In order to excel you need to shut out all distractions, but if you start to think of advice and coaching and support as distraction, something which doesn't concern you, you've had it.

It's a hard balance to achieve at the best of times, but as a guy far from home for the first time ever, in an alien environment where everything's so different from that you've been used to, it's almost too much to expect: especially at the age of 19. It was hard to see V put himself through it sometimes; he'd become frustrated and get really down on himself. All players experience a lack of confidence sometimes and V was no different. In spite of being a training-droid, he was after all human and would have periods of intense self-doubt. Our first game on ESPN, in the conference tourney, would prove a prime example. Vitaly started the game with a free-throw he'd shot thousands and thousands of times before, only to shoot a foot-short air ball. He looked destroyed; embarrassed and nervous, and so I walked right across to him, tapped him on the shoulder and said 'You straight V, come on.' He gained his composure and nailed the second one. It was the state of things to come. The season would be characterised by him finding it almost impossible to get really loose on teams because they would spend the whole week preparing how to stop us by stopping him, and by me struggling to find any kind of form within the confines of the new structure.

The focus on V, whilst stressful for him, was at least all about his own career. For the rest of us it was impossible to deal with. Even though he would have three or four guys on his back whenever he caught the ball, Coach would still urge him to shoot. He was a great player, but he would have been twice as good if the focus and pressure would've been taken from his giant shoulders: a pressure which had, in turn, forced most of our other starters into nothing more than robots and role players. We all had skills and they would still be called upon if ever the big man wasn't there, like in that now legendary game against Xavier in which the infamous

Shot was carved into Wright State folklore.

For me, junior season was up and down as usual, I did have some pretty impressive games, but a feature of my game which would always remain was beginning to come to the fore: I'd come to be known as Mr Versatility, there was already no danger at all I'd ever be known as Mr Consistency. I've always had an issue with pushing myself forward. In hindsight, a little more blind confidence and selfish play might've carved-out a different career. But when I did manage to come out from under V's huge shadow I could still show off the talents God had seen fit to bestow on me. I had a really good game against Xavier in Cincinnati. I loved playing the best team in the conference; it's a chance to really see where you stand as a player, to step-up and show what you can do. And I did, finishing a great game with 22-points and 7 boards. In our second encounter with the conference leaders, this time at our place, I had 16-points and 8 boards. An average of 19-points per game, against a team ranked in America's Top 25: quite respectable.

Whilst the rumour of the NBA circled around Wright State, my old boy Allan Houston was already carving out his career with the Detroit Pistons. I never doubted that Al would be a properly famous baller one day, any more than I doubted he'd ever forget his old friends once he was, and so when I next visited him I headed for Detroit. If I'd thought his celebrity was kind of funny before, now it seemed just plain big time. We were in a club called Legends in downtown Detroit when we found ourselves unexpectedly kicking-it with Montell Jordan. At the time his hit 'This is how we do it' was high in the charts and for some reason (maybe it was height, the dude's 6'8") we ended up necking shots of Goldschlager together. That cinnamony brew was going down a dream and we whiled the night away, Al, Montell and Widnes Del, getting bevvied-up and cracking jokes, Ta-neck back!

It was around this time that I found myself in even more impressive company, to me at least. I was playing in a pick-up game with Al and was already excited because Grant Hill (NBA Rookie of the Year, from Duke University) was supposed to be playing. I was only in town for the weekend and was due back at WSU the next day and his no-show was pretty disappointing. Nevertheless, we prepared for an informal scrimmage. There were a couple of Pistons playing, some local college kids and the odd American who played in Europe. Good company but nothing in comparison to the legend who then walked in. Calm as you like, as though he was just a normal person, Isaiah Thomas strolled into the gym and out onto the court. Now playing for Indiana Pacers and coming back from a serious Achilles Tendon injury, Detroit's legendary point guard, two-time World Championship winner, 12-time NBA All Star and out and out hero to me (who had spent hours and hours watching videotapes of him battling with Larry Bird and Magic Johnson) was stood in the same gym as me. He took the ball at the top of the key and, trying not to stare, I was on the other team looking around for someone approximately my size to guard.

'Yo young fella, I'm over here.' Was he talking to me? Was Isaiah Thomas talking to me? *'I'm right here young fella, come and guard me!'* He was. I walked towards him in a nonchalant fashion. Well in a manner which was as nonchalant as I could manage, which in hindsight was possibly not that nonchalant after all. I was nearly bursting at the seams with emotions: pride, shock, disbelief. I wasn't only getting to see an idol, I wasn't only about to meet him face to face, I was going on court to do battle against him. I thought of my boys back in Manny, if they could see me now they'd be scooping their chins off the hardwood.

He got me on the wing in one of those typically NBA style clear-outs, or Isolations, rocking the ball back and forth between his legs, and then hit a twenty-footer straight in my face. I'd seen him do it before, to Jordan and Magic many times in the NBA playoffs, and I couldn't believe he'd just done it to me. I shook off the shell-shock. Determined to show them what type of game this kid from England possessed, I told myself I must belong on that court with these guys, or else why would I be here? So I went for it. The first time I pulled up for a nice 3-pointer at the top of the key; the next time a guy who had been trash-talking since we got there came running out to block my shot in the same position as before. I pump-faked him, exploded right down the lane, and dunked it so hard in traffic! A voice yelled out *'Yo, we got a young Grant Hill here! We got a young Grant Hill right here!'* He was laughing as he shouted his props across the court; it was Isaiah.

I mightn't have been quite Grant Hill (at the time one of the NBA's top players) but then I wouldn't like to argue with a legend either and so I stored his massive compliment and went back to WSU a little taller than when I left. Added metaphorical height which boosted my confidence; saw me through to that ever-memorable encounter to come. 'The Shot' in that final game against the mighty Xavier would not only seal my name into Wright State history, it would be one of my most memorable moments on court. It was by far the highlight of my junior season, possibly even of my WSU career, and is something of which I have treasured memories. The day after 'The Shot', the Wright State media department had printed a hundred or so copies of a photograph taken by Nick Falzerano in case any Raiders' fans were interested in purchasing a souvenir. I'm told the picture sold out in minutes, it's a treasured possession for Raiders' fans of the day and a treasured memory for all involved. But in spite of our achievements as the season ended, I wanted nothing more than to leave Dayton forever.

I'd finished my season averaging a respectable 10-points per game, I'd hit the Shot against Xavier that would be talked about around WSU athletic circles forever more, and we'd made it all the way to the conference finals, but I was enormously unhappy. I'd averaged over 33-minutes per game, but I felt like I was being totally held back by the system that was now in place. I was really fond of Vitaly and knew all too well his potential and Head Coach Underhill's determination to see him through the draft, but I needed to think of myself, of my career. I knew it wasn't feasible to transfer schools now; I'd have needed the buffer of a red-shirt year for that and I'd used that option up already at Wright State. At the time, I spent much of my summers starting on the England Under 22 squad and was privileged to be coached by a great guy called Curtis Xavier. He was my biggest fan (with parents like mine, that was saying something), Curtis had really high hopes for me, I trusted his judgement above all else and so I called him for advice. I let it all out to my boy over the phone. I felt like I was playing in handcuffs. Any interest Head Coach Underhill might've once had in getting me to the next level had evaporated as soon as V's NBA potential had become obvious. Head Coach was driven by winning at all costs and now by getting V into the NBA. I've played under some tough coaches throughout the last twenty-five years but have rarely seen a man who could focus his energies so entirely on a single member of his squad. Luckily for me, Curtis Xavier talks sense. I had good friends on the National Team who would cut off their lanky toes to be in my situation; in a major college, starting, getting all the minutes, and I owed it to all the work I'd put in to at least come back and step-up for one final season. In the meantime, I'd be heading out with the Great Britain team that summer to the 1995 World Student Games in Fukuoka, Japan. Some much-needed props with my old boys would do me the world of good, I needed to quit moaning, to look to the future and to think that, even if your Coach does breathe every ounce of his energy into you, other people could still have problems, other people like V.

At Spring Break that year, the past had come back to haunt Vitaly in about as vivid a way possible. The vacation meant that WSU was like a ghost-town. Most people (us ballers included) tended to make the most of the first of the good weather to get away for a week or two of rest and, more importantly, fun. Vitaly was the only player who was staying on campus and as we had a potential recruit coming to visit WSU, V agreed to act as player-host (as I would do myself many times). The place was pretty deserted and so the tour can't have been that much fun. A potential freshman wants to see the facilities that might be on offer, but he also wants to catch some of the vibe of the place, something that only existed when there were students around to create it. After the afternoon's tour, Coach Brown took V back to his apartment at around 4pm and, as a thank you and also for some much-needed company, told him he'd be back by 6 to take him out to dinner. By the time Coach had returned home, V had already been on the phone and had left Mrs Brown in no doubt that he was in major trouble. About to call V to check he was okay, Coach was interrupted by a call from Head Coach Underhill who, in desperation,

Vitaly had also called. He was in a panic, but had managed to get across that his old Ukrainian coach had showed up at his door and demanded he take him back to Kiev right away. Managing to buy some time, Vitaly had gone with his coach to a restaurant called The Red Lobster, just off WSU's campus.

By the time Coaches Brown and Underhill made it to the restaurant Vitaly was visibly scared. The Ukrainian coach was an intimidating guy. He'd have to be, V was 310lbs of human-mountain but even he was terrified. He set off on a series of demands which culminated in his assurance that Vitaly would be accompanying him back to Kiev on a flight that evening and Coach Underhill listened to his tirade without flinching. Calmly, and with the authority of a man who had spent his entire career ordering young men much larger than himself around, Head Coach Underhill leaned in towards the Ukrainian: *'You are not in Russia now. You are in the United States and Vitaly is going nowhere.'* 6'10" of terrified kid left The Red Lobster sandwiched within the paternal protection of a pair of coaches. V was fought over, whether either of the Head Coaches involved in the tussle had his best interests at heart is perhaps another issue. But the Raiders' Head Coach was right; V was going nowhere, at least not if Ralph Underhill could help it.

A Senior (again)

The summer before I returned as a senior to Wright State for my final showdown had been spent on the international stage at the World Student Games in Japan. It had been a phenomenal experience and one which I felt deserved to be followed by an awesome season as I bowed out of Division One and on into... into what? By this point in my career it was clear to me that all those dreams of NBA stardom that dad and I had spoken about on those long drives to and from Manchester would remain just that, a dream. It was disappointing, of course, but I'd had time to get used to it. As I'd worked through high school ball and college ball, it had revealed itself slowly and so the pain of realization was more a slow burn than a swift stab. I'd lived two years in the shadow of Bill Edwards, an awesome player who I really respected and admired and even he hadn't reached the grade for the NBA. That, and numerous other knock-backs I'd seen around me, had led me to conclude that the NBA is entirely the reserve of those very, very few utterly exceptional talents. It had also led me to conclude that, whilst I wasn't one of them, I was someone with enough talent to make this passion of mine into a career, I just didn't know where yet.

Whatever the future held, the present held a return to Dayton: by now a place I considered to be home. Being a fifth year senior earns respect. I'd been on campus and on the Raiders team for longer than anyone else and had earned myself a kind of status, not only within college through making it happen on court for WSU, but also around Dayton from playing in pick-up games in not only the toughest spots in the city, but against the city's best players; Darnell Hahn, Chris McGuire, Eric Wills, Jervaughn Scales, De'juan Wheat, Renaldo O'Neal, Alex Robertson, Dwayne Bryant, Mike Haley, Bill Edwards and Tony Stanley. Street-ball was something I'd never experienced before I came to the States; it was also something that would (a couple of years later, through Midnight Madness) give me some of the abiding memories of my entire career.

I'd earned some respect with the coaching staff as well, and so at the outset of my senior season I managed to cajole the Raiders out of a feature of basketball which all players loathe - the most dreaded and feared words in any player's vocabulary: pre-season conditioning. I hated it, and never saw the point of spending that all-important period of time on other fitness activities when we might otherwise just focus on basketball. Pre-season conditioning would normally consist of running a timed mile on the first day, followed by a series of sprints on our indoor running track which was 220m and over-looked the four basketball courts of McLin gym. I appreciated that fitness, stamina and speed were essential elements in our sport but always wished the coaches would think of some way we might incorporate this type of conditioning into something a little more directly ball-related.

Throughout the previous years I'd kept my complaints to myself: never one to be openly critical or push myself forwards too much. And anyway I'd always been amongst the best conditioned players on the squad and so had tended to finish in the top three of every conditioning drill we went through. My record had earned me points and so with the confidence that comes with being a senior, I went to speak to Coach Brown to see whether for this six-week conditioning period, we could just 'play ball'. No crazy sprints, no hours and hours wasted on mindless running, just hard intensive ball. The rest of the team were behind me, I promised him and gave him my word that all the guys had vowed they'd work their asses off: they weren't bull-shitting just to get out of it, they genuinely wanted to focus on a different type of conditioning this season. College coaches (just like high school coaches) weren't allowed to be present in the gym when we played during this period, coaching wasn't part of conditioning and engaging in coach-player interaction during such practices was strictly forbidden. To my amazement Coach agreed, he sanctioned us 'just playing' on one condition; that we all played hard, always. I vowed I would get everyone to do just that and when I came back down stairs from his office and told the fellas what we'd managed to achieve, they were so happy. The mad props they gave me consolidated my role as a leader on the team and it felt good to feel I'd made it: a big fish in the Raiders' pond. Having someone believe in you is a real confidence boost and Coach Brown's decision made me feel he respected my leadership role (as well as confirming he was a really cool coach). He knew me well enough to know that I wasn't trying to pull the wool over his eyes; I'd work hard because that's the only thing I knew how to do.

It was to prove a difficult year. Vitaly was still our star and, as such, remained the focus of the Raiders' entire world. However, during the summer he'd decided he really needed to bulk-up (this is the guy who weighed in excess of 300lbs even before he'd entered WSU) and had focused his personal training programme on lifting. Not just any lifting, really lifting to excess and that, coupled with a complete lack of any cardio training at all, had changed him beyond recognition. If at the end of my junior season he'd been like a mountain, he was now bordering on being a planet. That tough-neck was enormous and as soon as pre-season had begun, it was clear that he was also in terrible shape. It was a real shame. He'd done what we all do, the thing he thought was best for him and his game, but it was a badly judged call, the extra weight slowed him down and smothered the natural talent which had previously radiated from him and throughout our entire team.

It would be two-thirds of the way into our season before V would manage to get back into shape and therefore get his groove back, but in the meantime him being effectively on court but out of the game changed absolutely nothing. I'd never had a particularly positive relationship with Head Coach Underhill (always feeling it was Coach Brown who championed me) and it had taken me some time to get used to the way in which the media would be an additional part of every relationship within the world of Big Time ball. I was confident that Coach Brown respected me as both a person and a player so, even if an off-the-cuff remark by him appeared in the press, I'd take it on the chin as constructive criticism; it was a different matter with Head Coach Underhill. Vitaly was his focus and he would be until Head Coach saw him drafted. Our first game of the season was a disaster and Head Coach pulled no punches when he spoke to the press. Wisconsin played in the Big Ten and enjoyed the additional honour of counting Michael Finley (the NCAA 1996 Player of the Year) amongst their starters. For all my versatility (the thing that would come to define me as a pro), I would be anything but versatile in my record of scoring in the season's opening games: nearly always leaving the court with only 6-points. Against Wisconsin I had the dubious honour of one of my worst shooting records too: an embarrassing 0-7 from the free-throw line. We lost and Head Coach Underhill wasn't happy. The next day the papers quoted his displeasure: I'd better be on my toes; a guy who can't hit his free-throws is in danger of the humiliation of losing his starting position to a freshman, he'd said.

It might be expected that a guy who'd already spent five years in the spotlight would get used to such knocks, but I never did. I had toughened up considerably; I'd had too, but had never managed to develop that rhino-hide necessary to let the views and comments of other people bounce off me like some lame back-board shot. Curtis had helped me remember I wasn't a quitter and I didn't regret returning to WSU to finish what I'd started. But one game in, it was clear that this year wouldn't be any kind of a final lap of honour; it'd be a slog. In spite of the awful shape of our star, Head Coach Underhill was undeterred: it was still all about V. I vividly recall a practice early in the season in which he'd said to me *'Don't even worry about shooting, passing, anything, you just REBOUND, and get the ball to Vitaly.'* It was exactly the kind of thing that would make my game just slump. It wasn't that I couldn't do it well; I could. In his more flattering moments, Head Coach would refer to me in the press as a tattoo-less Dennis Rodman. But in reducing my game to rebounding alone, I felt totally disrespected. It was a huge dent to my ego and made me feel like a scrub; like I was some one-dimensional stiff who didn't have the skills to do anything else. Sometimes his lack of faith in my game would floor me and I'd have to work to rebuild my confidence, other times it would get me swole'. I was far from one-dimensional and I would prove it.

The choice to be a sportsperson (of any sort I guess) is one which encompasses your entire life. Everything that happens on court affects everything that happens off court, and vice versa. There's no separation between work and life because your work is your life. For a person like me who's enthusiastic and honest, it's a positive choice, but for a person like me who's also unselfish and relies on other people's support and belief, it's possibly not. My season picked up once my mum came over to visit. Figuring she deserved some treat time, Gid had managed to sort it so that the two of them would come to stay for a couple of weeks. They'd see all the things around campus I'd been telling them about for so long, mum would take a little road trip to Niagara with Tiffany's mum whilst Gid hung-out with me and the guys and, most importantly, the two of them would get to take in as many matches as possible. I always stepped my game up when I had family in the crowd, as though I could feel them willing me on to the point that it would transform my abilities through transforming my self-belief.

I've always been a player who takes his role within the team seriously. Over the years, I met many ballers who would listen to what Coach said in practice and then disregard the entire plan as soon as his soles hit the hardwood in favour of playing his own glory-game. That wasn't me and so, much as it pissed me off, when Head Coach Underhill urged me to hit the boards and grab every rebound, I did exactly what was expected of me. In one particular game during my mum's stay, I'd been taking his words literally and by half-time had 10 rebounds. In the locker room, Coach Brown took me to one side. Rebounding like I was, I had a real chance to break a WSU record. The most rebounds in one game was a record held by Sean Hammonds. It stood at 21 awesome, but currently within my grasp and so it was on. I had a goal, something which always sharpened my focus; my mum was courtside, something which always boosted my confidence; and I had a real burning desire that before I graduated and left Wright State forever, I wanted to etch my name into the record books. I would etch my name (the glory of The Shot would ensure that) but it wouldn't be this day.

Back out on court the second-half began well. We were working together beautifully and when I skied for the boards, my teammates were clearing out the way. Over 10 minutes remained and I'd racked up another 4 rebounds, the record was in sight, only 7 more to tie, 8 to seize the crown. And then the horn sounded to alert the table to subs awaiting play and I was subbed out. I couldn't believe it. I hardly ever came out of the game! We were leading, it was going well, I couldn't fathom any reason why I'd been taken from the court and so I waited for a few minutes (if I ever did come off, I'd always be back on within a couple of plays). But the minutes stretched on and for one of the very few times in my WSU career I finished the game with the final ten minutes on the bench.

I'd taken to my role as team rebounder without complaint. Understood the role that the Head Coach figured I should fulfil and got on and done it to the best of my abilities. In a way, my attitude was suited to being the guy who focuses on rebounds; it's a role that requires a player to give himself up for the aims of the team. There was much talk after that game. Articles in the local press about the greater good of the team, about basketball being about more than one person's performance, the glory of one player. It's a debate that rages. But I didn't see my desire to achieve that record as being counterproductive to the team. I wanted it for me, but I would never have put that above what we might achieve collectively. I just wasn't that player and I never have been. It was the first in a number of 'nearlies' that season. Some of which made me more proud than others. During the last few months, I almost had two triple-doubles. A triple-double occurs when a player obtains double-digit stats in three different categories. But like a skint guy at the bar, I was always just a dime or two short: with 17-points, 10 rebound and 9 assists against Toledo and 17-points, 9 boards and 8 assists against Wisconsin Milwaukee, in my final home game. A little sneaky padding by the table would have seen me finish the season with at least some kind of record! Missing out on getting into Wright States' 1,000-point club, by only 12-points was the 'nearly' that hit me the hardest, possibly because this time there was no one to blame but myself. It's a regret that can be summed up in one phrase. I've heard it so many, many times from my peers through my entire career: *'Del! Shoot the damn ball!'*

Maybe it comes down to where I come from, or more specifically to not knowing where I come from. I had the hunger, it was revived even more by having mum in the Nutter crowd to will me on, but I didn't have that elusive thing that the really, really great players have: blind faith. I can't defend myself against the criticism that I never shot the ball enough, because it's true: I never did shoot the ball enough. Always too unselfish but then also always thinking what others might think or what they might say. Needing approval I guess, needing to be admired, respected. Just one more basket per game in my senior season would have easily seen my entry into the prestigious 1,000-point club. But there's no denying it, that need for approval was clearly stronger. Irony is, the guy whose approval it was I was craving, the elusive Cass, didn't even know I existed.

I strung together some good games during the final month. Mum helped a lot in being there; sat in the crowd with Tiffany, for once not needing to note down my stats in her little book. By now that was someone's professional responsibility. But in spite of my increased performance, and V being back to his old formidable self, we struggled to remain at .500. But come tournament time, just as we'd done the previous year, we managed to turn a mediocre season around into something a little more attractive. Once again we were fortunate enough to be playing the tournament in our own gym and, once again, with the Raiders' fans behind us through every second of the clock, we rallied. Producing our best basketball would face an immediate challenge, a brick wall that went by the name of Detroit Mercy. We always had tough games against them, but we always won. I, in particular, would find my game when faced by them with matches between us producing some of my most memorable dunks. In the previous season we'd met them in Detroit, and Al (by now one of the Pistons' stars) had come to watch me play. Our college careers (and his fledgling NBA career) had meant that the only time he'd ever seen me play was when we'd been one-on-one, two-on-two, three-on-three, just working-out during the summers, messing about and keeping in shape, and so I wanted to represent for my boy. As ever, a friendly face and a faithful heart in the bleachers lifted my game and the crowd was nothing but '*ooohhs*' and *'aaahhhs'* as I enjoyed not only the game-winning tip-in but a serious left-handed double pump gliding lay-up, where I took off on one side of the paint, ducked under three guys and scooped it home. I didn't let my boy down, but my career might have been a different story if I'd managed to transform that focus into one of not letting myself down.

A basketball game, like any other sporting match, exists only in legend (or in regret) once that buzzer has sounded and so, memories aside, Detroit were ready for us now. We had played them about five times over the last two seasons and, knowing from experience that they couldn't handle Vitaly one-on-one, every time the guy touched the ball they gang-banged him. Their defence was actually third best in the nation; holding teams to shooting under forty per cent. And coupled with that, V was having something that every baller has from time to time (some more than others): a nightmare game. But our game plan didn't change, it never did, we just kept pounding the ball into him regardless; living and dying with him. When you're off form, you're off form. Sports psychologists would make billions could they identify and eliminate the elusive thing which occasionally kills a player's otherwise impeccable game. That night against Detroit, we might as well have been pounding the ball into a fish. And so living and dying alongside V meant that this night we died. And so did V's NBA stock. It's incredible how quickly a career can be won or lost; I saw it myself when I managed to catch the eye of a guy who'd previously overlooked me just by slamming home a couple of dunks in a half-time mess about, and V saw it that night. He finished the game with 4-points and 9 turnovers and it would take him many, many hours of hard work in the gym after the season finished to get his stock back up at the NBA pre-draft camps.

My season, and my WSU career, my life in green and gold as a Raider, ended with the standing ovation which followed The Shot. It ended in a way that all of those mini-slumps, all of those confidence knocks, all of those balls I didn't shoot, could only have allowed me to dream of. It was time to leave Wright State, time to face the world, to see what it was that lay beyond the Big Time, to see what else besides the NBA was out there. To see if anything besides the NBA was out there.

A Pro

Whilst I was fretting and sweating about what was going to happen to me now I was no longer a Raider and no hope of the draft remained, another sportsman I'd never even heard of was fretting and sweating his own battle many miles away in the European Court of Justice.

In 1990 a little-known Belgian footballer reached the end of his contract with RFC Liège and looked to continue his career with the French team Dunkerque. A simple transfer scuppered by Liège's refusal to pay the requested fee left Jean-Marc Bosman trapped: unable to transfer he was effectively unable to work, unable to earn. His next move (his decision to sue his way out of the situation) took so long to come to fruition it probably didn't do the guy's career much good, but it did make him more well-known than the midfielder might otherwise have hoped to be, albeit not for the reasons he'd intended. Bosman interpreted his situation as being a 'restraint of trade' and took his case to the European Court of Justice. His eventual victory (in 1995) is officially known as the ruling in case C-415/93,ECR1-4921 regarding freedom of movement for workers; most people call it The Bosman Ruling.

Thousands of miles away, in Dayton Ohio, already missing ball and attempting to motivate my ass to complete the required classes (I wasn't going to leave WSU with a Golden Ticket to the draft so I at least needed to leave there with a Bachelor's degree), I knew none of this. Even if football had interested me, Bosman was too small-time a player to have received much notice, at least until now. I should've known, especially considering I'd end up owing the birth of my pro career to the guy; once again the timing would be perfect for me and Bosman's refusal to give up on his own career would directly influence the start of mine.

It was difficult for me to stomach, but there would always be England. WSU's failure to get back to the Big Dance meant the chance for vital exposure was lost; I might, after all, be heading back home. I was sure to secure some kind of pro contract in the BBL, English players with five years NCAA experience were rare, but that had never been my ultimate ambition. And then, just as my career looked like it would take a turn I'd always kind of dreaded, the Bosman Rule popped up and I was saved. It hadn't taken long for other sports to latch on to what the ruling meant for them and in terms of European Basketball, it meant a lot: essentially allowing any player with a European Union passport the permission to work in any EU country without being considered a foreigner. It doesn't seem much, but the ruling was an enormous deal. Previously teams could fill only two spots with players who weren't nationals of the team's country, and so those spots were always taken by Americans (high-profile college players like Bill Edwards or former NBA guys taking the first steps to retirement). What this ruling meant was that a Spanish team (for example) could now retain its two 'foreigner' spots for Americans and make another spot available for a player from any other EU country; Portugal, Italy, Germany, the UK, the pool of European talent was now wide open to them, and just in time.

One day I was in the wilderness, the next day my phone was ringing off the hook. A player like me, an EU citizen with five Big Time NCAA years up my jersey, was a dream for a European club: essentially American in terms of experience and conditioning but now recruitable within the ranks of regular European players. Pro Agents, never known for their reticence, clicked on to this within days of the ruling and so any Division One baller with the skills and the passport (a pretty limited bunch, back then at least) was pounced on and recruited fiercely. It was like winning the lottery. Possibilities started spilling from my phone almost hourly meaning that now I wasn't only pretty much guaranteed a start to a pro career, that career would be in the world of Continental European ball: okay, not the NBA but the next best thing.

It was surreal. Alien voices with thick foreign accents shouted stats and offers at me across the Atlantic, baffling me with information and throwing salary figures at me that were damn near rude. So many agents with so many different opinions all sharing one thing; the certainty that they were the guy to get me the best deal. It was easy to get overwhelmed, tempting to be carried away. Within the first week I had a job offer from Vitoria Taugrés, a huge Spanish top division team. Heading into their playoffs, they couldn't wait 'til next season, they wanted me then: $70,000 to head out right away. I couldn't believe my ears. Money had never been the most important part of the dream but it was a massive consideration. I'd been skint for that long that the number of zeroes they were throwing at me were blinding.

It was tempting, extremely tempting. I still hadn't decided on an agent to sign with but a couple of the guys I was talking to suggested that a move to Vitoria Taugrés (or anyone else) at this stage in the season could be disastrous. I needed to see the bigger picture, not just the string of zeros tied to the deal, general consensus seemed to be that it would be incredibly tough to gel with a team at this late stage and that any performance which wasn't seriously impressive might permanently dent my stock. The offer had come from a team within the top three leagues outside of the NBA (the others being Italy and Greece); a promising start, but general feeling was that my priority was to secure a decent agent and sit tight whilst he worked on securing me a contract for the coming season.

I was already leaning towards one in particular, Dejan Vidicki from an agency called Courtside. Dejan, a Yugoslavian working out of Amsterdam, was hard on me every day and convinced me that signing directly with a European agent was the smartest move as a US one would only have to sub-out to a European guy as soon as he hit the language barrier. It made sense, but still felt like a massive decision. The choice to opt for Wright State had been simple in comparison, I'd seen the facilities and jumped on board. All I knew of these agents were snippets of their reputations and the tone of their voices. Courtside's rep' read well: the largest European agency with an impressive roll of players and contacts across the continent.

Whilst I mulled my choices I shut myself away in Coach Brown's office (relieved to be away from the constantly ringing phone) and got to work on making my highlight tape. A really fun task. Luckily Coach had every one of my college games on tape and I had a good memory. I searched through all the games in which I knew I'd played well and recorded the most impressive parts. The editing left a lot to be desired but the final product was sweet, and five hours later I held in my hand 45 minutes of some serious performance against some tough competition. It didn't seem a bad result for five years hard slog. I mailed the tape to Dejan along with one of a normal game in which I'd played to my average. A single highlight tape isn't sufficient for a serious agent; most half-decent players can cobble together evidence of some cheeky moves, making themselves look great on a highlight tape without evidencing whether they have any clue how to actually play the game. The day after he received the tape Dejan called. He blasted his amazement and excitement down the phone and told me my tape had not only already been copied, it'd already been mailed across Europe throughout the network of agents Dejan worked with. It was on. In for a penny and all that, I dared to ask him what salary he thought I might be able to get. Considerably more than a penny it turned out; Dejan was aiming for close to $100,000 net.

I barely had time to collect myself, or finish the 40-ounce I'd cracked with Eric (Wills, my teammate and one of my closest friends), before Dejan was back on the line with offers already rolling in. The deal he was most positive about had come from a team in Italy's Serie A. It seemed inconceivable that this was a possibility, as I knew for a fact that the coveted league had never previously had an English player, but Dejan was certain they were keen. I tested the water: were they serious? What were they offering? A free apartment, $90,000 tax-free. And a car. What kind of car? What kind of car do you want? This was ridiculous: a Benz, I laughed. Sure, a Benz, no problem.

The team was Genertel Trieste. Struggling near the bottom of league A1 and (in spite of what I considered to be a massively impressive deal) a long way from having the league's biggest budget. What they did have was the need for me to fly to Italy and try out, immediately. I was spinning. A few weeks before it was game over and now I was expected to pack my bags and head straight out of Dayton. Dejan assured me that this kind of impatience was perfectly normal. If a team really wants a player, they want him now (before anyone else gets in there) and Trieste wanted to sign me bad. Italy was a major league and it would be fantastic for my career. I still hadn't signed with Courtside but I'd need to if I wanted to take up the offer of the try-out and as soon as I confirmed we were on, Dejan arrived, all the way from Amsterdam to Forest Lane Apartments. It felt like a privilege to sign responsibility for my career away to them. They were going to take care of all my basketball affairs, all I needed to concern myself with was my game.

In less than a week I was walking out into the arrivals hall of Ronchi dei Legionari airport and into the company of a young guy by the name of Gaetano Cusmano. If omens mean anything, the trip to try-out started well. I was wearing what I always wore, a tracksuit, basketball shoes, carrying a Nike bag and was approached by a little kid who asked me if I was Scottie Pippen. Was that how things worked in Italy? Did they hire little urchins to accost you in arrivals and flatter you into signing a deal? I knew nothing of Gaetano at the time, just that he was an Italian agent who worked with Dejan and was the ideal guy to broker the deal, not least of all because he was a native speaker.

If ever basketball needs an ambassador, Gaetano's the guy. The sport's been his life since he was knee-high to a grasshopper, challenging US Army Officers to a game on the street courts of Rimini; through being a player; a scout; an agent and a manager. He sums it up most simply himself: *'I have looked for happiness in basketball, and basketball has given me happiness'*. He's older now, of course, probably more reflective, but when he met me from my flight that day, he was painfully conscious of his age and inexperience. I wasn't the first player Gaetano had managed to get signed; he'd had a single success with an Italian baller the season before and had been recruited by Trieste to fill a specific gap. Gaetano knew I was that guy as he'd watched my tape. He'd called me directly once Dejan had explained the deal and I'd asked him right off 'Ok, when do I start?' It was naive, overly-eager, but was also right: *'That is the same thing I would say if I was in his same position'* thought Gaetano *'to play in a professional championship, to be paid for the thing I loved to do above all'.*

We were thinking on the same lines. I'd been so eager I'd barely stopped to check where Trieste even was. I'd never heard of it and already one thing was obvious, the place was beautiful. Situated just an hour from Venice, lesser-known Trieste is no less imposing; its Adriatic seafront (our first stop for pizza) lined with the most gorgeous buildings, and it was clear from first glance that this was my kind of place. Gaetano apologised for the speed of lunch, practice was in an hour and, mashed from jet-lag or not, I was expected in the gym with the rest of the players. This was business now. There was a potential $90,000 investment on the table and it was time to step-up.

If the view from the pizzeria on the seafront was something then the view from Genertel's gym was something else. I'd never seen a gym like it, with one whole side glazed and offering the most stunning view down over the roofs of Trieste and out over Navy battleships in the Adriatic. The scrimmage was pitched to me as fairly informal. The Americans who'd already been signed for the forthcoming season wouldn't arrive in Italy until the start of pre-season, but in addition to the team's other players there were a couple of English guys there on try-outs, Karl Brown (from Georgia Tech) and Kenny Scott (a BBL legend). As soon as I stepped foot in the gym, I knew in my heart that the job was mine. I could taste it.

The half-court three-on-three we played was a joke. The Italians were too big and slow, or too small and slow, for me and I was abusing them one by one. That none of them wanted to guard me was immediately obvious. Hunger for the job pushed past my jet-lag which only managed to pull a couple of my shots short. I wanted to prove everything they'd seen on that tape was no fluke, it was really what I could do; even with a belly full of margherita and a head full of confused time-zones.

At the time, 'margherita' was about the extent of my Italian but even with no knowledge of what was being said, I got a vibe of excitement from the team's General Manager and President who were watching intensely from the sidelines and incessantly talking on mobile phones. Gaetano explained that a friendly scrimmage against the A2 team Gorizia had been arranged for the following evening and would be my next opportunity to continue to impress them. Grateful for the chance to rest and attempt to recuperate physically, I still managed an additional sense of excitement; Gorizia featured Antonella Riva, a legend, in his late 30s and a scoring machine still killing it. As ever, the chance for a little feisty competition, someone really special to prove myself against, fired me up and despite the pressure, the lack of a crowd, and the fact that I wasn't in my best shape (a lack of training even for a couple of weeks flops you pretty quick), my 'teammates' fed me the ball and I hit a few 3-s, made some great penetrations and passes, and capped the evening off with a nice dunk. I'd finished with a moderate 16-points and around 8 rebounds and 7 assists and was pleased I'd managed to show myself as the living, breathing, jumping embodiment of my highlight tape.

As I headed out into the foyer after the game, I wasn't so sure that it had all gone well. Angelo Bagueira, the team's GM was arguing with Gaetano. Yelling at one another, the few pauses for breath were filled by the voice of Dejan shouting out from Angelo's mobile and adding to the kerfuffle. I was shocked; I'd thought things were going great. They were, Gaetano assured me, kind of too great. Angelo had seen enough, he wanted to sign me there and then, but Dejan had refused. He had other offers up his sleeve and was doing what a good agent does; trying to sell me to the highest bidder. Angelo was pissed, as far as he was concerned it was a done deal, they'd agreed a price which Dejan was now trying to renegotiate and I got scared. I already loved the place, I liked the team, I was more than pleased with the deal, I wanted to sign and I was terrified that renegotiation attempts at this late stage might fuck the whole thing up. I took the phone from Angelo and asked Dejan to chill, I was happy, I wanted to sign and the next morning I put pen to paper in Angelo's office and became a pro.

My visit had been scheduled for five days but I stayed an extra week. Trieste is a fabulous city, it was going to be my new home and so the opportunity to check the place out, kick back, soak up some sun, was too good to resist. When I landed back in Dayton, my cheeks smarted from a week of grinning like a Cheshire Cat and my pocket pulsed with the $5,000 cash bonus I'd been given to see me through the summer. Did I feel like a new man? I felt like a man full stop. A scholarship is a wonderful, wonderful thing, it buys your tuition, your books, your kit, your apartment, your food and your medical bills; it doesn't buy you any pocket money, nor does it allow you the option of finding work for extra cash (even if you did have the time to fit it in between study and practice and fixtures). It was the first time in five years I'd had any money at all and this wad was more money than I'd ever seen in my life. I walked tall. I was set for next season: I was a pro baller. I also still hadn't graduated and so by day I tried to stop smirking and concentrate on my books and by night I let myself be a 23-year-old with $5,000 burning a hole in his pocket. For the first time I could treat my friends and that wad of notes saw me right as I hit the clubs and allowed myself a little flossin'. It could only be a little. Degree under my belt, I was expected back in Trieste on July 23rd and the last thing I needed was to land there out of shape.

A quick stop back in England was all there was time for. A little catch-up and some celebrating that the dream (most of it at least) was now blooming into a career was capped by an article in the local paper. Dave Bettley of the Widnes Weekly News had followed my career and written some great articles in the past and it was especially satisfying to share the good news with him. The headline read *'Delme's £65,000 Slam Dunk'* the picture featured a still grinning me, proud in my new Trieste kit, the skinny little gold chain with #32 that I'd worn since the days at Claymont High still round my neck. That grin is a grin of pure pride. I'd achieved what I'd set out to achieve and hopes of the ultimate NBA prize had been rekindled. There was no reason why, in a couple of seasons time once I'd made my name in Italy, an opening back in the States might not present itself. At least no reason I knew of. In reality there were actually too many to even count.

Pre-season was shocking. We were running at 8am on a track half-way up a mountain; completing combinations of sprints: 8 x 800m, 6 x 400m,

8 x 200m, 5 x 100m, 10 x 50m. The likes of which I'd never seen before and have never experienced since. We'd break off in the heat of the day and reconvene in the evening for practice. The little weight I had dropped off me and the heat meant that resting in the day was almost impossible. This was no joke: suddenly the Benz in the driveway and the money in the bank seemed well earned.

I was exhausted but none of it mattered, this was the life I'd always dreamt of and here I was 23 and living it. Perhaps living it a bit too much. Our coach Furio Steffe was only 31, incredibly young, especially for a coach in A1. He was under enormous pressure to prove himself and keep the team from the threat of relegation. Another factor to Furio's age was the connections he had: eyes everywhere, meaning that a young player who was under the impression that it was okay to get out and about around town and enjoy some of the nightlife Trieste had to offer, was about as wrong as he'd ever been.

It wasn't only a huge transition moving from the cosy world of college into a life of fending for myself, the transition to a whole new country was also enormous. I'd always liked to party but had also always kept things in context. I'd never gone wild because I'd always respected ball too much and I didn't go wild now, but I was young and completely unaware of how exposed my life now was. It seemed ridiculous but I was kind of famous now, at least in Trieste. Everywhere I went, people knew who I was and man did they love their ball! They were glad to see me and seemed to welcome the sight of me enjoying myself, but it quickly became apparent that no matter where I went, what I did, what I drank, first thing in the morning Coach would know everything. He wasted no time in laying it on the line. I was used to curtailing my social life around ball, I'd been doing that for ten years already, but this was something else. It wasn't that Coach expected me to stay in the night before the match (I'd have always done that), he wanted the night before that and, to add to the deal, the one before that too. I didn't want to seem ungrateful or unprofessional but three nights before was extreme. It wasn't like I was even drinking more than a couple of drinks if I did go out, you can't play basketball (or probably any pro sport) at this kind of level without seriously looking after yourself, but the deal was set. We played on Sunday afternoon so Thursday, Friday and Saturday nights were off limits.

Worst thing was I was lonely. I'm a people person, always have been, and I'd spent the past five years of growing from boy into man surrounded by the kind of close-knit camaraderie that's a given in team sports. At WSU the Raiders were a team on court and off. We lived together, partied together, worked out together and that fraternity of support and fun had been a massive part of my life. Sure we fell out, there were fights, but at least we were a team. Life in Italy was something else entirely. The Italians on our team fell into two camps: in their late 20s and settled; or just 18 or 19 years old, neither of which I particularly fitted with so I anticipated the arrival of our Americans (somewhat after pre-season - a vet' move if ever I saw one!) in the hope that they'd not only prove good for the team, but also good for me.

First to arrive was Darnell Robinson, a 6'10" monster who had won a national championship with Arkansas and had been drafted by Dallas Mavericks as 29th pick in the 2nd round. He'd also had a stint on the books of Philadelphia 76ers but, in spite of the fact that he could run the floor, dunk, use both hands and shoot the 3-, he never managed to play in the NBA and had instead headed out to Europe to earn his living. He was a year younger than me but wasn't going to be any kind of brother to kick-it with as he'd arrived with all his moves and a fiancée and a baby daughter. Darnell's record was impressive, he'd be good for Trieste even if he wouldn't do much for my social-life, but our other American was what can only be described as a true vet': Steve Burtt from Iona, a tough-talking 34-year-old New Yorker who had seen and done it all before and proved to be one of the most dominating ballers I ever witnessed play.

The guy was a beast, a points-machine who'd led in scoring in every league he'd ever played in. After spells in the NBA he'd played in both Greece and Italy's A1s; he was Big Time. At 34 he was, in basketball terms, no spring chicken and he dominated our league (one of the toughest in Europe) in terms of scoring. In only our third game of the season he dropped 46-points. His most disappointing score sheet for Trieste saw a game total of, wait for it, 24-. Meaning his average points per game for the season would finally stand at an almost unbelievable 35-! He was older and focused and had seen it all before, he had kids and was well past the stage of coming to a different country and wanting to socialise with other players. I was a fun-loving guy still and soon managed to work out a way to have some chance of kicking-back off court and enjoying my newfound wealth. Sunday was game day so Monday was our day off. No practice meant that Sunday night was the only chance to have some fun. I'd heard from some American players on other Italian teams about Aviano, a US Air Force Base at Vicenza. We'd got chatting and (aware of my frustrations) they'd invited me to join them when they headed to a club out there which on a Sunday night was always jumping.

It was a lifeline. It seems silly that this should matter so much to me, but I was young, miles from any friends and really missing the college life I'd left behind. It soon became a ritual. After the game I'd drive to Vicenza, go to the club, stay in a hotel and return to Trieste on Monday ready for Tuesday's practice and feeling a little saner and a lot happier. Sometimes I'd meet guys from other teams up there, sometimes people I met and had become friends with who lived in Vicenza, other times guys I was friends with who were based at Aviano, once again the Air Force playing some kind of role in my sense of belonging (or lack of).

Life would, of course, have been sweeter all round had things on court been going any better than things off. They weren't. As everyone had expected, Steve Burtt was dominating the hardwood and whilst this was great for him (and good for our score-line) it wasn't giving my game much space to shine. They'd been expecting big things from me, at least 15-points per game, but I found buckets hard to come by. In my highlight tapes my game had been showcased alongside a pass-first point guard who would throw me lobs and hit me on the break. The team at Trieste was neither that deep nor that talented and so Steve stepped-up and having a player like him as our point guard was not a great fit for my type of game. I was a rookie learning the league and the European game and, on a personal level, things could've gone better. Steve's talent, heart and game was ridiculous, I never played with a better guard my whole career, but still I felt frustrated. For me, things might've been a lot different with a true point guard for me to play beside.

I did have my moments though; some particularly satisfying games early in the season and then proving myself in a real test which came in a tournament at Grado. The top-ranked US college team, Cincinnati, were on a pre-season tour of Italy and we were to meet them in the tourney. I was excited, as even though their home-turf was only an hour or so from WSU, I'd never met them in college and they were renowned as a tough and physical team: a real challenge. At the time they featured players such as Danny Fortson, Damon Flint and Melvin Levert and had a clutch of starters with American Footballer builds. Aside from this, I'd been in Italy for a couple of months by now and was looking forward to seeing some familiar faces. There was a good crowd at the tournament and the delayed start due to Cincinnati's travel problems only added to my anticipation.

Even allowing for their travel-related fatigue, seconds into the game Steve Burtt was delivering Cincinnati a master class in the difference between men and boys. The leap from college baller to pro is massive. You finish college thinking you're the man; you're the oldest and strongest on your team and each bucket you've made has brought a bucket-load of respect. And then you're a pro up against guys who are 10 or 12 years older than you, who were doing this for a living when you were an Under 13 and it's a different story. Steve dropped 24-points on their best defensive guards and that was in the first half. Feeling his work was done he chose to sit out the final half. We were up at half-time but it had been a close match. With Steve chilling on the bench it was time to show what I could do. I wanted to earn my props from my Ohio brothers.

They tried to full-court press us but my teammates kept finding me open in the deep corner and I knocked down 3- after 3-. The last time I pump-faked the defender flew past, leaving me to explode along the baseline and try to jam it. Danny Fortson was having none of it and floored me. I was a pro baller for fourteen years all told but that foul stands out as the hardest hit I ever took. It was instinct to jump back up to confront him, but I thought twice. Cincinnati were more of a footballer's than a ball player's build and Fortson was 6'7" and 280 lbs, it would've been like trying to retaliate against a Cadillac that had knocked you down. Nonetheless, I'd put on my finest show for Trieste and left the court with 22-points (19- of them scored in the second half). After the game, Bobby Huggins shook my hand and said he remembered me from Wright State. I remember you from before that, I told him, when you came to Claymont High to scout me. Basketball is huge but it's still a small world.

Mr Versatility was yet to be titled but Mr Inconsistency was flaunting himself all over the place. I proved I could pull it out of the bag when Steve was off court and proved it once again that Christmas when the Americans had been given leave for the holidays and the rest of us met Team System Bologna in a four-team tournament. With Steve and Darnell out of the picture I was now the main focus of our team and I thrived on it. I was giving Bologna fits in spite of them playing both their Americans. I scored 20-points and played a well-rounded game. But the consensus that the Americans were the main focus meant I took a backseat, a decision (subconscious or otherwise) which plagued me my whole professional career. As a team we had no rhythm, we were going nowhere. And then, with eight games of the season left to play, the powers that be fired both Steve and Darnell and relegated me from starting to the bench.

It was a massive shock and it came at a pivotal moment. To avoid relegation, Trieste needed wins in seven of the remaining eight games. A couple of new players were drafted in from elsewhere in Europe, one of whom, Teo Alibegovic, had played at Oregon alongside Gary Payton. He was tough, approaching the end of his career but 6'9", a lefty with severe class. But even Teo's impressive average of 25-points in the remaining games of the season, coupled with the stepping-up of Massimo Guerra following Steve Burtt's departure (racking up an unbelievable 37-points in our first game without Americans), couldn't save us from relegation.

I'd been on teams who'd lost before, no player is on the winning side all of the time, but this time it felt different. My frustrations on court had added to those off and even though towards the season's end I'd begun to dominate practice, I'd already been told it was too little, too late, I'd had my chance and would be sitting out the season on the bench. It was time I lost my cool. I'd always stepped back and taken coaches' decisions before but this was my job now. Sitting on the bench now might mean never securing a contract again and I lost it. Some of the Italian players seeing I was out of favour were taking the piss, trying to foul me a little too hard in practice and sending an already terrible atmosphere amongst the team into meltdown. I phoned Dejan to get me out of there. Gaetano had been to a number of games and had already been in contact with Coach, but it was no use, as he puts it himself:

'*There was too much pressure on the team. The coach was young, they lost many balls, they had too many stops, there was a bad chemistry around the team...the only reason for everybody was to save the team* [from relegation] *so they hadn't time for Delme anymore.*' Dejan sympathised, it was a shit situation, it was also (as I'd told myself at the outset of the season) business; he agreed Trieste were losing me money having me sat on the bench. I was running the risk of other teams having no faith in me for the next season, but it wasn't the time to do anything crazy. Dejan said to hang in there, get the money I was still owed. I took his advice and was floored when, one day, Angelo (the GM) called me into his office. I had a bit of an attitude and was expecting a bollocking. Instead, Angelo said he wanted to discuss the possibility of me signing a three-year extension to my contract. He'd always believed I was a project, he said, and he still believed I'd be one of the best players in the league in a few years' time. How could he say this when Coach had me glued to the bench? Well, that one was simple: it was Coach who wouldn't be back next season.

A Mistake

It was 1997, I was 24 years old and I can vividly recall the limitations of my mentality. Whether it was due to a lack of a father-figure, someone to guide me and advise, or whether the way I felt was just normal for someone of that age, I don't know. Either way, foresight was something I had no sense of at all. The terms of the contract which Angelo outlined for the season ahead revolved (in my mind at least) around the $10,000 pay cut he expected me to take. The shock of him wanting me to return for the next season was immediately superseded by the shock of this financial implication. Although my stats for the season hadn't been that great and I hadn't performed to what I (and I guess Angelo) knew to be my full potential, it still felt like a kick in the teeth. I couldn't see past it to ask what the remaining two seasons of the new contract might bring financially, mainly because I couldn't see past it at all. The politics which had shaped the atmosphere of the team in Trieste had made my mind up for me already. Whatever my problems had been, I'd always been treated with an amount of fairness; work hard and outplay your teammates in practice and you'll earn your court-time. I'd finished as third all-time in minutes played at WSU and there was a reason for that, those minutes were earned. That hadn't been the case in Trieste and it didn't matter what Angelo was offering; I was going.

Financial advice is something every baller needs; it's absolutely vital for young players but is also something that is often completely lacking. When contracts started to be discussed, I'd been hypnotised by the numbers of zeros offered and each dollar added up to transform my attitude. I'd never had any money in my pocket, ever, but I did have what I'd now describe as a 'poor way of thinking'. It would be many years before I'd managed to learn enough to be able to alter my mind-set into a 'rich way of thinking'. Books I later became interested in taught me that a person's attitude to money is as (if not more) significant than the amount they actually have. That year in Trieste my attitude was laughable (I'd even bought Mercedes rims to put on my team car!). The size of that first contract had seduced me into thinking that money would always roll to me now and, rebounder that I was, I would always catch it. My attitude meant that (even with the drop Angelo had stated) he'd still be paying me $80,000 to play for the next season, but the dent to my ego that the $10K drop caused meant I couldn't see that the remaining salary was still pretty decent money for throwing, catching and running about for a living. Maybe I should have put all my dissatisfaction and unhappiness aside and played on, just for the money. Or maybe I should have made a move no one would've predicted and willingly returned to England.

That pro sport becomes your life is inevitable but that was something I'd always seen as a positive. Establishing a career from your passion had seemed too good to be true. It was. So it turned out was the offer which had been placed on the table by the team of my old home-town, Manchester Giants. In the time I'd been Stateside, English ball had moved on and teams such as the Giants were proof of how much. They played their games in the 19,000-seater Manchester Evening News Arena, a space which was as close to NBA facilities as you could imagine. I told Angelo I wouldn't be taking up his offer and left Trieste, season all done, on March 22nd, one of the earliest check-outs I ever experienced. The year had been a huge disappointment and I felt desperately in need of some time with friends back in England to unwind, get my head back together and attempt to take stock of where my career went from here. I managed to catch the BBL finals at London's Wembley Arena where I'd been hooked-up with a nice court-side box and concentrated on hanging-out and taking in how much the English scene had changed.

From the minute I landed back home, I found myself being wooed. Manchester Giants' Coach Jim Brandon was after me hard. I'd heard he'd been interested when I was still at WSU. At that time I hadn't even considered a move back to England, but now things were different. I'd seen that money (although I was still interested in it) didn't bring happiness alone and I'd also seen that the overall set-up of a team was in fact the most important thing. There was already a concrete deal on the table from the Belgian team Antwerp who were looking to sign me as a package with English legend Roger Huggins, but the Giants were offering a contract which was, to my amazement, rivalling even this; serious money, a nice gaff and the added chance of a great adidas contract. On top of it all, it was in Manchester. I'd never thought I'd think this way but a big part of me just wanted to come home.

My experience in Italy had tarnished everything and left me with the fear that all Continental clubs might be the same. But I'd agreed to a try-out at Antwerp nonetheless. Roger Huggins, who was already there, had assured me on the phone that I'd love it and the club's president had also called me direct on the night before I was due to fly out. Sensing my hesitation, he offered me an extra $5,000; taking the money on offer up to $75,000. Even less than Trieste had offered me to stay. As long and as hard as I thought of that decision, as many people as I asked for advice and as many pros and cons I mulled over, I turned Antwerp down. Manchester were offering me the moon on a stick (comparatively at least) and the opportunity to be surrounded by my friends and family for the first time in seven years was all I could see. After wanting to be away from Widnes so badly for so long, all I wanted to do now was come home to Manny. The deal they were offering was too good to be true: literally, it turned out.

Unhappiness had blinded me. My agents were warning that a move from Italy's Serie A to the English League was unheard of for a reason: it was precisely the kind of move that could kill a guy's stock. But the long-term of the dream meant nothing now; I couldn't see past my need to be part of something real again, to be in a place where I really cared for the team and wanted to get them to win something major. I knew Dejan was right. It's just that at the time I didn't care. Italy had killed my love for ball and I needed to get it back. I signed for a pretty hefty sum but not before I'd spelled the situation out to Jim Brandon: I was tired and would be taking three weeks off. Nine months in Italy doing two-a-days meant that before I picked up a ball again, I'd be having a holiday. It was still early summer and Jim Brandon agreed, no ball for three-weeks and then back to business. I put pen to paper and things went from potentially promising to bloody awful.

The Manchester deal was close to what I'd been offered by Antwerp, most of the salary was made up of bonuses which would come with winning, but I had no worries on that score, I was pumped and the promises I'd heard about the Giants meant that the other players would be too. The owners of the team were big-time boosters from Indiana University who were staging a try-out in Indiana in a few weeks' time. I'd made my plans clear, I was having time out, but Jim Brandon assured me it was no problem, he wouldn't be expecting me to play just to be there to help him choose the team. I was going to be Stateside anyway. I'd planned on some time catching up with friends and relaxing, even if I hadn't planned on the star-studded turn my break would take.

I headed out to Allan's new place in New York as my first stop. He was looking forward to showing me round his new gaff, complete with a kitchen which overlooked an indoor pool. It was a temporary place for him and his wife Tammy to stay in whilst they were finalising plans for their dream home which they were going to be building. Even this temporary place was naughty and I'd barely had time to look around when Al asked whether I felt like flying to L.A. When would you not feel like flying out to L.A.? Especially when it's to accompany one of your best friends as he makes a cameo appearance in a rap video. Al had just taken a call from his agent who'd asked him to fly out to California where New Yorkers Salt n' Pepa were filming a video. Did I mind, asked Al? Mind? I picked my chin up off the floor and he booked us two first-class seats to Cali'.

From the stresses of my own stuttering career, via beans-on-toast at my mum's gaff, to reclining back on a flight to an L.A. rap video shoot. If I thought this was surreal, I was in for a shock as we checked into our Hollywood hotel. I glanced around hardly able to believe my luck and my eyes rested on a familiar face. The nine difficult months I'd spent in Italy had been made a little easier by the recorded videos I'd been sent of my favourite show at the time 'In The House' starring LL Cool J, who was sat now right in front of me in the lobby of the hotel, just reading quietly by himself.

It's weird how little things can help to keep you sane in the most challenging of circumstances and those videos had done just that and so I couldn't just let myself go up to my room without saying something. I didn't want to mither the guy but I figured it was as good a time as any to approach him, seeing as he was sat by himself. So I did. I said I just wanted to congratulate him on a great show and let him know how it had helped to keep me sane living in a foreign country. He was really cool, down to earth, and thanked me for what I'd said. I walked away in a weird sort of daze that this was now the kind of thing that happened to me. It was going to get weirder; someone came to Al's room and casually mentioned that one of my favourite artists at the time (the now deceased singer Aaliyah) was in the lobby. The skinny Widnesian tough-neck in me wanted to bound on down there but the newer cooler Del wouldn't let him and so I never did get the chance to meet her.

Being just a random English pro baller, I wasn't sure how this whole shooting-a-video thing was going to work, but I hadn't expected that every day we'd to be up at 7am in order to be ferried by mini-bus to the set. We'd been told that the video was to also feature some other familiar faces and so, as we jumped onto the mini-bus that first day, I wasn't surprised to be able to nod to the guy sat in front of us and laugh 'What's up man?' It was LL. Before he could think I was some kind of crazy stalker, Allan also said 'hi' and explained I was visiting him. As soon as LL heard I was English, that was it, and we travelled to the shoot with him asking all kinds of things about England, a country he said he loved having visited when he was younger.

Although it had been an amazing visit, the long days on set just hanging around had been rounded off with one memorable night out at a club where we'd rolled up for the VIP treatment in a nice Limo and had kicked-it with Salt n' Pepa and Queen Latifah, it had also been the longest time in my adult life in which I hadn't touched a basketball. I was out of shape, it's frightening how quickly the phenomenal levels of fitness you reach when practising twice daily at pro level is lost. But it didn't matter, there was time to turn that around. Once this three-day camp was over, I was back to England, back to my own pre-pre-season conditioning, back to work. As soon as I arrived in Indiana, it was clear that things with the Giants had changed and any afterglow of celebrity was wiped away in a blink. For a start, Jim wanted to know where my practice gear was and when I reminded him I was just here to help him select players, he said that the owners were here and I needed to prove my worth, now. For the first time in my life I'd kicked-it and not worried about fitness. I'd never let my foot of the gas before but I'd needed a break. Now I had no choice. I borrowed some gear and lumbered around the court, not impressing myself, or the owners.

Although on the surface the facilities at the Giants were top-notch, a quick peep underneath showed a different story. The team had acquired a mansion in one of the most expensive of all English residential areas, Wilmslow in Cheshire, a very affluent location which was home to many of Manchester United's world-class footballing millionaires. The building had been converted into several plush apartments and, as I'd stipulated in my contract, I had a place to myself. Unfortunately for me, living in the apartment beneath mine was a guy called Jay Goldberg, the Giants' General Manager, on hand to ensure that any scrap of privacy I thought sole-use of an apartment would give me was lost completely. If I moved, Jay Goldberg knew about it.

The fitness scare I'd had in the summer had only been a temporary blip and I remained as focussed as ever on my physical condition, but still I was young, on home turf and determined to make up for the unhappiness of the previous season by enjoying myself as much as I could. But any late-night shenanigans were immediately reported back to Coach and caused tension between us from the off. At the time I saw no reason why my social life should be any more curtailed than necessary as long as it wasn't affecting my performance. But then maybe I wasn't playing that great, even in practice. Basketball had been my life for so long that I was fully aware of the importance of keeping in shape and I never once forgot that, in spite of any partying which might've occurred.

Unfortunately, something which was strengthening rapidly was the tension between me and Coach Jim Brandon. When he'd been recruiting me I'd been promised the earth, something I'd been promised before by people who'd been more willing to keep to their word. He'd assured me that the squad was being built around me but had subsequently recruited some big-time players, which meant we were so deep. I would've been a very good role player and sometimes break-out and have a huge game, but he wanted more, and the chance I thought I had of seeing what might be accomplished on home soil after all those years away flopped, and I was fired four games in. Of the four played, three games were lost and I'd inexplicably only clocked-up 27 minutes, not per game, in total. 13,000 people were in the crowd for our first game, I'd hardly got on court and had been seething since then. I take some responsibility. My boy Jon Ramey was over from the States at the start of the season and we'd been enjoying every aspect of affluent Cheshire life. Okay, we were kicking-it! I was young, I felt I had a season's unhappiness to make up for and my focus shifted for the first and only time.

I guess 'fired' can be ambiguous: I wanted to be released and they were all too keen to release me. Dejan had been right all along, it was the worst move I could've made but I'd been too young, too stubborn, too unhappy to appreciate that. Dejan had also been right about the dangers of the contract I'd signed. The Giants didn't only drop me after four games, they'd also worded my contract to ensure that (in firing me on the last day of the ten-week period since I'd signed) they were only obliged to pay me for those weeks and nothing else, a devastating quirk unique to British contracts. If this season was a lesson in the harshness of life as a pro' that final insult was the thing that hammered this reality home.

After three weeks of I-told-you so's from Courtside, they managed to secure me a month-long trial at Besancon. There was already a fellow English chap over there with the French team, a 6'11" wild guy who could really play called Spencer Dunkley. Spence was like a stretched Yorick Williams and had warned me already that, in France, they work you hard.

He wasn't wrong, after a brief appearance in two games for them (and plenty of their legendary hard training), we had a break for National Team and I flew back to the UK. I got a call from Courtside whilst preparing with the England squad. Dejan had been pissed-off by my recent choices but had since gotten over any atmosphere and had called to say he'd secured me a guaranteed contract in Leuven, Belgium. I'd have to leave immediately following National Team responsibilities, meaning there was no time to return to France, but what the hell. I headed out to Belgium to see how they did it over there, a couple of months into the season and already on to my third team.

Although geographically so close, the world of Leuven ball was a million miles from life in France. Besancon refused to pay me any of the money they owed but then I'd end up getting accustomed to this kind of shenanigans. So many ballers are owed so much money from so many pro teams who seem to run some kind of sideline in wriggling out of paying their players whenever possible. It's ridiculous. But things had been so bad this season that I was almost beyond caring; life seemed much more my style in Leuven and I felt happy enough. For a start, serious two-a-days were a thing of the past and we even had a mid week day off, and all this for the same money I was being offered in France to bust my guts in practice for no court-time. The team's Americans were cool; Calvin Talford was the highest jumping cat I'd shared a court with. From East Tennessee State, Calvin was a NCAA Slam Dunk Champion and I swear it was like the guy could levitate. The other was a serious shooting guard from Northern Iowa, Jason Daisy. I knew one or two of the natives from playing in an International Under 22 tournament in Finland when I'd dropped them off for 31- and so there were also a couple of familiar faces there to sweeten the move.

I was settling in and really starting to enjoy practice, which myself and the two Americans easily dominated, when the precariousness of ball reared its head once more and the coach who'd recruited me, Jon Van Crumbre, was fired. It's an age-old story, but the new coach came with a set idea about the players he'd inherited which this time left me as one of the ballers with no love. I'd be scoring a comfortable 30-points in friendly games against division two teams, but come the weekend, would barely get on court. It came to a head in a game against Belgium's top team Oostende who we were killing by 50-. With three minutes on the clock I was still on the bench and as Coach went to sub me into the game, I refused to move. We argued, I went on court and scored a rapid 6-points before the game was wrapped up. In the row that followed he spelled his situation out to me: there's three months of the season left and then you'll be gone, he assured me. I'm focussing on developing my younger players, you've had your time.

When at the end of the previous season Angelo had warned me about turning down his offer, he'd said you'll end up earning 30K in Belgium next year if you're not careful and his prediction turned out not to be too far from the mark. The season was a flop and only one challenge remained; the European Qualifiers, taking place at the scene of my early-season disappointments; Manchester's M.E.N Arena. I was apprehensive about going back. If I'd managed to turn the season's bad start around, it would have been a different matter. But since leaving Manchester I'd lurched from one disaster to the next and the thought of bumping into Jim Brandon again, now his lack of faith had been proved right, was sickening. I talked myself into a positive frame of mind and decided to play as hard as I could to get some good minutes on the English National Team and prove to everyone that Jim Brandon had been wrong to cut me.

I did what I'd always done and worked hard in practice. It paid off. I started the game at the M.E.N in front of 5,000 (mainly Israeli) fans. I played well, and caught the eye of Bob Gonnen (an American Israeli) who placed a call to Courtside which secured my future for the season ahead. When I came face-to-face with Jim Brandon in a corridor after the game, I'd played so well he could only congratulate me, but the satisfaction wasn't enough to wash away the horror of the season I'd had. Trying, as ever, to take some positives away and learn from what had happened, I was at least comforted by the thought that I'd seen the worst that ball could offer. It had to get better than this.

25

26

WSU

WRIGHT STATE

32

GO RAIDERS!

27

WRIGHT STATE 32

28

29

WRIGHT STATE 20

30

MCC

Delme Herriman

38

39

40

41

42

43

50

51

52

53

WITH LOVE
WE REMEMBER
RAY (OZZIE) OSBORNE
DEVOTED HUSBAND AND FATHER
DIED 14TH MARCH 1993
AGED 49 YEARS
SAFE AT LAST

A Journeyman (Europe)

I'd never cried after losing a basketball game before. But this loss meant that we also lost the championship. I'd already been gutted but when I'd looked around the locker room for our leader, Tony Miller, and found him curled up in the showers crying his eyes out, it had been just such a disheartening sight. Convinced he'd let the Den Helder squad down by not playing his best, he was heartbroken, and seeing the rock of your team break down like this was just too sad. It was a major disappointment. I'd been so excited to join a championship squad. We'd had an unbelievable season; 3-1 up in the playoffs best-of-seven series before a game at home to seal it all which we inexplicably lost by 20-. We went on to lose the following two, finishing 4-3, losing our crown and hitting us all with the full-on devastation that our last game together had been such a disappointment. I'd really enjoyed my season, had had some great times with the guys, especially Tony and Chris Mims. It would also be another six years until I'd manage to be part of a championship-winning squad.

Den Helder is a weird place out on the end of a skinny limb on the northern tip of Holland. Getting there takes one long road: one way in, one way out. The closest real town, Alkmaar, home-town of my WSU boy Mike Nahar, is a good 45-minute drive away. Den Helder is home to Holland's biggest Naval Base, a small mall, a few bars, a couple of clubs. It's a little town with a great tradition and it's crazy for basketball. It's also kind of isolated. I'd been met at the airport by Chris Mims, a cool, cock-diesel 6'6" light-skinned cat from University of Tennessee, Chattanooga, who, two years previously, had been to the NCAA's 'Sweet Sixteen'. Big Time. He was now something of a Den Helder Celebrity.

Chris took me on a tour of the town, something that was already a common fixture of my career: arrive in new country, be met by player, have the tour, meet the team. It didn't take long in Den Helder. The highlight of the tour in hindsight was a casual introduction to one of Chris's friends who worked in a phone shop, Adele. She'd pretty soon be my girlfriend. She'd bring some much-needed stability to the season as on-court frustrations would turn into off-court naughtiness and we'd attempt to keep a relationship going for five years, across a series of countries and time-zones, teaching me some of the harsh impact that pro sport can have on any idea of settling down.

Whatever Den Helder lacked in terms of night-life or a beautiful climate, it made up for in the town's love for basketball and there was still a real buzz about last season's exploits. Bringing the Dutch Championship home had meant that all five starters had returned this year. Great for the team's stability; they were a tight group, all a similar age (around 25), and were welcoming of a new player (we were soon hanging out a lot and having some right laughs), but their secure places in the squad would have an inevitable impact on my court-time. Of the four Americans we had, I was most looking forward to playing alongside Tony Miller, who hailed from close to my old stomping-ground Cleveland Ohio. I'd followed Tony through high school and had seen him in the State Finals in Columbus. He'd gone on to star at Marquette University, where he'd finished as All-Time Assists leader, an honour significant enough to place him sixth All-Time in the history of the NCAA: a true point guard who could pass the rock. As a team we also had great defense: with myself, Chris and Tony giving our offensive players fits. Our go-to guy, Nii Nelson Richards, was tough, and if a team managed to get past us, they'd then find themselves having to deal with our 7' centre, Erwin Hageman. As well as myself, there was another International coming off the bench: 6'7" shooting machine Okke Te Velder, alongside another impressive player, Jeroen Barth.

It was a strong team with a good record and I'd been brought in by Coach Gonnen as his defensive stopper. Not wanting to alter a winning formula, he kept the same starting five, but could see that I should have taken the three spot where the reliable but defensively-challenged John Duggan played. In addition to the likelihood we'd dominate the domestic league, Den Helder also played in the Saporta Cup, a Pan-European Cup

Winner's competition which pitted Europe's most exciting clubs against one another. We were grouped with Italian Powerhouse (and future 1999 Champions) Benetton Treviso and I was excited about returning to Italy to face them. Being in the Cup was great fun and meant that our time was really varied. Sometimes playing up to four times in a seven-day stretch, we'd often play a domestic game on a Saturday night only to fly out across the Continent on Monday morning to meet some Saporta Cup team. It was a lifestyle I loved and playing so much came with the added bonus of having to practice less; we practised on court.

A pattern was already emerging to my career; getting minutes in the pro game was tough, especially in a successful team with an established core of players. It was massively frustrating for me; something which was also emerging into a pattern. Being on court had always been my outlet. As a young guy, I'd never really needed a way to blow-off steam as I'd always done that on court. Without that safety-valve I'd find myself other, less productive, ways to break loose. It came to a head during the Tulip Inn tournament: we'd played two or three games already on back-to-back nights, and I'd hardly been off the bench. I needed to release some tension and so I drove alone to Amsterdam (about an hour away) for a night out at 'The Challenge'. It was the night before our last game of the tournament. It did me good but driving home some hours later, the Dutch signs confused me and pretty soon I was lost, heading in the complete opposite direction from home on my way to Rotterdam. It was 5am before I got back. Dawn on game day, not a sensible move, and also a move which would come back to haunt me later in the season.

The Dutch lifestyle was good; it suited me, and getting to play in a nice town hanging with a close-knit group of guys was, I realised, much rarer than I'd imagined. It was the first season since Wright State that I'd had a group of friends around me and we all made the most of it, playing hard in practice and games and just as hard off-court. Although I'd always enjoyed a challenge, it was a good feeling to go into every domestic game knowing we were going to win, that we were number one. Amsterdam were a close second to us but we raced out to seventeen consecutive wins, we were top of the league, it wasn't unusual for us to beat a team by 30- or 40-points, hammering one poor team into the court winning by a 60-point margin. When I'd been able to get into the flow by getting good minutes, I'd played really well and had finished the season with a few 18-point games.

Things were going well on court and off court my life was settling down. At 25, guys I'd been to college with were already getting married and having children but my lifestyle of not knowing where I was going to be from one season to the next (one month to the next in my second pro season) meant that even if I'd wanted this, it would have been impossible. But mid-way through the season things had started to get serious between me and Adele (the girl from the phone shop). It was a tough decision for both of us. Even without the reputation ballers have, it was likely I'd be leaving Den Helder at the end of the season but I sensed something special in her and we decided to try to make it work. It grounded me a little and, finding my role in team, I was grounded on court too. I knew now that I'd be first off the bench and, once on court, would average 25-minutes a game. At least it was consistent and I really enjoyed playing alongside Tony, a true pass-first point guard, Den Helder's leader and nowadays an assistant coach at the University of Southern California.

Things were going well and unsurprisingly, were also about to blow-up. We'd travelled to Austria to play a Saporta Cup match in which Coach left me on the bench for 39-minutes. It was a close game but a minute's playing time was a joke. I was pissed. I knew my input would've helped us avoid the narrow defeat and had been looking forward to playing against another English guy, Ray Carter, who I'd just met and was on the opposing team. Ray (a future National squad teammate) and I had hit it off right away and had already arranged to meet for drinks after the match. It was a Tuesday night and with playing responsibilities over all, tomorrow meant was a flight back to Holland. So when we got back to our hotel in Oberwart the team headed to the bar for a few drinks. We were having a laugh, I started playing a few of my cheeky jingles on the piano, and then out of nowhere Coach decided we were all on a curfew.

Okay so we'd lost the match, and okay I admit I was already pissed at him because of the bench-sores on my bum, but putting a curfew on us just seemed petty. I'd already arranged to meet Ray Carter at a bar in town, so I went. I'd been good lately, more settled off court, practising hard as always and still not getting played in these important games. I felt I was owed a little fun. It was only a little, it turned out. The bar was pretty ginger, and definitely not worth the punishment next day on the bus to the airport as coach called me up to the front. He was fining me $250 for breaking curfew and asked why I'd ignored his orders, so I told him: one, I am a grown man; two, it was the night after the game, not before the game; and three, I'd been working really hard and felt he was completely disrespecting me and the team in keeping me on the sidelines.

Coach was clearly unhappy with me, he didn't like me speaking up any more than he liked me deciding things for myself or (from his point of view) taking things into my own hands. It might've blown over a little quicker had this incident not coincided with another little shenanigan I'd by now thought I'd gotten away with. Remember that night out in Amsterdam? Remember the drive home when I went round and round that tabernacle getting my ass lost? Well I'd also managed to clock myself up a little trio of speeding tickets. All from the same night and all detailing not only location but time of offence. Coach called me in from the weight-room a week or two after the Austrian fine and confronted me. The tickets (from a couple of months earlier) had just arrived at the team's office. He wasn't daft, one at around 3am, another an hour later and a final one around 5am on match day as I was desperately trying to make up for what I'd done by high-tailing my ass back home. Kind of understandably Coach Gonnen got my agent (who lived in the same town) involved; I told them both the same thing, I was in the wrong but had only been out those times because I'd been so frustrated at my court-time. The thing I'm guilty of is having a stubborn rebellious streak, but I'm not a moaner. A guy who's playing shit and not delivering in practice deserves no court-time, but doing that to a guy who's working consistently hard and out-playing opponents is just a betrayal, a message that the guy's not worthy.

It's business though. These things have to be gotten over and they were. When we played Ray Carter's Austrian team on the return leg, I started, played 35-minutes, had a naughty dunk in traffic and held the leading scorer of our whole Saporta Cup group to way below his average. This time we won by 27-points and any night-out was a sanctioned one. We'd had a phenomenal year, but ultimately we'd failed to capitalize in the play-offs just when it counted, a final result which meant the squad as it stood would be disbanded. No pro team sticks with a formula unless it's a guaranteed winning one.

It had been a really enjoyable season for me. By far my most successful as a pro and, as well as being gutted to have just missed the chance to be on a championship-winning squad, I was sad that we were going our separate ways. It's terrible to spend a season on a team with no social life, almost as bad to have that and then have to wave it goodbye. We'd had some great times hanging out, especially Chris Mims, Tony Miller and me, hooking up some mean Chicken Caesar Salads and kicking-it together, taking one of our Den Helder's youngsters, Niek Staal, under our wing teaching him how to party.

Season over, I took solace in the next best thing and headed off to America to kick-it college style. Except by now, college style was changing a little itself. My old teammate Eric Wills had married my old college friend Tiffany Gover (who'd sat in 'The Shot' crowd with my mum) and people were becoming a little more settled into adult life. We were all getting older, changing, the Kid n' Play flat-top of my Uhrichsville days had matured into a more close-cut 'do which I'd been (for the last few months in Den Helder) growing into a nice little 'fro. I felt kind of fly as I landed in Cincinnati that summer, strolling through the airport like some Continental member of the Commodores. At least I did until Eric and Tiff met me in arrivals and fell about laughing. It was clear the 'fro needed to go when my boy Bill Edwards walked straight past me at the Cincinnati summer league. He'd no idea it was me; probably not the 'do he expected from a guy who has tea with the queen.

My summers were in as much of a pattern as my seasons by now, perhaps even more so. I'd play nine months on the Continent, fly to the States to stay with Eric or (in the early days) my old roomy Jon Ramey who'd swapped ball for financial advising and had secured a nice condo from his new lucrative career. Still in Dayton, Jon's crib had a main apartment upstairs and a separate annex underneath with a weight-room, a living room and an en-suite bedroom. I had my own key and came and went as I pleased, a bonus for Jon whose new career didn't include the bonus of months of summer vacation, and an ideal base for me. It was a running joke that Jon (a white dude) had me shacked-up downstairs in the 'Slave Quarters'. We had many great times over the summer and I was so grateful to Jon for letting me stay as long as I wanted. A great friend in the big house whilst me and the darker-skinned lads were down in the 'Quarters'! A consistent feature of my summer was, of course, basketball: always wanting to solidify the rep' I'd carved out in Dayton as much as the local ballers wanted to test themselves against a pro. I'd handle my business on court there, get my respect and leave for the Continent with batteries recharged.

The summer time following Den Helder had a twist though, for the first time I was cutting the States a little short to enjoy a nice holiday to Greece with my girlfriend. It'd been years since I'd holidayed away from ballers and was a good break before a return to the UK (my mum's house now my only real base) and news of what next season would bring. My agent was talking about an offer which had come in from a team in Germany, a guy called Joe Whelton had been making enquiries. I knew Joe from being the Manchester United coach back in the days of Jeff Jones and Will Brown, I also knew he was always on the lookout for English players. But the world of pro ball is never straightforward and it would be October before I'd find myself in Giessen, meaning that I'd been away from a team (out of work) for six months. By the time I got to Germany, Giessen had played four games. I'd seriously dented my savings from last season's wages and the Italian player they were now cutting was still practising alongside us, despite knowing I was there to take his job and his nice apartment.

The Italian was cool about it. It probably sounds ridiculous but this is life for a professional baller. Players are regularly fired at a moment's notice, losing the nice car and tidy gaff that went with the job and flying back to their parent's house: from hero to zero. Waiting around all summer long, not knowing when, or if, your agent will call you with a job, let alone what that job might entail once you get there. At MTV Giessen, it was the job that was the issue: my agent had sent me there as a four-man, a power forward. Coach Whelton knew my size (or lack of it) for that position and stressed that I could guard the big stiffs they had over there in Germany, but it was my first real experience of playing inside and I hated it. I felt like I was playing in wellies; setting pick and rolls, banging with the big boys and, for the first time in my balling life, I started to lose confidence in my outside shot, rarely looking at the hoop from outside.

Aside from the difficulties of adjusting to a new unfamiliar position, both my Giessen teammates and the coaching in Germany were great. We ran a very structured 'Triangle Offence', similar to the one run by the Lakers with Kobe Bryant, and I loved it. It's a formation which gives everyone on the team an equal opportunity to get involved and score, ideal on the Continent where all too often an American would just take over and jack-up shots. Because I understood the offence quickly and I could guard these bigger players, I was inserted into the starting line-up pretty much from the off. As a team we were so patient on offence, rarely taking a bad shot, that the opposition would just hate playing us and, after games, the amount of players who would approach us to compliment our style of play was ridiculous. Credit goes to Joe Whelton, himself a standout point guard at the University of Connecticut.

I had some great teammates in Giessen. There was basketball royalty: son of the NBA's famous Rick Barry, Richard 'Scooter' Barry, who was the eldest of a dynasty of four Barry boys carving their way through the NBA: Drew, Brent and Jon. 'Scooter' had achieved the ultimate accolade in college basketball, having won the NCAA Championship in 1988 with Danny Manning and the Kansas Jay Hawks. Another of our Americans was Joey Beard, a high school McDonald's All-American who'd go on to Duke and, at 6'10", was the most athletic white guy of his size I'd ever seen. He could run the court as fast as me and then 'windmill' dunk it at the other end. He was a great player for us and eventually went on to sign a million-dollar multi-year contract for Italian giants Treviso. Joey was also a funny guy. He'd make me laugh by saying he'd be so nervous any time he took a free-throw in a game that he'd 'shake like a leaf'.

I clicked at Giessen with Tom Johnson, a Canadian National Team player who looks like the Lakers' Rick Fox. We had something in common; he was adopted, like me. Unlike me, Tom was eventually successful in tracing his father who, low and behold, lived and worked as a musician in Manchester. It brought up thoughts of my own dad which had never really gone away. I stored them in the back of my mind, travelling across Europe not knowing from one week to the next where I'd be. It wasn't the right time to seriously look, but it would be one day. Tom was a great shooter who didn't only find his dad, he also went on to be a very successful coach in Belgium.

The teammate I spent most time with at Giessen was my boy 'Long Shanks'. 6'10" Stephen Johnson, a year or two older than me, who'd attended the University of California, a big-time school where our English Team guard Richard Midgely, and Jason Kidd, attended. 'Shanks' had a nice BMW with some massive rims on it and pretty soon we were chilling a lot after practice, just hanging out; something which eventually wound up getting us into some serious professional trouble. It was a Sunday game, something I've always hated for nothing more than the impact it has on any Saturday night potential. Going out was still a release for me and after a week of doing two-a-days and the settling influence of a steady girlfriend all the way back in Holland, it was something I needed. Saturday morning practice was over before noon and the day until we met back up (9am Sunday morning) stretched out ahead, tempting me. I took a nap after practice and woke up around 5pm, fully alert and already bored. I knew that just kicking round my apartment alone would mean I wouldn't be able to sleep that night and so I called 'Shanks'. We were agreed: we'd go to this very nice cocktail bar we knew for two, three 'bevvies' at the most, and then we'd call it a night.

What is it with maths on a night out? We quickly agreed that the two should be three, but then that became five and before we knew it we were seven drinks in, kicking-it in a club, chatting to a nice young lady who 'Shanks' tried to impress by smoking a ciggie. It goes without saying that the pair of us played shit the next day, losing the game by just a few points. I should have known better. On all fronts, I should have known better. If the last few years on the Continent had taught me anything, it's that if you go out, you'll be found out - the last few years, it seemed, had taught me nothing. Monday was our day off, I spent it in bed and was woken in the morning by a call from Coach Whelton: had I really been in a club on Saturday night? There was no point lying: I had, I was home by one. Okay, there really was no point lying, especially since he called me an hour later to ask whether, when I said '1am' I actually meant to say '3am'. I did. He wasn't happy. The third and final called exposed me completely. Like all European Coaches, Joe Whelton had spies everywhere: when I said '3am' I was lying, wasn't I, it was more like 5, and you were sipping on Hennessy and one of you was smoking a cigarette! Even by Coach's standards, this was impressive spying. Turned out spies weren't really required, not when the nice young lady we'd been chatting to was actually the Club President's daughter! Coach Whelton was so pissed off, he talked of fining, he talked of firing and before he hung up he suspended me until further notice.

If I hadn't already regretted going out (which I did), the five days I spent in my apartment banned from practice would have hammered it home. I'd been pretty good before this happened. I'd been enjoying the place, the team, the set-up and I'd blown it all. Coach called Friday morning, he wanted us at practice that night where we were to apologize to the rest of the team. Whilst the guys scrimmaged against each other at practice. 'Shanks' and I had to jog around the outside of the court continuously until we were subbed into the game. We were subbed back out and had to keep on jogging, round and around. The next day we were to play a huge game against Leverkusen, Germany's second-to-top team, and I was just starting to get a little worried about how tired all this jogging would make me for tomorrow when Coach called time on practice. The second I had to think we were off the hook was over pretty quick; the team could relax, there was after all a big game tomorrow, 'Shanks' and I would entertain them by sprinting up and down the court. I swear I nearly collapsed and just as I was about to start throwing up backwards, there and then, Coach called time proper: punishment served.

It didn't take a genius to work out that the game against Leverkusen was make-or-break time. I was nervous. Would Coach play me or not? If he did, would I fall flat on my face? Get fired? Be back home by Wednesday drowning my sorrows in my mum's cheese-on-toast? Whatever happened, beating them would be damn near impossible, even without the pressure of all eyes being on me and 'Shanks' after our little escapade.

Although versatile, I was still a little inconsistent. But one thing that was consistent in my game was that, when my back's against the wall, I come out firing on all cylinders. We weren't on the bench for long, unspoken team etiquette said Coach would have been wrong to start us, but our stature as athletic players, both long and lean, meant he couldn't keep us benched for long. I came in and played my best game of the season. Stat-line; 24-points, 9 rebounds. But most importantly, a win. 'Shanks' had a monster game too with 18- points and 16 rebounds. A performance which got the pair of us off the hook. It's amazing what a good win can do. I'd paid the price for my misdemeanours and stayed out of trouble for the remainder of the season. It had scared me. This career I'd longed for all my life was being jeopardized by my need to party: I thought I was a young guy, that I should've been out there kicking-it, enjoying my youth, but as if to send me a message about the passage of time, a back problem appeared which left me hobbling around like an old codger (like Mrs Overall[xiii]). It had been niggling all season and was eventually diagnosed as a slipped disc. I'd never experienced it before but, still, as I lay before a game having a pain-killing injection, I couldn't blame Coach Whelton for thinking he'd been sold a 'dud'. I'd need to sort this out, especially if I wanted this career I'd finally got to last. Next season I'd need to focus on stabilizing and strengthening my core. I wasn't getting any younger.

We were well prepared for the playoffs, but standing at seventh in the league meant we'd have to face Leverkusen again, who'd finished in second place. We lost two games to one, finally being finished off almost single-handedly by a great player called Chuck Evans and his massive 38-point individual haul. Facing Chuck here would become yet another example of how small the world of basketball is: many years later, he'd not only become my teammate at Everton Tigers, he'd go on to be Head Coach.

I liked the league in Germany, their arenas, their style of play and my coach so much that I was willing to overlook the small amount of money on offer to stay. I fancied the chance to come back for a second season in my natural position, small forward, but it wasn't to be. There was already an offer on the table which was extremely tempting. For a start, it was back in Holland (much easier in terms of my relationship) and was with a new team set-up at the professional football club NAC Breda. The money on offer was sweet, especially for Holland, close to double that which Giessen were able to offer. The Coach seemed cool and the whole thing as a package just seemed to make sense.

It was the year 2000. A new millennium, a new start. After just a few seasons as a pro I was already becoming a journeyman, travelling from one team, one country, to the next with no roots whatsoever. It hadn't mattered so much before but by now I was starting to crave the security that a long contract could bring: in terms of settling down a little, but also in terms of being grounded so that I'd get the chance to grow as a player and a person. A move to Breda seemed like it might offer this; the chance to be part of a new team from the outset was also tempting, as were their top-notch facilities. I had a huge two-floor apartment to myself hidden away off the main road and accessed via an entrance I called the 'Bat Cave'. It was a nice set-up all round. Breda is a beautiful city, back on familiar territory and also close to Antwerp, another lovely place, should I need a change of scenery.

It soon became clear that another benefit to being in Breda would be my teammates, some really great guys. Quentin Hall had made the 'Elite Eight' (a massive achievement) when playing at Gonzaga. Put simply, the guy was a star, not to mention a character: 5'8" in his socks, larger than life, and with the confidence, demeanor, and aggressive style of play of a man a good deal taller. Then there was Nicola Simic from Belgrade, an outstanding 3-point shooter who, like me, would remain at Breda for another season. He liked the place so much, he's even spending his retirement with wife Sandra and their kids just outside of the city. We weren't short on decent shooters. Sjoerd de Jong, a New Yorker with Dutch heritage, was also pretty handy. It was a decent crew of players but it was a diverse squad which took time to gel on court. We had a couple of big 6'10" guys, the first was Q's right-hand man, Rod Platt. He'd played at Loyola but in these early days of his career was too raw and found it near impossible to put the ball in the basket. He was huge and it earned him the nickname John Coffey (from 'The Green Mile'). Give the guy his due, mind, he worked hard and it paid off, improving his game immensely which also resulted in a long career, currently in the Czech Republic.

Breda also had another giant, he never really produced for us, but at the time it was the least of his worries. Rob Gibbons, an Irish-American from New Jersey, who'd played ball at Illinois State with my boy Steve Hansell from the England National Team. We befriended one another right away; it was the right friendship at the right time, especially for Rob, a guy at the lowest ebb a guy could be at. Rob had arrived in Breda to channel his mind into something positive, his four-month marriage was in tatters and his devastation was written across him like a neon sign. Rob's issues went from bad to worse, his court-time was virtually non-existent, and a serious blood-clot he developed in his thigh added to his woes. But Rob's a unique kind of a guy, the first baller I'd met who kept a journal, and certainly the first I'd met (the first ever?) who would spend his evenings doing stand-up comedy in local clubs. The Irish in him mixed with the sadness in him and created a little cocktail that liked to drink and, through hours and hours of chat about all kinds of deep stuff over the year, we cemented a lifelong friendship.

Rob's recollections set me to thinking about everything else that basketball has brought into my life. I found it through a love of sport and the luck of being Gid's brother, but the triumphs and frustrations on the court are only a tiny part of that which basketball has brought me. I was looking for belonging through basketball and the belonging I did find came through the friendships I made along this journey. When I'd first thought about writing this, I'd asked old friends and teammates for any thoughts they had about my career. I was at first a little put out by how few had focused on strictly ball-related stuff. But Rob (the only properly literary-inclined baller I ever knew) sums it all up and reminds me that whilst sometimes ball feels like all there is to life, it's really life that's all there is to life: *The people in your life that help you through tough times, not just by listening but by helping you make sense of all the crap that is in your head, are more valuable than we ever could know at the time. I have always believed it's the people you meet and the experiences you have that make for a great journey. Del was a part of mine, and our friendship is one that I have held close no matter how much time passes between us. He's one of those friends that I don't have to talk to every day, or month for that matter. Yet whenever we do get to catching up, it's just like those old days back in Holland. Those nights where we talked about everything, laughed and drank and laughed some more. We talked about the world, the women in our lives, the state of craziness in some way or another that we called life. Memories die slowly, some don't die at all, and I for one, am very happy for that'.*

Although on court things were often difficult (I was still stuck in the power forward spot) there were also enjoyable games, not least of all those against my old team Den Helder. I'd always want to step-up when facing the team of a former coach and meeting Bob Gonnen's lot would be no different: I set my mind right, I wanted to score. The fact that, unlike a lot of players, I didn't usually go into a game with this mind set might go some way to explaining why I'm not sat on a yacht in the Caribbean writing this, but sometimes I'd just get this all-consuming urge to prove my worth and this game was one of those occasions. I dropped 25-points, grabbed 8 rebounds, but left the court unsatisfied: we'd lost. They were second in the league, we were seventh, but it wasn't the point, the re-match would be a different outcome. We were at their place, I dropped 22-points and 11 rebounds and as I left the court, Bob Gonnen approached me: *'We're flying off to a Saporta Cup game tomorrow, want to come along? We could use your help.'* he joked.

By the end of the season my average points per game stood at 11-, the highest of my professional career and not too bad considering how little I actually shot the ball. Playing with four Americans meant it was hard to get a good look, especially for a player like me unlikely to just jack one up because I am open. It was clear at the end of the season that Breda were looking to keep me and so I sat down with my coach, Jos Wolfs, to just come out with it: what did he think I could do at this stage to improve my game, to take my play up to the next level to where I felt my talent meant I should be? The answer he gave was about the last thing I expected to hear him (or any coach) say, it shocked me and tapped a raw nerve: *'Only one thing,'* he said, *'find your father.'*

I was floored. I knew Coach Wolfs was aware I was adopted and that I'd attempted before to find my biological dad. He was an open-minded guy and had once set me up to have my tea-leaves read by someone he knew. It had been interesting, pretty accurate, and must've alerted Jos to the fact that I was also pretty open-minded about the spiritual side of life. He had a theory. Jos believed that the emotions felt by a mother during pregnancy can be absorbed by the unborn child. It seemed feasible. He went on: a young girl hiding not only her pregnancy from her parents but also the identity of the child's black (and married) father must've suffered unbelievable strain: a level of anxiety that the baby would've no doubt shared. He saw in my play sometimes a level of nervousness that was disproportionate in a player of my skill and firmly believed that there was a direct correlation between my current situation and my situation in utero. Finding my father would ground me, he thought, in my life and on the court. What my game needed was roots, the one thing I'd never really felt, and there was only one way I was going to secure them.

Although I was able to relax over the summer in the knowledge that next season I'd not only be back in Breda, I'd be kicking-it in a new naughty gaff (right downtown, studio apartment, 12' ceilings), once I was back in Holland the usual craziness of pro ball would kick-in pretty much as soon as I landed. There was a meeting, the first of many it turned out, in which the bombshell was dropped that budget mis-calculations at the football club meant if this season were to happen at all, every one of us needed to take a 25% pay cut. Just when things had finally seemed to be settling down, here I was again; dissatisfied, frustrated and wondering whether I'd have hungered after my dream so hard had I known things would turn out like this. My good friend Femi Abodunde, who had roomed with me and Nahar at Wright State, was coming over to spend six weeks with me and it was perfect timing. Femi is the guy I go to for advice on life and he couldn't have timed this visit any better. There were plenty of heated debates between the squad and the chairman; discussions are bound to get lively when they involve money, especially a lack of it. We must have spent hours and hours locked in those talks. It would mean a monthly loss of $1,000 to me, but also something more, it meant the start of a creeping feeling that this was just the beginning of the end of things at Breda. We took the cut: at that stage, season virtually underway, what was the alternative? But our off-court woes were a distraction, one that inevitably trickled onto the court: our performance suffered, and so did our record.

We were pro's, though, and this was after all pro life in a nutshell and so we sucked it up, ploughed through the season and got ready for the playoffs. Finishing seventh meant we'd meet Groningen, a great team with some naughty Americans: Lamont Randolph who was a beast inside, and an outstanding guy by the name of Mack Tuck. Thanks to a great game by my boy Mark 'Booger' Sinema, a really athletic 6'5" power forward, we managed to knock them out of the playoffs only to fall to my nemesis, Amsterdam, in the semis.

Even if we had finished the season in a stronger position, there was no escaping the feeling that Breda's ship was sinking. I got onto my agent to see what he could do for me. There were issues with trying to sell me in

Belgium, he said, because they thought I couldn't score. Then send them the tape of me scoring over 20-, twice, against Holland's second best team! But it was no use, there'd be no love for me there, I'd messed up by not going to Antwerp in 1997 and, even if the ship I was on was sinking, the Belgian one had already left the dock. By now I was being represented by Jan Lughtenburg who suggested I should attend a 'pro exposure' camp in Budapest. It would mean paying my own flight but that wasn't the only thing that pissed me off. What had I been doing for the past few seasons if not getting exposure? I'd played full seasons in some of Europe's biggest leagues, averaged double-figures in Holland, and played for my National Team every year in the European Qualifiers. Couldn't a good agent sell a player with a resumé like that?

I had no choice. I might be impulsive sometimes, naïve, a little stubborn, but I'm not stupid; unless I was willing to take my chances in Breda (and I wasn't), I'd need to do some impressing. The majority of players at the Budapest camp were fresh out of school, most were yet to secure an agent, some of them were also damn near rude! Jan had told me that there was a general feeling that I was a baller who just didn't score; I needed to prove them wrong. I finished the first game (with Vincent Krieger running the point for us) with 21-points and I hadn't even taken a jump-shot. I'd gotten in the flow, had a couple of tough rebounds that finished with me going coast-to-coast and getting 'And Ones' and the word from Jan was that scouts were impressed. There'd be something in the pipeline he assured me, even some good-money early-talk from Paris Saint Germain. It sounded great. It spurred me on to a solid camp and at the end of it all, with 15-points per game against some major competition, Jan had me a job offer. It was in Breda.

There was no choice but to go back. Well, there was a choice, but I wasn't quite ready for a second English comeback yet. Over the summer things in Breda had gone from bad to worse. The club's negative finances had been taken over by a new businessman who'd keep the club afloat by cutting players' salaries even further. This was my third year on this NAC team and the third year my wages had dropped. When I'd left Germany I'd thought this new team would flourish. I'd been wrong. I'd also thought my wages would go up. Wrong there too.

Everything surrounding pre-season was a mess. We didn't only have no apartments, no new cars; we barely even had a gym to practice in. Housed in a rented place, way out of town on a caravan site, we had two intense two-hour practices a day. It must've been a lean season all round as the team Coach had managed to assemble was bordering on an All-Star squad: Groningen stars Lamont Randolph and Harvey Van Stein and a rebounding machine by the name of Angelo Flanders (who was a little bit like Newcastle's Leonard Stewart) had joined us whilst myself, Quentin, Nicola Simic, Kurt Schwamp and Mark Sinema had all returned. We were stacked; practices were intense and exciting, we forced ourselves to see past the shit money and focused on a vision: beat Amsterdam and win the Championship. We raced out to eight wins in a row, things were looking good, and then our money stopped. Pay day came but cash didn't arrive in bank accounts. Meetings followed. Everything was up in the air. The new owner pulled out and it looked like the whole thing might fold. Coach asked us to stick it out, see it through, but after the fourth meeting without progress, my patience was as shot as my finances. Coach was a good guy with big dreams and good intentions but he was clutching at straws, there was no way this team could continue with out proper financial backing. After a long heated debate, Coach asked who'd stand behind him and it's a credit to the faith held in him that some guys agreed. Other guys had family in Breda and so also wanted to stay; others were all too painfully aware that three months into the season, other options had pretty much dried up.

I, on the other hand, had made up my mind. I'm a very easy-going person, I have a reputation with my friends for sometimes being a little too soft but when it comes to my livelihood, my stubbornness comes through. Coach went around the table asking people if they were in or not and there'd been a Mexican wave of head-nodding. It came to me and I said 'No'. The room hushed with shock but I went on: I've had enough of the bullshit and the false promises, I'm packing my stuff. There was an argument, but I stood firm: I'm taking my chances. I packed my things into my little white car and headed off to the only other Dutch place I knew: Adele's place in Den Helder.

The fickleness of the world of basketball doesn't only stretch to last-minute sackings, it turned out that all that talk of me having blown it in Belgium had also now blown over and a couple of weeks after walking out of Breda, I was not only signed by Aartselaar, a second division team near Antwerp, I'd also managed to hook Nicola Simic up with a place on the squad. Second division meant that we only had to practice twice a week and so could just drive there and back without moving house again. That practice was very poor was no surprise, but when your pay check suddenly stops coming, you have to do something. I bumped into my old teammate, Hans from Leuven, there and we had some fun, but playing at that lower level was frustrating. I forced myself to get on with it, to think that at least I was earning, and to focus on getting out of there, quick.

A call from my agent saved my skin. Ten weeks of the season remained and I'd be spending them in France at St. Etienne. It was already late March but as the French season continues longer than in any other country, I'd be playing until mid June. I didn't care, so grateful was I to have found a place on a higher level team. The news got better; I'd be rooming with my old friend and England teammate Mike Martin who also played for St. Etienne. We'd spent time together on England tours but these only ever lasted for a couple of weeks so this was the first time we'd had long periods in one another's company and we became pretty close. It's funny how you seem to just find people when you most need them, just as with Rob Gibbons back in Breda, Mike was going through a tough time. The strain that living away was having on his relationship with his wife and son, hundreds of miles away across the English Channel, was causing Mike to question whether being a baller was the right path for him at all. Any baller will tell you, maintaining anything like a normal relationship with someone so far away is virtually impossible.

Mike's talent was purely home-grown. His late start in ball had meant he'd missed any opportunity of an NCAA college, had played a few years in London and, after the exposure of being snapped up by the National Team, he'd been scouted and offered a good contract in the second division of France where the standard was very high, probably higher than in the BBL. Mike had finally made it into Europe and I was proud of him. Going to the States doesn't only help you hone your skills and develop your game, it also allows really young guys the experience of living a long, long way from any friends and family. It's often hard (especially at such a young age) but I appreciated now the life experience it had brought. It was tough for me and Adele to keep our relationship going, but at least we'd had periods of time living close by one another, and I was, after all, more than used to living on different continents from the people I loved.

Although brief, my time in France was a good experience, the French reputation for practising hard hadn't changed, maybe I just appreciated getting to practice more than I had before the precariousness of pro' life had hit home. In France there's no such thing as a light morning shoot around; any shoot around is a full-blown, full-court one-on-one. But yet again I'd been sent to a team as a power forward. Even at the ultimate weight I'd achieved (around 208 lbs), it wasn't my optimum position. I had to battle with Mike and George Phillips on a daily basis, both of whom were chiselled to the max and tipped the scales at 235 lbs. Even though I tried to tell them otherwise, the guys on the team thought it was my position and would kind of roll their eyes when I told them I was actually a guard. So day after day, month after month, I would be on the block. My outside skills and confidence were slowly wearing away. I earned my minutes at St. Etienne through hustle and defence and because I was more experienced than Mike. It was frustrating for him, not only because sometimes Coach would play me over him, but also because Mike's a true baller, and a true baller always wants to be on the court.

I'd been brought in at the role of defensive stopper and it was a role I was getting accustomed to as I also played it on the National Team. I'd also been drafted in to St. Etienne to replace a player who'd been injured at the same time as a new coach had arrived. With just ten games of the season remaining, the team was already on the brink of relegation without all this turmoil and so the aim now was the save St. Etienne from going down and just get on with the job I was paid to do. I did, and after ten games we were 7-3 and out of the danger zone. Job done.

Although basketball was by now very much a job, there were of course memorable games which were still challenging and fun to play in. One which stands out at St. Etienne was a French Cup game against Pau Orthez who not only topped Pro A (France's elite league) but dominated it with a winning margin of 20-points per game. As second division relegation threats, St. Etienne versus Pau Orthez had the makings of a potential on-court massacre. Their starting-five included two players on their way to the NBA: Boris Diaw (Phoenix Suns) and Michael Pietrus, but we stepped-up. With myself, Mike and George Phillips all having a stand-out game. The gulf of difference between our teams was massive, reflected in the type of salaries players were receiving with even our top player being paid just a fifth of that of Pau Orthez's. You won't be surprise that we lost but we held them close and, at close of play, the gulf had lessened with only 9-points separating us.

My ability to remain optimistic (sometimes beyond the realms of believability) is probably the personality trait to which I owe my sanity. Season over, there was no way St. Etienne were offering a contract; to them I was a power forward and so was also too small, but I kept the faith and entered the summer with the belief that I'd be getting a call any day. August moved into September and the realization moved in that even if the call did come now, I'd be joining a team after the start of the season. It was becoming a regular occurrence, one I'd never enjoyed. The lifestyle was starting to get old; waiting around all summer long, effectively homeless and so camping out at people's houses, not earning for three, four even five months and so never getting anywhere financially as I was always having to support myself through such times by spending any savings the season had brought. I was getting to the time in my life when I was thinking more about the future and with no permanent base, no way of securing one any time soon and no money, I wasn't sure what that future would bring. When I'd dreamt the dream I had no idea of its harsh realities;

it's probably good that I didn't. And then the call came, my faith was restored and I packed my bags for Austria.

It wasn't only the fact that Wörthersee Piraten were six games into the season that made me a little wary of the move, nor that the team's coach had a reputation as a hard ass; I'd always hated cold weather and the thought of basketball mixed with lakes and snow seemed a mix too far. But it was a job and Austria seemed like a nice country to live in. Still, I couldn't help thinking it would be a backwards step in terms of my basketball career. I was wrong.

There wasn't time to check anything out, at least not now, and before I knew it I was in the gym taking a few shots on the side so as not to interrupt the session which was already in progress. Coach Rick Brooks, whose bellowing voice was a complete contrast to his skinny-looking frame, said *'Is this him? Warm-up now. Let's see what you got!'* I was accustomed to coming straight from airport to gym but I'd never come across a coach who didn't even come over to greet you before. Coach Brooks wasn't even unfriendly, he was kind of intimidating; quite an achievement with such a frail appearance. *'Let's see what you got,'* he repeated, calling me out in front of the whole team, *'I heard you can play D.'* And with a final shout of *"Boogey' you guard him.'* That was it, game on.

The 'Boogey' in question was around 6'4" and built like a tank. The older of two brothers on the team, he was the Austrian National Team's enforcer, not that I knew any of this at the time. All I knew then was that this guy was trying to punk me right off the bat. He tried to play very physical with me and every time he got the ball, Coach would yell *'Take him Boogey, take him!'* But it didn't work. I locked him up and matched his aggressiveness no problem. I may not have the 'juice head' build of a 'Boogey' but I was just as strong, if not stronger, on the court. Nervousness made my shot a little off but pretty soon Coach lightened-up and seemed satisfied with what he'd got.

Although it was probably the weirdest introduction to a team I'd had, it was clear from the off that everything about this squad was professional.

I moved straight into my fully-furnished apartment and boy what a place! The Club's President owned a small family-run hotel out on the lake in Reifnitz. Although twenty minutes from the centre of town and accessed through a forest, the place was unbelievable and included two self-contained apartments in the grounds, one of which would be mine. The set-up here was a million miles from anything I'd experienced before. On every other pro team I'd been on, if a player needed anything, he had no chance of getting it unless he was prepared to kick up a fuss, boycott practice, stamp his feet; this was a different world. If you needed anything at Wörthersee Piraten (a VCR for your apartment, let's say), you not only got it by the next day, you also got an apology that sorting it out had taken so long. The team organization couldn't have been better and my gratitude for that almost outshone my frustrations at being stuck playing power forward again, but not quite.

My agent had yet again sent me to a team who needed an athletic four man. That was all he had for me and so of course I went. But still I felt like I was wasting my talent and time. The best part about my game is my ball handling and passing but playing inside takes away a lot of my effectiveness. It was the same old story. By now I guess I should have been used to it, but it's hard to explain how demoralizing it was to once again, for the fourth year in a row, be stuck playing inside, banging with the big boys. There was a little hurt pride in there too. I hated that my peers would actually think of me as an undersized power forward, but it also meant that getting to play the point for England in an International tournament in Austria in the coming summer would feel extra-special.

If I'd had my doubts about the standard of basketball in Austria before I'd arrived, my mind soon changed when I saw the pedigree of our point guard, Thomas Kelly. He'd played back-up point guard at Michigan State when they went to the Final Four, his court-time only sometimes limited by future NBA guard Mateen Cleaves. The standard of play and the popularity of NCAA ball can be proven by the stat that one game in Detroit between Michigan State and North Carolina drew a crowd of 78,000. That's college basketball, folks! 'TK', as we called him, was tough. He was a quiet guy I remembered from when I played in Holland but man could he play. He was very strong, had a fearless attitude, and was incredibly quick. Our two other Americans were NCAA Division Two All-American, Eric Brand, and a raw power forward from Oregon called Rob Johnson. With former Croatian International Nenad Vidicka, two England Internationals (myself and later on Refiloe Lethuyna), and an Austrian International in 'Boogey' (real name Joachim) we were pretty stacked and managed to hang around the top four positions in the league.

Austria would prove to be an experience which was all about hard work for me. Coach Rick Brooks' tough non-nonsense attitude was legendary in Austria and he had a solid rep' for working his players to death. He told us: *'You guys are going to be the best conditioned team in this league!'* and he damn well made sure we were. He pushed me especially hard, having missed pre-season conditioning. He didn't let up until I was amongst the best conditioned players on the team. When Refiloe turned up not in the best shape halfway through the season, Coach let him have it, yelling and making us all play really hard until Refiloe was damn near dying. Coach Brooks was the only coach I ever had who would stand under the basket during warm-ups to make sure you were going at full speed. He wanted nothing but the best and wouldn't stop until he got it. I remember one game in which he wanted me to press full-court and, just because my man caught the ball 90ft away from our basket, he let me have it; like I just lost us the game or something!

The guy with the bugged-out eyes and the crazy thirst for perfection was a completely different character away from the court. Coach Rick Brooks was caring and thoughtful, the kind of guy who would do anything for you. The first time I really saw this side to him was during a break in season when he invited me and a few other players up to his home in Slovakia where we went out drinking and had a blast. After this we began to have some individual sessions during morning practice and, one-on-one I was able to showcase both my guard skills and my shooting. He (like most other coaches in Europe) hadn't seen me play as a guard in the NCAA or in Italy and was really shocked to see this other side of my game. He came to practice the following day and said to me *'Del, you need to watch Sea Biscuit.'* I said 'What the hell is that?' He came at me deep, I was taken aback, and he said *'Just watch the film, and when you have, let me know.'* I spent the afternoon sat at home in front of a rented tape.

The film was about a horse. A race horse who was smaller than other horses and lacked some self-belief, he'd fallen from grace with his owner (who also owned a Triple Crown winner whom he favoured) and was mainly used as a front-runner. Eventually, Sea Biscuit was bought by a trainer who not only believed in him, but understood him. Matched with a Canadian Jockey (also down on his luck), Sea Biscuit's career finally took off and his legacy began. In 1938 he won 11 out of 15 races, including one with phenomenal rewards which in today's money would have netted his owner $2m. Sea Biscuit became an American legend and was National Champion many times over.

So what the rass did this all have to do with me. I'd never even been on a horse, I'd been on a donkey once at the Beach in Rhyl, North Wales, but even though I was only about seven years old, my legs were so long my toes had scraped the sand as the poor thing had hobbled along. Turns out Coach meant it as kind of a metaphor. He'd already flat-out looked at me straight in the eyes, after watching me put all types of moves on his starting guards in a morning practice, and said; *'Why aren't you making $140,000 somewhere?'* My thoughts had immediately returned to Trieste, to how different my career might have been had I had the foresight to have looked past the money and stayed in Italy. Coach Brooks told me: *'I always knew you had more talent than any player I ever coached and I coached some good ones. I felt you could have been wereever you wanted to with basketball but didn't seem to make the right choices.'* With this kind of faith behind me, I might have been able to salvage something more in Austria. But I was already 32, getting older and getting to the stage where flogging my ass to death in practice for the kind of money I could earn back in England was starting to feel no longer worth it.

For the time being though things were going well on the court. Coach had everything taken care of; there wasn't a detail small enough for him not to cover and when February rolled around (the time when most teams cut back on the tougher side of life, like two-a-day practices), Coach shocked us all by cranking everything up to a whole new level. We were going into the playoffs in tip-top shape and so, for two weeks, we went into training overload. After a full evening practice, ending as ever in a half-hour scrimmage, we'd now complete a series of sprints: ten lengths of the court in one minute, five times, with only a one-minute break. Any baller is familiar with a 'suicide' (running to the free-throw line and back to baseline, then half-court line and back, etc) but this was practically two 'suicides' back-to-back, without a break, five times. A week of this and we were like walking zombies. The height of it all came after a midweek two-hour scrimmage; Coach pushed us to play our hardest, only to make us finish off again with five sets of sprints there and then. He was trying to break us and see how tough we were. At the following day's practice we could barely move, and then out of nowhere I produced a naughty tip-dunk in traffic. It amazed everyone, especially me; Coach laughed *'If you can still jump like that, I'm obviously not working you guys hard enough!'*

Pushing us to the limit physically had meant we were not only in great physical shape but also great mental shape. I was going to need it. As things had started to strengthen for me professionally, cracks had begun to appear in my life off the court. Adele and I had managed to somehow keep our relationship going throughout the past four years. It had been really tough at times, pro life only allows space for weirdly-placed free time, in the middle of a week day, say, but rarely ever evenings and certainly not weekends. But playing in Holland and Belgium had meant the miles between us weren't insurmountable, as long as I was willing to cover those miles in my car. Austria was a different matter, with a settled life, a job and young children in Den Helder, relocating was out of the question for Adele, and our relationship was exposed. We argued a lot over the phone during the first few months and then, over Christmas, She called it off. I was devastated and for the first three months or so had trouble sleeping; waking in the middle of the night in a pool of sweat. Mentally I was a mess, I focused everything I had onto the court and was probably saved by the sheer intensity of Coach Brooks' expectations.

Even though it seemed impossible, basketball went up another notch with the arrival of playoffs. We couldn't have been more prepared, Coach had seen to that. But there's not much you can do about nerves, which had a massive impact on some of our players. But not 36-year-old Nenad who, after a season of chilling, decided to elevate his game back to Croatian National Team standards and played some outstanding ball. Some players are like this, able to literally relax during season only to pull it out of the bag when it matters most. Others expose the cheek of this by committing that extra mile when it's unimaginable that there's an extra mile to give. One such player was Andreas Kuttnig.

Really young, around 21, Kuttnig was our tenth man, charged with the unenviable role of guarding Thomas Kelley everyday in practice. A tough assignment. But Kuttnig was a tough competitor and the more I watched him play in the junior games, the more I could see he had serious game. When I got to know him better, I realized his work ethic was nearly on par with Vitaly's: working an extra four hours a day during season, and in the off-season doing sprints, lifting, shooting, ball-handling drill, everything. If he hadn't put in six-hours of work in a day, he thought he hadn't done enough. We spent a lot of time together as the season in Austria progressed and it's great to see that all Andreas' hard work has paid off. He's still with the team, and is now a permanent starter.

We were knocked out of the playoffs by the new team of my boy from Breda, Rod Platt. But I was in no rush to leave. After the way things had been going personally, I needed some time to take stock, just working-out and enjoying Klagenfurt's social life. I'd moved from my place out on the lake into town and spent time enjoying myself. One weekend the whole of sleepy Reifnitz was taken over by a 'VW' Rally. Turns out the otherwise beautiful but incredibly quiet town on Wörthersee Lake is, for one weekend of the summer, a Mecca for every 'suped' up chromed-out Volkswagen imaginable. The place was unrecognizable, with huge marquees housing makeshift bars and clubs and revellers everywhere you look. I bumped into my former WSU teammate there, our 6'11" centre Steno Kos, and made sure

I took the chance to enjoy myself in such a beautiful setting. It was crazy that one of the wildest parties I'd ever been to would be right on my doorstep in the quietest place in which I'd ever lived.

It was time to go. Not only to leave Austria, but also to leave the Continent. As the season had progressed I'd made my decision; this would be my last season of playing in Europe. It was an amazing season to finish on, one that had taught me a lot, but the Continental market which had been so buoyant five years before was getting increasingly tougher to find work in, even for players not the wrong side of 30. It can get very lonely out there. I wasn't the first player to want to come home for this reason and I certainly won't be the last. I was heading for England, I'd need to find a team, but for the first time in my career I'd begun to think beyond ball. I needed to start thinking about what I'd do once I retired from playing basketball. I would need to start the groundwork. Before I headed back to my mum's, a 32-year-old man more than a little lost, I made one last detour to Holland to try to save my relationship. But, like my time on the Continent, it was over. Time to move on.

A Patriot

As a National team starting-five the line-up was kind of naughty: John Amaechi, Roger Huggins, Steve Bucknall, Karl Brown and me. Major talent and all with the added bonus of plenty of time in the American game under our jerseys. Not bad for a country still so new to basketball. That we'd all played so long in the States was proof that opportunities in England were still limited and that a baller looking to make a life in the sport was still looking across the Atlantic.

I'd played alongside John Amaechi in Manchester when we were both teenagers: he'd just picked up a ball and was terrible, but within six years was starting for the NBA's Cleveland Cavaliers. Enough said! Like me, John was now playing in the big leagues of Europe, as was another of our starters, Steve Bucknall. Although I'd followed Steve's career avidly, I'd only actually met him a few months before our first Men's team practice. I'd recognised him in a German airport en-route to Trieste. Steve Bucknall is an English basketball legend. After captaining the University of North Carolina, he became the NBA's first British baller, a stint which included half a season with the world famous Los Angeles Lakers. I've never been backward in introducing myself, but it was a little surreal to shake his hand as I recalled him so vividly from starring in a UNC - Duke game on one of my cherished college videos. It was great to meet him, especially prior to seeing him on court in practice. I explained that Coach Laszlo Nemeth had recruited me after coming to watch me in a summer scrimmage and I'd be joining the squad at their next training camp.

Another English legend featured in Laszlo's new starting-five; Roger Huggins, one of the nicest guys you'd ever wish to meet, who was at the time holding it down with Sheffield Sharks: dominating English ball, winning every major domestic trophy and doing the whole thing with a constant smile on his face. Another player more than a little familiar with the American scene rounded out the line-up: Karl Brown. A star at Georgia Tech, one of the most big-time of all Big Time colleges, Karl had even played in the Final Fours (the only English guy to ever do so) and I'd seen loads of him on college tapes. Without doubt the most talented and experienced starting-five I'd ever featured on, but we still managed to lose our first game.

At our first practice I'd been really excited; it felt like an achievement to even be on the same court as the best players in the country and I wanted to get my props right off. I hadn't known at the time when I'd met Karl Brown in Italy that he and Steve Bucknall were really close friends and so my assurances to Karl that I was more than a match for Bucknall one-on-one had, of course, got straight back to him and he was ready for me as I arrived at practice with a shout of *'I hear you've been talking shit, young fella!'* I was 23, fresh out of college and raring to go. On one of the first plays Steve was guarding me and, determined to make an impression, I flashed to the post on the right-hand side of the court receiving the ball from the National Team's most capped player, Ronnie Baker. With Bucknall on my back, I quickly spun to the baseline and dunked the ball hard, on the other side of the basket. It got me noticed then and there; Ronnie Baker coined a nickname for me; *'Sauce!'* (a tribute to my mad flavour). I was honoured to be on court with these guys, overwhelmed to start alongside them and felt I'd finally arrived.

Although we lost that first game, to receive my first cap (against the Czech Republic in Leicester) was quite a welcome home. It was the first time I'd played in England for six years and, to celebrate, the whole family had come to watch the game. The loss mattered in the way that any loss matters. No one ever wants to lose or is able to easily accept it (if they can, they're in the wrong profession), and nothing was going to completely take the shine from this experience, but it did become clear from the start that building a National Team has unique complexities: our clubs were scattered across Europe, we'd meet for a two-day practice prior to a match and then expect to click as a unit out there on court. National Team was going to be a whole new world of experience.

Getting over my admiration of the other players (and the fact that I was now sharing the hardwood with them) was my first hurdle as I'd watched many of them from afar since I'd first found basketball. One such player was Ronnie Baker. I'd literally grown up watching Ronnie and his twin-brother Stedroy dominating at Brixton Top Cats and, for a long time, Ronnie had been a National Team mainstay. Players were petrified to guard those Baker boys and their speed was legendary; they were English Hoops Royalty. But when I met Ronnie, he was nothing like I expected a player with such a rep' to be. I was shocked by how quiet and humble he was, especially considering his record as the highest-capped player is unlikely to ever be topped. It was reassuring to see such successful players who were also managing to be just really nice guys; rolled together, Ronnie and Roger Huggins didn't have a bad bone between them.

Our captain at the time was Peter Scantlebury, another really nice guy whose amazing career has seen him come full-circle in the world of English basketball; first as a player (second only to Ronnie in number of International caps), then captaining the side, going on to become Assistant Coach and ultimately Head Coach (steering us to our Bronze Medal victory at the Melbourne Commonwealth Games in 2006). Scants was a massive support to me from the start and, along with the other guys, made me feel really welcome as part of the elite of English ballers. He recalls that very first practice, too: *'Everyone could see Del had talent and was a very gifted athlete but for some reason things did not click for him at the start. Maybe it was the huge weight of expectation on his shoulders. However, as time went on he established himself as a regular in the England squad and he proved himself to be a very reliable and a great part of the squad. In particular, he would use his athleticism on the defensive end and showed his versatility by being able to defend players from guards to forwards. He also used his versatility at the offensive end by being able to play in three positions. I think he found his niche in playing a role on the team rather than being the star player.'*

A pattern to our year quickly emerged. To attempt to make Europe's top-16 we'd play qualifiers, meeting in November for a 10-day stint and then again in February. The time in between was spent fulfilling our various club responsibilities. We had some big guns on our team, players like Amaechi, Bucknall, Spencer Dunkley and Andy Gardiner; guys who liked to shoot, leaving me the role of defensive stopper. It was great for Steve Bucknall as I was stepping into the role he'd played in at college and in his early pro career, allowing him to conserve most of his energy for the offensive end now. Him stepping back to let the young buck do the dirty work was fine by me. Anything that got me good minutes at this level, and might secure a win for the team, was all cool.

National Team brought something unique to my basketball career, a sense of pride and honour at getting to meet and to play with so many cool teammates. Each year there'd be new faces on the squad as guys just graduating from college and finally getting the long-deserved 'nod' arrived, and others who'd been waiting on paperwork could step-up having finally got their English passports. It was also an amazing chance to travel to loads of different countries and face some really impressive opposition.

In my first year I flew home from Italy to play against Russia at the Guildford Arena. We had a good squad. Amongst our starters was Spencer Dunkley, 6'11" of real talent who'd been drafted in the second round of the NBA. The Russian team were stacked. We were neck and neck throughout and it was a rough game. In the first-half, Ian McKinney's head met my lip on our inbound play, sending my tooth straight through my top lip, leaving me to spend half-time with a paper towel over my face having my lip stitched through a little cut-out hole, and playing the second-half with a blood-soaked jersey like some warrior of ball. The game went right to the wire and with two-seconds to go we were down by a single point. Amaechi took the final shot: it missed. I jumped. Tipped the ball and, with a fraction of a second remaining, it was in. But the refs blatantly disallowed the basket and we were left gutted.

It was phenomenal to face such major competition. Many teams we met were outstanding, but a difference between them and us was immediately apparent: our team had funding issues. Lack of investment in the sport had been one of the things which had driven me Stateside and which had been so shocking when I'd first arrived there and saw the financial gulf between English and American ball. In the early years we'd had a very small Nike deal; we'd each been given two or three sweatshirts, a couple of t-shirts and a single pair of boots. In terms of American ball, this was laughable, especially considering that in the decade I played for England, they were the only pair I was ever supplied with! (It was even ridiculous in comparison with the four pairs I received in just two summers of playing with Midnight Madness!) But it wasn't only equipment that was an issue. Playing for National Team was an honour but sometimes it was an honour which actually left players out of pocket. Travelling to meet up with the team was reimbursable but being reimbursed took months and months and sometimes never happened at all. Players were given a per diem (daily payment) which stood in 1996 at £25, and in 2006 at (guess what?) £25. It's just as well we were all so proud to represent our country. When we met up, we'd practice for four hours (making the most of the little time we had) and would travel by road crammed into small mini-buses or vans. There was none of the pro sport glamour some of the guys were experiencing at their clubs, but there was a real team-spirit and also a huge amount of respect for our coach, Laszlo Nemeth, who went out of his way to support the team more times than I could count, often paying out of his own pocket for the team to eat when the realisation dawned that the deal which had been provided by English Basketball was inadequate.

Laszlo Nemeth is one of those coaches who embody the best of his sport. There wasn't much he wouldn't do on a practical level to support the squad and had even been forced to defend our race. Unofficially, Laszlo had received word from the powers-that-be that there was dissatisfaction with the National Team's racial balance. Bluntly: too many of us were black. Laszlo, a white Hungarian, massively supportive of his new-found English 'brothers', refused to back down, never bowed to pressure and never considered race to be relevant in the selection of players. He simply did what every good coach does, continued to select the best man for the job. Although he was complimentary about my game, recalling: *'I realised immediately that I see on court an outstanding athletic talent, who was elastic, could jump and was quick like the lightning.'* Laszlo is also a coach who recognizes the off-court things which are essential in making a player successful: *'England basketball team operated at the time on a shoe-string budget and to play for the country often cost money for the participants. Delme's incredible commitment came alight when he joined the program and never abandoned it, and even returned without hard feelings when I cut him on one or two occasions. These are the human qualities what made him a permanent member of the squad. His commitment and readiness never were in doubt if I called him for National Team duty.'*

The under-current that those behind the scenes at England Basketball were on a different page from the coaches and players would be frequently obvious. From issues of not respecting the commitments made (most heart-breakingly relieving Laszlo of his National Team duties, just before his ten-year mark, meaning that his English citizenship alone wasn't enough to qualify him for a state pension), to an over-riding sense that we were simply on our own. One of the worst occasions was a game scheduled to take place in Russia's CSKA Moscow Arena in which our entire squad consisted of just seven players, the others on lock-down at home due to a lack of organization concerning visas. It was a joke. We were so desperate to conserve our under-manned squad's energy that we were even reluctant to run all the way to the half-court during lay-ups. Unsurprisingly, we got battered, but Yorick Williams managed a great game, scoring 24- of our limited points.

Managing to remain committed under such challenging circumstances was something Laszlo excelled at. It was also a blessing to have him on side in some of the Eastern European countries we'd regularly visit, with five languages and an understanding of the workings of such places, he was indispensable. Once in Minsk, Belarus, our Assistant Coach Tony Garbelotto lagged behind the rest of us crossing the road on the way back to our hotel and was accosted by a couple of cops in a boot-leg Skoda who inexplicably began to demand money from him. Laszlo, fluent in Russian, managed to square them off and Garbs escaped being dragged off to the cop-shop for nothing more than walking too slowly (or secretly laughing at their Skoda). It was an eventful trip all round, trips to such places where there seemed a Mafia kind of whiff in the air were often like this. One night a group of my teammates were woken by a ruckus outside their window. On the street below a woman was screaming out, she was being beaten by a group of men and, unsure what else to do, the guys called down to reception to ask them to call the police. The reception-guy spoke English and listened to their concerns before assuring them he wouldn't be calling for help; instead, he'd be doing exactly what he recommended they now did: minded their own business. The Minsk trip wasn't particularly unusual (we'd even previously stayed in Eastern European hotels where the lobby staff were armed guards) the food was worse than usual though and was nowhere near sufficient to feed a team of 6' and 7' ballers. Laszlo and Garbs always thought ahead though. They'd brought us emergency supplies, a stash of Pot Noodles, in their suitcases.

Representing our country as ambassadors of ball was not only less than glamorous, it was often simply crazy. But we were soldiers who loved the sport and the honour of being the England squad and so we sucked everything up and focused on the task at hand. We completed the Minsk trip with a victory, playing a solid game in front of a hostile crowd, tough but really enjoyable. The lack of glamour rounded the trip off nicely for Roger Huggins who (needing to get back to the UK for his son's birthday) was forced to travel back across Europe by train. A 6'8" black guy, travelling alone, unable to speak the native language of any of the countries he travelled through didn't escape attention for very long and was stopped and incomprehensibly interrogated at every border. Fear and frustration aren't generally associated with the perceived luxuries of professional International sport, but they certainly exist, for British ballers at least. It didn't dent his commitment, though, and next trip out, Rog' was back in his England jersey.

Being part of the England squad was always a massive honour, usually a great laugh and full of weird paradoxes. In my second year of representing, in a game versus Israel at Manchester's MEN Arena, I was guarding an Israeli player who earned $500,000 a year, whilst I was struggling for, fraction of that figure in my own pro life and being fed Pot Noodles by Coach Nemeth to keep my energy up. It was a game I really enjoyed though. I played excellent defence, hustled hard and it was that which brought me to the attention of Bob Gonnen, an American-Israeli coach, who'd then called my agent and sorted my contract with Den Helder. For me, this highlighted one of the side-effects of playing for the National Team. Although pretty much no one outside of basketball knew anything about us (probably didn't even know there was an England Basketball team) and any exposure was limited to a few sentences in the sports section of a small number of newspapers, people in the know would get to see us play against the best in the world and this would often lead to other professional opportunities opening up.

The 'having a laugh' side of National Team cannot be underestimated and was one of the things the guys loved most about meeting up. We'd get a break from club responsibilities a couple of times a year and became like a family – one which worked extremely hard on court, and played even harder off it. A couple of us were nicknamed 'The Night Cats' by Laszlo. He found our fondness for kicking-it off-court kind of amusing, and so we always felt we shouldn't let Coach down and lived up to our off-court reputations whenever possible. One of the first laughs would be when a new player arrived in the squad and the solemn inauguration ceremony would take place; standing on a chair surrounded by the rest of the team attempting to sing the National Anthem without knowing many of the words. It was a ceremony undertaken by the current Great Britain team captain Andrew Sullivan when he was still at a New Jersey high school. I knew he was going to be a player from the off when he dunked on Amaechi off the 'vert'. He went on to Villanova University, dominated at the Newcastle Eagles for several years and then deservedly signed a big contract in Spain.

Sometimes by the time a player was called up to the squad, it would feel to the rest of us (and no doubt to them too) like a long-overdue capping, one such call-up was Yorick Williams who, once the nod finally did come, didn't disappoint. That tough-neck could shoot the lights out and had

224

grown from our days back in Manny into an outstanding defender. In an early game against Slovenia he held their star guard to just 4-points, contributing significantly to our overall 4-point victory. International level can be crazy at times; our win over Slovenia was followed by a merciless 40-point beating by Italy, only for Slovenia to then batter Italy a week later. If the game stats were up and down, at least one thing was consistent; our level of talent. Yorick arrived at a similar time as a guy from Birmingham, Steve Hansell. After attending a junior college Stateside, Steve went on to Illinois State and turned out to be our starting point guard over Ronnie Baker. I'd played with him before both on the Under 19 squad and at the World Student Games and he subsequently went on to a great contract with the Italian team Bologna before spending most of his pro career in Greece. Another one of our stars at this time was a young guy from Leicester, Andy Betts. Andy was, like most of the England players of this era, a great fun-loving guy. He was 7'2" of potential who went on to Long Beach State in California, and was drafted second round in the NBA. He's still playing in Spain now.

Another new member joined us on our 2000 tour of New Zealand. Fresh from Georgia State, Julius Joseph was a division two All-American whose game could be described in one word; TOUGH. He turned some heads in New Zealand, was a fearless shooter, strong, aggressive, tough on the block and an out-and-out warrior. He would become a stalwart of the team and we went on to play together for many years, culminating in us standing together on the podium receiving our Commonwealth Bronze Medals following our last-ever game for England.

In a similar position, as a mainstay of the team, was Chris Haslem. When he came to his first practice in Hungary I was struck by his size, 6'11" and about 285lbs. Chris, a fellow northerner from Southport, had played on a team with my brother before securing a scholarship to the University of Wyoming. He was a great post defender, very strong with an outstanding touch on his jump-shot and a complete lack of shyness when it came to pulling the trigger. He had a long and successful career playing in Europe's best leagues before coming home to finish his career in the BBL with Everton Tigers.

It was unusual for a National Team player to not have at least some level of American experience. To compete at International level, it's vital to have the edge that only playing in the NCAA can give, but Mike Martin arrived in the England squad looking to smash that expectation. At 6'6" Mike's built like a gladiator; a gladiator with Hops! I'll never forget his first practice in Coventry; he caught the ball on the right base line, drove hard to the basket and hook dunked it with authority on the other side of the rim. Seriously impressive, especially considering he did all this on a 6'10" guy and another who stood at 7'. With Mike's arrival, National Team practice jumped to a whole new level. He was hungry but very raw and hadn't had the chance to get Stateside as he'd been 21 by the time he'd first picked up a ball. That Mike could perform like this with so little grounding in the sport was terrifying; only one other guy could dominate practice by dunking on people this way, fellow Mancunian Mike Bernard. He played college ball in Florida and had a good career in big leagues in Europe. He's 6'9" and a beast. At a tournament in Egypt he dunked on three guys at the same time, Ta Neck-Back! In addition to these guys, our two power forwards were Kojo Mensah-Bonsu and Refiloe Lethuyna, both tough players who played serious college ball. Kojo out at Washington in the Pac 10, and Refiloe at Miami of Ohio. Chris Pearson from Davidson was another serious talent.

As well as getting to play alongside the country's elite, National Team had other positives, one of which was the amount of fun we had. A number of my teammates were as interested as I was in getting out and kicking-it hard once our playing responsibilities had been fulfilled. There are numerous memorable nights from this time in my career and often at the centre of these was one of my favourite teammates, Ray Carter, who, like Silas Cheung, was essentially American but had been born in the UK and therefore claimed by us. Ray had a very similar character to mine. He loved to crack jokes and have fun (not to mention the odd cheeky drink). He was right up my alley. Oh, and he could ball too. On the court the guy had no conscience. I'd never seen anyone shoot the ball from so deep before, and with both him and Yorick on the court at the same time, anything could happen.

If playing alongside the elite was a thrill, playing against the elite of the rest of Europe was a challenge I relished and these were always the games I enjoyed most. Teams like Spain, Croatia, Italy and Slovenia were tough and I had a lot of respect for them. It wasn't like we didn't hold our own, we certainly had as good a defence as any team. It was in creating a fluid offence where we struggled. There was definite potential though and that was frustrating. Had we had more chance to practice in the summer, or had we all played in the same domestic league, we'd have got it together. But sadly we didn't and the flow the other top teams enjoyed seemed to stagnate between our two best players, Bucknall and Amaechi.

There were moments of greatness though; games which I'll remember forever and which seemed to hold a different level of significance from those played professionally at club level. One such game was a home clash against the huge Hungarian team. It was significant before our toes even touched the court; because of Laszlo being Hungarian but also because in order to qualify for the summer championships, we not only needed a win, it needed to be secured by a minimum of 7-points. Failure would mean the torture of having to attempt to re-qualify in some obscure country in the middle of the summer. It was a huge game, made huger still by the number of players we were without. It was the extreme of a skeleton squad; we'd no Steve Hansell, no John Amaechi, Andy Gardiner, Julius Joseph, Silas Cheung, Ray Carter, Mike Martin, Mike Bernard, Chris Pearson, Tony Dorsey or Chris Haslem. It was ridiculous but we soldiered it out to make Laszlo proud. After three minutes we'd also lost Roger Huggins, out for the remainder of the game with a back injury. I got the nod and entered the game at the power forward spot. As well as being seriously under-manned (even our Assistant Coach Peter Scantlebury dressed-up), Hungary were enormous. In addition to a 7'2" guy who played in France, they had a number of guys who stood at 6'10". It was a battle; a game which went all the way down to the wire where we managed to secure not only a victory, but also a victory by the exact 7-points we so desperately needed.

I hadn't really thought too much about retirement, figuring I'd play as long as I possibly could, but by the end of 2004 I was 31. In sporting terms, not a spring chicken, and it was then that we heard that an England squad would be formed to play in the 2006 Commonwealth Games in Melbourne, Australia. The squad would have only twelve spots, considerably less than the number of regular faces we had, and from the off one thing was clear; whoever got to go Down-Under had better be prepared to bring back a medal. Even with eighteen months to go, coming home without one was definitely not an option. There was a sense of this being a real make-or-break moment for English basketball. I don't recall it being spelled out to us, but I do vividly recall the immediate knowledge that a medal-less return from Australia would destroy any future basketball funding.

As is probably clear from the sheer number of players I've mentioned here (and believe me, this is only a fraction of the entire squad over my years), we rarely played two games with the same guys on the bench, let alone the same starting-five. I figured that criteria for picking the team would come down to chemistry and commitment. The preparation schedule which had been put together included plenty of time for training and playing together and so seemed to finally deliver the kind of backing that might make us a great team. However, it wouldn't all be plain sailing. A closer inspection showed that each trip featured a different squad, not because Coach deliberately wanted to rotate, purely because of players' prior commitments or their reluctance to spend too much of their summer break away on long trips.

The first tour in 2004 saw a skeleton team head off to Japan. So many players were missing that the tour included only four guys who eventually made the final cut. It was my second time in Japan and it was a real pleasure to return as I especially loved the hospitality of the Japanese. We were to travel a little once over there, playing the Japanese team in three different locations, and I was excited to be captaining the squad. Being captain is a pretty clear-cut honour, he's simply the guy with the most National Team caps. But nonetheless, for me it was the fulfilment of a childhood dream. As it was summertime and these were just friendlies, I was shocked by the size of the crowd at our first game, with 5,000 turning out in spite of it being televised. Our first loss, was however, followed by another two and whilst the whole experience had been pretty amazing, I was disappointed. This was nowhere near the capability of our real team, had our mainstays have turned out. However, their absence did make the trip a great opportunity for some new players to enjoy a spot on the team with Chris Sanders, Junior Williams, Keith Jarret, Lijah Perkins, Dave 'Tin Tin' Watts and a guy called Phil Perre (great at getting in the passing lanes) all making their debut. But I couldn't dampen down a little hint of annoyance at the thought of the usual guys walking back in at the last minute to claim their Commonwealth Games spot, in spite of the rest of us committing and working for our places 7,000 miles away from home.

There were many complexities to selecting the Commonwealth squad, in particular a ruling that, to be eligible, a player must be currently competing in that country's domestic league. The Games meant a month away from your club and European teams (ineligible to compete) would be reluctant to release players for that amount of time. This gave the selectors a massive headache as all England's best ballers were playing abroad. For the first time ever, English Basketball saw a problem and threw money at it to fix it. Earmarked players were lured back into the domestic league by a massive cash injection which buoyed-up salaries and meant clubs could offer players close to the type of cash they were used to earning on the Continent. It was a good decision which showed a real commitment to the squad, but it came too late for me to benefit from as I'd already returned to England and was now playing at Chester Jets. Not everyone was so positive about it though. The money was intended to guarantee the return of six players, with the squad's remaining six essentially receiving no incentive, and was intended to be kept secret. But we ballers were pretty tight and soon everyone knew who the six funded players were: Mike Martin, Germayne Forbes, Steve Bucknall, Andrew Sullivan, Julius Joseph and Robert Reed. Officially, the 12-man squad was still undecided, unofficially at least, half of it was already selected, six spots left and I had to have one.

By now I'd played on the National Team for close to a decade, across Europe's pro scene for eight years, and had endured all those crazy Eastern European trips. In the eighteen-month preparation period leading up to the Games, I was one of only two players who'd attended every trip and played in every game. My commitment was beyond question. I even did this when times were otherwise pretty hard; I'd been gutted to have just missed the funding opportunity as things were difficult for me financially. I'd never earned mega-bucks in Europe but wages in the BBL (especially at Chester) were a fraction of those on the Continent. I could do one of two things, cry and bitch, or just take every opportunity I had by the horns and make sure I got on that damn plane to Melbourne.

The final opportunity to play in Europe before the squad left in March 2006 came in the summer of 2005 with the longest trip we'd undertaken in which we played a series of ten games throughout Portugal, Austria and Bulgaria. It was a great opportunity for me to return to Austria where I'd played the previous season in Klagenfurt, for Wörthersee Piraten. Visiting Kapfenburg's gym, I got to see the tribute which had been placed there to my former teammate Amadou Cisse, who had died that summer in a car crash with his mother in Senegal; a great guy and an outstanding chef.

On this tour the team seemed to be shaping-up into what felt like winning form. No one knew the final twelve places for certain yet but in our games against Denmark, Austria and a Big Ten College All-Star team, the squad as it stood were looking pretty strong. We spent many nights in our hotels chatting and racking our brains as to who would, or wouldn't, be selected come March. The team wouldn't be announced until a month before departure and so all I could do now was play hard for Coach Scantlebury. It was a challenge. I was playing a lot in the position of point guard, my favourite, but one that I hadn't played properly in for the past fifteen years and was now playing in at International level. I was suffering a weird elbow infection which had made the joint swell badly and meant that any little knock was torture. But I did a credible job and loved every minute of it. My deepest wish had been to have played the point in College and into my early pro career like 'Penny' Hardaway and so I was going to relish this chance now, to make up for that disappointment.

Germayne Forbes shared point guard duties with me. I'd instantly liked him when we first met at the training camp in Portugal. The Portuguese camp was serious with practice four times a day; lifting weights at 8am, 45-minutes conditioning at 9, followed by a two-hour team practice before a break and then another two-hours training in late afternoon. Germayne's fun-loving mood lightened a lot of these practices. He is a really cool cat and can play too, having plied his trade at Gonzaga University and later transferred to West Georgia. This dude can flat out stroke it. He has an un-guardable crossover which sets him up for an on-the-money 3-pointer. It was a memorable trip with my boy from Liverpool, David Aliu, also making his debut. Dave was a great guy to have around. We'd known one another for years, and from a team perspective, his naughty shooting made him an added bonus.

The tour culminated in Hungary with a convincing victory over a really strong Macedonian team with an outstanding point guard. It had been a great summer of basketball for me and a trip that I'd really enjoyed. I'd started in every game, captained the team throughout the tour, even when John Amaechi played (due to the caps rule), and felt honoured to have led the guys, even with someone older and with years of NBA experience on the squad. John's a cool guy; I have a lot of respect for what he's achieved both on and off the court and it was great to have the chance to captain a squad he was part of. When it came to the cut, this meant my chances were pretty good. But not all the players had been on the tour, significantly some of those clearly destined for a place like Steve Bucknall, Andrew Sullivan and Mike Martin. I'd gotten stuck into the four-a-days, had done everything Coach asked of me and played hard. All I could do now was hope my dedication would pay off.

The waiting was hard, issues at club level meant that I was now playing in EBL Division One when most of the other squad prospects were playing top-flight domestic ball. I could only hope that my game wouldn't deteriorate in the six months leading up to the Games and that Coach Scants had already seen enough of me to believe I was a prospect for

Melbourne. We had a couple of final training camps, one over Christmas and another in the New Year, and each session saw more and more additions to the squad. This would be the most major event in English Basketball history, everyone felt they deserved to be part of it and competition was fierce. It was the only time in my International career that I ever really questioned if I'd make the final roster.

I knew, in spite of my 100% attendance and my recent captaining, that if push came to shove, playing in the EBL would be held against me. I had a lot going for me but still things weren't looking good, especially since a new surprise addition to the squad had arrived; Newcastle Eagles player/coach Fabulous Flournoy. Fab and the Eagles had dominated English Basketball throughout the previous five years. He's the ultimate competitor and team player, a person you'd far rather have on your team than not, and in spite of his nationality (Fab's American) his dual-citizenship made him eligible for the single 'dual' slot on the squad and a real threat for my spot. He was very versatile, could play a variety of positions and had outstanding defence. Sound familiar? I was convinced they'd only take one of us.

The final practice arrived. Coach told us prior to the morning session that he'd be announcing who would be flying to Melbourne after practice and I'd had a sinking feeling in the pit of my stomach. There'd been a couple of late potential additions; Yorick Williams, one of the country's best scoring guards, had joined us but he was coming back from a serious ankle injury and hadn't attended any of the preparatory tours. Six of the guys were guaranteed to go (seven including Amaechi) and of the fifteen still remaining, it was easy maths to work out that by the end of the day three people's hopes and dreams would be dashed. Was it my time? I'd already been gutted by missing out on the funding (something that'd also happened to Steve Hansell who was ruled out of the squad because finances had forced him to remain in Europe) and although I'd enjoyed the hours I'd put in when I'd been holding down the fort in the other main players' absence, I had been doing it for a reason. Surely there'd be some justice.

232

Scants called us individually to an empty court for a debriefing. I took a deep breath and prepared for the worst. It had been really close, he said, but, in a month's time, I'd be on that plane to Australia. A sense of unbelievable gratification went through my bones. Half the squad had been spared such agonies, their places had been set from the off, but for the others who'd been borderline (scraping around for those last five or six spots), it'd been very stressful. It was an absolute dream to get the chance to represent England in the Games, one that came true for me that day and one that was broken for others that day too.

The broken dreams of some were hard to bear, even for me. I especially felt for Dru Spinks, the only other player who'd been on every trip of the Games build-up, and Yorick, because he was arguably the best shooting guard in the UK and a really good friend of mine too. But there was little time for empathy. The successful squad were ushered through to a conference room where we were shown a video and given an information pack about what we might expect from Melbourne. It was immediately obvious that this would be a trip like no other. Even if we'd still had Laszlo there'd be no need for his suitcase full of Pot Noodles, this trip would be big-time. We'd be travelling with a 520-strong contingent made up of rugby players, athletes, swimmers, gymnasts; not to mention the massive support staff of doctors, physios and coaches. It was a really exciting time; the closest thing to the Olympics you can get and a chance to really represent against countries such as Canada, Australia, New Zealand, Jamaica, Nigeria, India, Pakistan, Ghana and the Bahamas.

The schedule looked sweet; we'd get time to acclimatise in a holding village where we'd stay in a nice hotel for a week with the rest of the English contingent, and then it would be down to competition. The place was amazing: everything I'd hoped it would, be and waking each morning at seven with the sun beaming in made me start the day with a smile on my face. There was a real sense of camaraderie through the England contingent and it was great for us ballers to get to mix with the other athletes here to represent for our country. Some of our teammates were even kind of famous. The level of exposure which British track and field athletes get is far beyond anything us ballers experienced at home and so they were familiar to us, even if we weren't to them. Some, like Long Jumper Jade Johnson (who went on to win Silver) and Darren Campbell (Olympic Gold Medal sprinter and familiar face being the cousin of Trevor Campbell, an old friend of mine) were really cool. Ballers tend to stand out, mainly due to our sheer physical presence, and we got a lot of respect from other sportspeople in the holding camp where we were staying awaiting our transfer to the Commonwealth Village.

Being in Melbourne was a dream. A beautiful place with just the kind of weather I like and a real once-in-a-lifetime opportunity I was determined to make the most of. We'd also come here to win and so morning practices at a local college were deliberately tough. At the first practice my legs felt like shit, like I'd somehow left them back in England along with my jump-shot which (due to jet-lag) had left me, as everything pulled-up short. Jet-lag cushioned any worries and thankfully my jumper arrived the next day and, surprisingly, I was 'wet' the whole trip, missing hardly any jumpers at all in practice and making an already awesome experience potentially all the sweeter. It was the first trip I'd been on in which we were treated like the best in the country at what we did. As a minority sport we were still surrounded by this make-do attitude, but here (where all participants received the same) we were treated like royalty. At the side of the court at the first practice, there'd been a table laid out for us full of fruit, chocolate, Gatorade, muesli bars and all sorts of treats. We couldn't believe our eyes, we never got anything like this and so when we were told to tuck in, we did (making sure we loaded some extra goodies into our bags). At the next practice, the table had been replenished and was just as bulging as before. We'd assumed the first one was a never-to-be-repeated welcome, stocking us up with nutrients just to begin with; we hadn't clicked-on yet that (for the month we were in Australia at least) a suitcase of Pot Noodles would be just a memory.

After a week of intense practice, our first test was a friendly against a local professional team at the university where we'd been training. From the off, the toughness of the Australians really struck me. They were physical and strong, perhaps down to all that fruit and Gatorade, or maybe they were just so bloody healthy because of all that sunshine and fresh air. Nonetheless, we performed well and progressed to our next pre-Games challenge in which another pro team gave us all their strength. Another tough game and this time in front of a large crowd. Every guy was in his zone now. We'd come to Melbourne to win and we were of one mind: we were going home with a medal; all that was undecided was what colour that medal would be.

The transfer to the Commonwealth Village (where we'd stay for the remainder of our trip) couldn't have come at a better time. Outside of practice and the friendly games we'd played, a little boredom had set in and we were all keen to move on to the main facilities. The 520-strong English contingent made the hour's drive to the Village in a convoy of coaches and, as the sun beamed down and the massive security gates swept back, we saw for the first time the mini-city that would be home to over 5,000 athletes from all over the world. Our accommodation was amazing; brand-new houses with four twin bedrooms on the ground floor and the same upstairs with a shared living room and bathroom on each. They were tiny but adequate for what we needed; we weren't planning on spending too much time cooped-up indoors in such a beautiful place. When I say tiny, I probably need to stress how tiny. Rooms that are probably palatial for gymnasts are a bit of a squeeze for ballers and when I extended my wingspan (bearing in mind I'm only 6'6", 5" shorter than some of the squad) I could practically touch both walls simultaneously. You were in some serious trouble if your roomy had major morning breath.

Accommodation was for sleeping. An athlete's obsession with his or her stomach meant that the food hall was the hub of the Village's social scene. A huge tented structure, it served every single type of food you could imagine, was open 24/7 and operated an all-you-can-eat policy, in that supplies were limitless and free to all participants and staff. For a guy like me, struggling to support myself on the wages my 33-year-old ass was raking-in, it was a dream. Deep freezers filled with ice creams, a steak cooked to your specification at 2am, and (most importantly for us guys unused to the 90° heat and so spitting feathers after each practice) a Gatorade cooler whose door was gratefully opened the minute we entered the hall, to treat our oesophagus to as much rehydration as it could handle.

It didn't take any time at all to settle into Village life; it was a dream come true and was shaping up to be the trip of a lifetime. I was rooming with Mike Martin; we'd gotten really cool when we'd roomed together at St. Etienne. He's a guy who recognises me more as *'Mr. Genuine'* than Mr. Versatility, but then we've connected as much off-court as we have on. Mike's my boy and having one of your best friends to room with is the one thing that can make an excellent trip even better. A month's a really long time to be sharing a room with someone who gets on your nerves, even when the room's not so small you might accidentally elbow one another in the night.

Melbourne is a beautiful city and the Games' planners had been doubly kind to us by constructing the Commonwealth Village in one of the city's most prestigious inner-suburbs, Parkville, so close to the coast that St. Kilda became our spot. After practice sessions and between games there'd be some time to chill. And if there was time to chill then we'd be out at St Kilda, a beach resort with nice restaurants and bars. Heaven. Having left the UK's freezing temperatures, we'd arrived in Australia's late summer heat and Germayne Forbes, Julius Joseph, Robert 'Big Ginge' Reed, Mike Martin and myself would sit and take it all in, sipping on a 'cheeky pint' of Australia's finest and listen to Germayne kick his flows. We were always together and were already enjoying some great times just chilling on the veranda of our favourite restaurant overlooking the beach. I couldn't help sparing a thought for all the guys back home who hadn't made the cut. It was already an unbelievable experience and we hadn't even played our first game yet.

The team were agreed, nothing less than Bronze Medal would do. Every guy had the same mind-set; we were bringing it home. All those months of committing to long trips in dodgy locations were about to culminate in the biggest chance the team had ever had and no one was going to blow it. We stayed focussed, we stayed professional, we came to do a job and that's what we were going to do. Scants worked us hard, but practice was full of competitive fun, from trying to dodge Richard 'Bam-Bam' Windles' sledge hammer-like screens, to competing in endless shooting games. We had a squad full of talent but it was a weird mix; veterans who'd retired from the game or were about to; young guns hungry for recognition; and hard-working role players who'd come to do a job like they always did. I suppose it was inevitable that such a hugely varied group would separate off into cliques, probably also inevitable that this would blunt the chemistry of the team.

We'd been in Melbourne for a fortnight and were itching to start our campaign and claim our first scalp. Game one was Barbados, coached by true BBL legend Nigel Lloyd. We pulled off a good win in spite of some of the guys' nerves (this was, after all, the most exposure the England team had ever had) and I was left personally disappointed at not getting on court. Keep cool, bide your time, I thought. We beat South Africa in a rout, and lost by 20- to New Zealand who did their traditional Maori war-cry (the Haka) before the game. It was an awesome sight, seeing the Tall Blacks go for it in their pre-match ritual, but I'd seen it many times before so it didn't faze me. What was fazing me was my court-time, with twelve guys it's hard to juggle minutes but, even so, I was getting frustrated. I was a vet'. I could contribute a lot. I just needed to get on that damn court more.

Before we knew it the semi-finals were on us. We'd come through well and were to face Australia, a tough side ranked 9th in the world. They outplayed us. A loss to Australia meant that any chance of Silver or Gold was lost, but the opportunity to still score us a medal remained. The game for third and fourth positions was against Nigeria and a huge crowd turned out to see who'd scrape that final podium spot and who'd be left forever haunted by the cruellest place to finish: fourth.

There were around 10,000 on hand in the beautiful light-blue arena and electricity was everywhere. Everywhere, that is, except in the tunnel where it most needed to be. We stood stretching-out waiting to be called on court suffocated by the weirdest team vibe I'd ever felt. Each man entirely quiet and locked in his own little world. I knew there were nerves floating about and understood; this was it, what we'd all been dreaming about. We needed to pull ourselves together as a team go out on court and kick some ass. I'd seen enough; I wasn't letting this opportunity go, I'd invested too much. I stopped stretching, and said, 'What's up guys? Let's go. Let's do this shit!' I raised my hand for us to huddle, they all came in and finally, for the first time in the Games, we had a good united team shout. We were ready now and, as we took the court, I felt chills down my spine.

Our new focus was short-lived; a technical error meant a 45-minute delay which left us vexed and getting cold. Mentally this was a problem; we'd enough issues trying to focus as a team and now it was affecting individuals too. Whatever happened now, by the time tip-off came I was just relieved the waiting was over. Our leading scorer and star player of the Games, Andrew Sullivan, was out having gotten injured in the previous game, meaning our starters were John Amaechi, Mike Martin, Germayne Forbes, Julius Joseph and Steve Bucknall. After the first quarter we were tied 15-all and Coach Scants started the second with an injection of new blood: myself, Fab, Andrew Bridge, Robert Reed and Germayne. We clicked on all cylinders, scored a good 6-points each and blew the game wide open. Pretty soon we were up by 27- and I smelled victory. I'd finally got a chance to prove myself in a big game, it was all working out and it felt great. Robert 'Big Ginge' Reed started working them out inside and the rest of us contributed greatly, leaving Nigeria no answers to our newly balanced attack.

The game was over before half-time. They didn't have enough weapons to make a comeback, so the last twenty minutes just dragged out. I always liked a battle on court and this sort of finish (although the victory we so needed) felt a little like an anti-climax. When the final whistle blew, sealing our Bronze Medal, it was a significant victory on many levels: for Peter Scantlebury, as Head Coach; for Bucknall, Amaechi and Ronnie Baker, who'd been stalwarts of the National Team even before me; and for me, the culmination of a lot of hard work and a well-deserved end to our England careers. Stood on the podium dressed in my England tracksuit, awaiting the Bronze Medal to be placed around my neck, I was bursting with pride. Thinking back over the long road I'd travelled, from the lonely trip in Japan, to Portugal's four-a-day practices, to questioning whether I'd even make the final twelve. It was a great feeling to experience such pride and I spared a moment to do what I always did at such times: wished my dad had been alive to have shared the moment.

With the pressure off and both the Men and Women's basketball teams going home with Bronze neck-wear it was time to indulge in the thing we did second best: party. Australia's convincing triumph over New Zealand in the final added an additional air of celebration to the party which had been thrown in all the athletes' honour and we got to soften the walk of shame (as we trudged home in the morning light in last night's clothes) with a visit to the Village's 24/7 Food Hall. One last day remained to explore all that we'd missed of the Village whilst we'd been focusing on practising and competing: the Pool Halls, the IT suite and the Xbox Lounges, where huge bean-bags lay before massive screens. There was one thing left to do; we needed to kick-it one last time down at St Kilda. We clinked our glasses in the sunshine and drank in all that Melbourne had to offer. It was the best of life, the best of ball, and the perfect way to round off my ten-year stint as an England stalwart, time which had given me memories I'd always treasure.

A Journeyman (England)

The general perception of a professional sportsperson (in England at least) seems to be based on the life of a footballer and so the expectation is that a pro life brings huge rewards (many of them financial) and the kind of security that means a really, really early retirement. It might be the case with NBA ballers (although one or two of those haven't been strangers to financial ruin in the last few years) but it's certainly not true of English ballers, none I knew anyway. Some of the country's finest talents receive accolades on court on Saturday night and then bowl up to the day job come Monday morning. I remember how my chin hit the floor when Mike Martin casually mentioned the job in Footlocker he returned to summer after summer, and I'd always been aware that another of our most talented ballers, Yorick Williams, supplemented his income year-round with his part-time job in a homeless person's hostel. I guess I'd had it pretty easy. I was back in England for good, jobs and money would need sorting soon enough. For now I needed a place to live.

Although my mum had always been cool about me returning home whenever I needed to, did my washing, made me cups of tea and talked with me for hours on end about the triumphs and the frustrations of basketball, I was a 32-year-old man, I was used to a young guy's lifestyle and so I needed to sort something more permanent out now that I was back in England to stay. Both Rick Brooks and Steve Hansell had been on at me for a long time to invest some money in property (even if I wasn't going to live in it myself). I'd avoided the issue, scared to commit to a mortgage whilst money was such a precarious commodity, but it was time to take the plunge. I figured wherever I ended up playing, the place to buy was Manchester, somewhere I knew well and which could be a base to come back to with friends and family nearby. I bought a two-bed new-build apartment and for the first time in my adult life had a place to keep my stuff (at least the stuff that wasn't strewn across the spare rooms and attics of Europe and America in various teammates' houses). All those years of living in club's apartments rent free, bills paid, soon hit home. My initial £800-per-month mortgage payments seemed like a scandal and the need for a job became more urgent. But it felt so good to finally have a place I could call home that it made up my mind: I needed to find a team close to home or nowhere at all.

Luckily enough, Chester Jets were not only one of the finest teams in England, they were also based just a forty-five-minute drive away and so I took my career into my own hands and gave them a call. Chester had spent the past few seasons snapping up all the major domestic trophies going and so (at this by now kind of late stage) they'd made all the signings they'd planned on making. I spoke to the team's coach, Paul Smith, a really cool guy who, in spite of the now inevitable financial constraints, managed to scrape together a small salary and committed to freeing up more money as soon as possible. I made it clear to Paul that I'd heard all this before, that I was more than happy to sign under such circumstances (the mortgage, remember?) but that if further money hadn't been secured by the end of the month then I'd have to walk. He understood.

If living in my own place and settling down to a more domestic kind of life (a more grown-up kind of life) was odd, playing for a team who had no pre-season conditioning programme was even odder. The 2004-'05 season tipped-off with a scrimmage in Wrexham, North Wales, (a few miles outside of Chester) against Newi Nets, two divisions below the Jets. I was relieved to see we put on a show, winning by 50- or 60-points, and also relieved to see how nice our team looked. But best of all I was running a lot of point guard. Coach was a really mellow guy, he had a lot of confidence in me and being free to stretch into my own position at last was like having my limbs unbound so that I could finally run free: pure bliss.

Chester Jets didn't only have an impressive squad, we also had a coach with the right attitude who talked, even from that first scrimmage, about how we were going to win the Championship and also about how every game was the most important one of the campaign. A winning attitude which was the perfect complement to a very talented team. First up: Billy Singleton, a true veteran winner from St. Johns; next Calvin Davis, a 6'8" silky smooth power forward from Texas A & M; Sean Myers, a Trinidadian genetic freak, 6'6", 36 years old, and still performing windmill dunks; DJ Harrison, a 6'7" inside-outside player from Colorado University (if you're reading this, you owe me a suit!); Trey Moore, a former Harlem Globetrotter from Mississippi State University; Anthony Martin, a cat-quick guard from New York; Phil Brandreth and Marvin, with the squad rounded out by a pair of local talents, John Simpson and Richard Murphy.

There was a good vibe amongst the team and we raced out to top of the league, 4-1. But a month had gone by and there had been no sign of the pay rise. I was too old for this. The time when I was willing to hang around giving teams the benefit of the doubt was long gone and so, after leaving the court following another win, I spoke to Coach and told him I'd be leaving. It seemed ridiculous to be a starter on the country's number one team and to be making the kind of money I could get at McDonalds. It might seem like blind pride, that any basketball job was better than none, and I admit I was reluctant to go. My love for the game was still hanging on in there but at these rates I doubted how long that could survive. I'd said I was going to walk and I did. But to where? It was the first time in my life that I'd quit basketball, mid-season, with no intention of finding another team, and I was lost. It was a crazy time for me, but it strengthened my resolve. If I'd ever been able to rely on basketball, on always finding another role on another team somewhere, those days were gone and I needed to be pro-active: this was my future now. I set up my own coaching programme in schools, just starting locally and earned myself some much-needed mortgage-money by working part-time in one of the Children's Care Homes which were run by Jeff Jones.

Working nights in the Care Home was the first proper job I'd ever had (I'm still not really counting having been a paperboy). A lonely shift at an awkward time was rewarded with more decent money than I could have earned elsewhere and I spent many a long night at that Care Home thinking, is this the life for me? It wasn't, but neither was playing sport at such a high level without any decent recompense. I was starting to wonder whether this was what the future held, how my career would come to an end, just withering away like a ball left to bounce idly across the court, when Paul Smith called. It had only been a couple of weeks since I'd left and there'd been some articles in the local press regarding my leaving because of financial reasons which had been leapt upon by the Jets' loyal fans, and somehow Coach had found some extra money to secure me a 25% pay-rise. Enough to lure me back? Enough to make me meet the team in Leicester the following night to play in a cup game? Just.

How much the injury sustained by Calvin Davis (meaning he'd be out for a month) prompted the discovery of that 25% I'll never know. But although I still had pride, I also still had that mortgage and even though I hadn't touched a ball in three weeks, I rolled up at Leicester ready to play. Basketball had always consumed me and it felt a bit weird having to switch my mentality from Mr. Care Home to Mr. Versatility in order to focus back on ball again. It didn't take long. I fitted straight back in and found, to my relief, that there was no animosity from the other guys about me having walked away. Only a baller can truly understand the difficulties faced by a fellow pro. There was something special about this unit and I felt it reflected in my own commitment levels. Time to focus on winning that Championship.

We ran out to fourteen unbeaten games on the trot. Trey Moore, our star player, had NBA game and played the point, with me starting at the two spot. My defence was pretty tight but Trey gave me fits every day. Soon he was trying to score too much in games which left me to step-up to the point and him naturally dropping back-to-back 40-point games. Both Calvin and Sean Myers weren't far behind him. They carried us a lot. In one memorable game, Calvin dropped 34-points and 24 rebounds on Sheffield. And so the Championship was within our sights, the only obstacle between us and that trophy came in the shape of the-up-and-coming Newcastle Eagles. As player/coach, Fabulous Flournoy had done a great job with them and the Americans they had were tough. Jeremy Hyatt from NC State, Charles Smith and TJ Walker were all exceptional players. They also had Andrew Sullivan from Villanova via The Netherlands and already starting to dominate.

Newcastle had been hot on our heels the entire season. There was only one title and there'd only be one team of champions. The Jets faced the Eagles in nearly all of the major finals and everything came down to one last game; the last of the season. We needed a win in our final home game against third-placed London Towers. We took to the court and simply every little thing fell into place: blowing them out by 20-. It was a really solid game for me and I dropped 17-points. Northgate Arena would be regularly packed-out with a small crowd of fiercely loyal and extremely rowdy fans who blew the roof off that tabernacle when we won. The place went nuts. We'd brought home Chester's first league championship and within all the experiences of my pro career, it was the best feeling I'd had. It was amazing to finally accomplish something at the professional level after all those seasons of trying. Surely this would be it now, the chance to secure a long-term contract, to play out the last few years of my career close to home. What happened next all but killed any love for basketball I had left: in spite of backing the country's finest (and reigning) team, Chester Jets' sponsors had reached the end of their three-year deal and rather than renewing, had decided to pull out. There was no money left. Any team members who stayed would be taking a significant pay cut.

I was really grateful to have had the opportunity to play at Chester that season and so proud to have helped them secure their highest achievement, but it had come with a huge financial cost, one which seemed now to be destined to go unrewarded. Stable two or three-year contracts were a rarity in England, but still I'd thought that such an achievement would have secured me something. It hadn't: so I signed up to Jeff Jones's second division Manchester Magic. Even if there was no money in it, I still needed to play. Selection was looming for the England Commonwealth Games team and if I was to be in with any chance of going at all, I needed to focus on maintaining some level of fitness. But I also still needed to earn. One day at my mum's house, my sister casually mentioned the possibility of getting work as a Supply Teacher (just like she also once casually mentioned the possibility of writing a book together). I was sceptical. Was it something you could do with just a BA degree? Turns out it wasn't, but the only other thing required was a CRB (Criminal Records Bureau) check to make sure you were okay to work with kids and we were on. I was amazed how straightforward it was. What it lacked in regularity it made up for with a great level of pay. All I needed to do was be ready and waiting on a call at around 7.20am and if I wanted to work then they'd give me the address of some random school and I'd be off. I got wise to the whole thing straightaway and after a couple of days doing general supply (which meant covering classes during any subject, essentially babysitting kids who were used to running rings around Supply Teachers), I decided I'd mainly take P.E. jobs. It was a lifesaver and was so flexible that there would be nothing in my way should I be selected to go to Australia with the England squad for the month-long Commonwealth Games trip. The flexibility proved to be useful immediately. A surprise call from my old friend Allan Houston meant I'd be unavailable for work for a few days. I was heading to New York.

I was still committed to playing for the Magic, which after a frustrating first few months was getting better, but a fortunate gap in our schedule meant I was able to accept Al's invitation to the party to mark his retirement from professional basketball. It was one of the best and most surreal experiences of my life: one day I'm supervising a raggedy gang of kids in a game of rounders at some under-funded high school in Crumpsall[xiv], the next I'm being met at the airport in New York by Al's chauffeur and bodyguard 'Champ' who drives me through Manhattan in a stretch limo, late autumn sunshine bouncing off my toothy grin. Al had booked me on a Sunday evening flight at short notice and so, literally the night before I'd been playing ball in some shitty gym in London somewhere, and now I was being whisked to the doors of the Marriott Times Square and being checked-in to my huge suite. How could life change so dramatically in the space of a few hours?

As I called Allan to let him know I'd arrived, I almost had to pinch myself to believe this was happening. The windows of my suite overlooked Times Square where a huge poster of Dwayne Wade dominated the skyline; Al was to arrive from Greenwich later on that evening. For now, all I had to do was kick back. I'd been touched that Allan had wanted me to be here so much that he'd flown me out to New York and felt honoured to be treated once again like a part of his family. I headed over to the lounge bar situated on the hotel's 48th floor and overlooking the beautiful New York skyline. It was such an amazing setting and when Allan arrived I felt like this was going to be a really special night. We went to meet the rest of his family in another suite Al had rented which was damn near naughty. This place was ridiculous; a sprawling duplex apartment with pool tables upstairs and massive couches in every room, it made my gaff in Manny (which was setting me back a king's ransom - ta-neckback!) look like a little mouse hole. The surroundings were only outshone by the pristine company as in the suite were Allan's family, his dad, Wade; Alice, his mum; his sisters Lyn and Patty; cousins; grandparents; agent; everyone. Before we headed the couple of blocks downtown to the venue which had been hired for the party, Wade made a speech in tribute to his son. It was really emotional, perhaps because I'd felt like a part of this family myself for the last fifteen years or so, ever since I was that cheeky skinny tough-neck from Widnes. Perhaps because having your father stand up and profess his love and admiration for you is something I suspect I'll never have.

We mosied on over to the party and saw Al's career off in style. Huge TV screens lined the joint, recapping some of Allan's greatest career moments including his 53-point outburst against the Los Angeles Lakers. It was a night I'll never forget and the trip was topped off with a couple of days of relaxation at Allan and Tammy's recently-completed house in Greenwich, Connecticut. The place was like a castle, with an NBA-sized half-court in the basement complete with overlooking weight-room. It was great to spend time bonding with Al's kids, Remie and Allan, a right pair of cuties who'd inherited their dad's liking for a bit of the old cheeky English phrasing.

It's a tribute to how much I like and respect Allan that I felt no jealousy for what he'd achieved and what he'd now got, not least of all a secure retirement full of new challenges. But it did spur me on to want to create a solid future for myself, I just wasn't sure how I'd do that yet. In the meantime, there was a life I needed to get back to. On the court with Manchester Magic, the season's bad start had picked up and begun to turn around. The Americans we'd had were too one-dimensional and we'd lost a few games we shouldn't have. Halfway through the season, changes were made and our imports inplace were upgraded: Troy Sledge, from New York, proved tough and Kenny Roberts, our point guard, also got into the stride quickly and had some great games. Imports in place we won ten of our last twelve encounters only to fall in the semi-finals to Steven Gayle's Worthing Thunder.

It was to continue to be a year packed full of contrasts: from living it up in New York to cleaning my own place for the first time, from the disappointments of EBL 1, to the immense highs of England's Commonwealth medal-winning campaign in Melbourne. I'd never had a season which had contained so many varying experiences. But reality was settling in and a more normal life seemed on the horizon. I was covering a general education class as a Supply Teacher at Springhill High School in Oldham when the P.E. staff got wind (via my ever-promoting friend at Select Education, Dave) that a Commonwealth Bronze Medallist was in the school. It wasn't an everyday occurrence and it was one they wanted to make the most of. They asked whether I'd mind spending my lunchtime conducting a little basketball session with the kids. I'd already been doing some schools coaching looking to get a little business off the ground and so I agreed. Within the hour the Head of P.E. was offering me a job for the last three months of term. Once the surprise wore off, I knew I had to accept. I needed some security but was wary about committing to something outside of basketball for this length of time, about how I'd get along doing a 9-5 job for the first time in my life. Nonetheless I accepted and the next day, just like that, I was a full-time P.E. teacher.

Although it was good experience, was mostly enjoyable, and above all paid the bills, I knew I didn't want to do this full-time. I also knew I needed to get back to playing. I was closing-in on retirement but I wasn't quite ready for it yet and I certainly didn't want my career to just fizzle out like this. The school was good enough to allow me a couple of days leave so that I could go to Paris to play in Europe's best street-ball competition, the Quai 54: another massive high in a roller-coaster of a year. I was over there representing Midnight Madness alongside some major competition including a team from New York who'd won the Rucker Summer League tournament. We were knocked-out in the quarterfinals but, as ever with Midnight Madness, it was an unbelievable experience: thousands of fans, great music, barbecues, an amazing vibe and some serious ballers. Some of the funniest experiences of my life have occurred when away with the Midnight Madness guys, two of them on this same trip. We'd taken being eliminated from the tourney as the cue to kick-back and headed to second-row courtside to watch the rest of the drama unfold. Years of experience had enabled us to sneak a couple of cheeky brews through in our backpacks and we figured the perfect accompaniment to the party atmosphere, the people dancing, the jokes, would be to get a little bevvied-up. My boy Dangles had got his party calculations a little wrong, though, forgetting that a combination of drinking a little too quickly, an empty belly and the sun beaming down on your head can have very specific consequences. He was sat next to me clowning around, rocking back and forth with laughter, when he suddenly bent double and 'yakked for Britain' all over the floor. It would have been funny enough there and then, without Dangles sitting back up and allowing a single moment of surprised bemusement to cross his boat-race, before going right back to necking his bevy like nothing had happened. Shame.......!

There's probably no sympathy between any groups of young guys, there's certainly not between ballers as the incident which resulted around ten minutes later with one of our entourage (a well-known street-baller with a nickname involving the word 'crowd') proved. He'd been chilling along with us, soaking up the party atmosphere, when his brews and his dancemoves carried him away. That cat was breaking out every move in his repertoire, really giving it some and getting low until, suddenly, he just disappeared. He'd been fine the whole tournament but his knee chose now, just as he was breaking out his finest shapes, to give out on him, literally. It seemed like a joke until the guy was stretchered out of that tabernacle. Next stop the emergency room, to have his knee returned to where it used to be. Okay, it still seemed like a joke then. See, no sympathy. I am kind of sorry he was in so much pain, but it didn't stop any one of us from dying on the floor laughing at the time!

Even though the season which saw me secure that Bronze medal (something which had never even figured in the outlandish dreams of my childhood) went on to be topped by an amazing trip to Chicago as one of the UK's Elite Street-ball team with Midnight Madness, come the start of the following season, the only lead I had was with Leicester Riders. I'd spent some time in the summer down at Crystal Palace working Steve Bucknall's Essential Skills Camp and it had been a great experience. I'd worked out a lot there with Sterling Davies, from the Scottish Rocks, and it had helped me out and led to a contract at Leicester which I simply couldn't afford to turn down. Besides, my former National Teammate and Georgia Tech Alumni, Karl Brown, was to be the coach and there'd be more than a few other familiar faces on the squad with both Yorick Williams and Dave Aliu also signing. The Riders had a great guard, Terrence McGee, Barbados baller Andre Alleyne and Connecticut's Rob Paternostro (a great small point guard) rounding out the starting-five. Other solid players would join the squad a little later such as Sean Myers, Adam Williams (a Welsh International) and Darren Mills who both had game, in spite of their limited court-time.

You might by now be wondering why I was still putting myself through all this. You certainly will when I reveal I was stuck playing back inside. You'll be beginning to think it's some cruel joke when I go on to reveal that, just as I was settling into the nice house I was to share with 'Big Show' Barry Lamble and Darren Mills, the club's finances flopped and 50% pay cuts were handed out all round. This was getting like Groundhog Day. If finances were precarious on teams on the Continent, on English teams they were more so. It would've been frustrating enough to have seen this as a fan of the sport but as a person still trying to make a living out of this, it was just beyond ridiculous. Karl had done a good job, had worked us hard the first few months, but it was to no avail since now (due to unpaid bills) the team didn't even have a facility to practice in. Not wanting another team to fold, I headed back to Manchester (as did Yorick) to make some money through our more regular work and we spent the rest of the season not practising together at all. We simply drove ourselves to fixtures, dressed-up, had a brief discussion about the opposition and then played. Although quickly getting out of shape, and having a set-up so unprofessional you wouldn't believe it if you saw it in some ball-themed sit-com, we finished the season a remarkable seventh, losing to the all-conquering Newcastle in the Semis. And this was top-flight English ball.

Some experiences would stand out as so unbelievable that they would completely highlight the state that lots of English basketball was still stuck in. After Midnight Madness, where everything wasn't only intense and exciting but also really well organized with every single person involved totally committed to making the whole thing be the best it could be, situations like the one we were in at Leicester seemed just pitiful. It would be a downer to return from something as big time as the Commonwealth Games, where every little detail was perfect, to some of the lousy experiences the season would bring, but there was no other choice than to just go on. Through Select Education I'd managed to land another three-month job with Manchester's Federation of Special Schools. The school I was sent to was Meade Hill in Crumpsall, one of the city's three sites where kids whose behavioural issues had gotten them excluded from mainstream schools were sent. Such schools are tiny and are so hidden away that anyone not directly involved would be unaware of their existence. As well as coordinating the school's P.E. programme, I did some work as a mentor there and began to experience the joy of paying it forward. I like to think that I helped some of those Meade Hill kids, if only in a small way, and it led me into thinking about all those young guys I'd known who'd managed to keep themselves out of too much trouble by channelling their energies onto the court.

Another summer rolled around and I had no team set up for the season ahead. Chester were still struggling financially and leads were almost non-existent when I took a call from Henry Mooney, a guy I'd known for years, and it began to look as if I might just be able to delay my retirement a little after all. Henry is well-known and respected in his home city Liverpool. He's one of those unbelievably committed guys who, week in week out for years on end, quietly going about voluntarily keeping a team alive. Amateur basketball is full of guys like Henry but guys who've shown this level of commitment for as long as he has are a rarity. Henry's been keeping ball alive in Toxteth for over forty years! He asked me to come along to a scrimmage in Aigburth[xv] and hinted that there'd been some developments in Liverpool (a city which, despite its size, had never had much of a pro scene) that might interest me. It was August and with nothing much else to do, I headed to the scrimmage with my boy Dave Alui who'd left Leicester before the financial stuff had hit the fan and had just returned from a dominating season over in Iceland where he'd been second leading scorer at 23-points per game.

It was funny being back in Liverpool. Although only twelve miles from Widnes, I'd always affiliated myself with Manchester but there were loads of familiar faces at the scrimmage, guys I'd played against when I'd been home in the summers for the last fifteen years. I spotted Henry and he pulled me to one side to give me the lowdown: Everton Football Club (one of the biggest names in all of Liverpool, well half of it at least) had long had a successful Premiership team and were looking now to start a new BBL squad. It was a complete shock to me. Football clubs supporting basketball teams wasn't that new an idea, Manchester United had done it all those years before and it was big on the Continent, but I was sceptical. I'd heard talk of things like this before, had been burned a few times myself by promises which transpired into nothing and I didn't believe it would happen. For this to have any chance of getting off the ground, Henry would need names and wanted to know if I knew anyone who'd still not signed so close to the start of the season. He was serious. Maybe this was going to happen. Not wanting to miss the opportunity, especially one so close to home, Dave and I were first to sign: local boys covered. It wasn't only our local connections that made us a good start, we'd proved our skills having both made the Midnight Madness Top Ten, twice. Next we managed to secure Calvin Davis, who was also now kind of local as he lived nearby with his English girlfriend. Calvin was a great signing and was one of my all-time favourite teammates to play alongside. By now it looked as though the team wouldn't only actually come into existence but that when it did we might be kind of naughty. I threw my enthusiasm into it and started to help Henry to recruit. I called John Simpson, my boy from the Chester Jets Championship team, an outstanding defender with a great talent, and he agreed to sign. Next on my hit-list was Chris Haslem, my old boy from National team. Chris took some convincing having, like me, heard it all before. But I assured him it would be a great situation, something he now agrees with having since signed a nice three-year contract with Everton Tigers.

Henry worked the University of Connecticut Basketball camps each year and from this knew a great shooting guard from Connecticut; Tony Robinson. We still needed a point guard so I took the opportunity and worked on convincing Everton that the guy we needed was my boy Tony Miller. Tony had been in contact with me over the years since Den Helder and talk would often turn to jobs. Like me, he'd been represented by Courtside and, also like me, was unhappy about the way they'd handled some of his career moves. I wanted to help him out and I also wanted to play with him again, but I still wasn't sure how much sway I had in terms of who was signed and who wasn't, and so was pleasantly surprised when they signed him. Only two Americans had been signed as our other import, Mohammed Nhang, had been unfortunately injured before the season began.

Everything was happening so quickly. It was a complete learning curve for me as it was the first time I'd been involved with a team from its very inception but was excellent experience for the future. Before we had chance to breathe, we were heading out onto the pitch at Everton's

Goodison Park ground to be introduced to the football team's fans. It was a reward for Henry, who'd done a great job in helping to make all this happen, getting to see his old Toxteth Tigers transformed into the new Everton Tigers supported by the Premiership Football Club he'd been devoted to since childhood. The crowd at Goodison that day was 38,000 strong and I was unsure as we stepped out onto the pitch whether applause would rain down from the stands or bananas. There was an underlying opinion in the world of Premiership football that Everton was one of the more racist of clubs and putting together a basketball team was in part a move to erase such a perception. As the team, 80% of them black, stepped onto the pitch, those Evertonians made a step towards erasing that myth entirely and they welcomed us with resounding applause. It was as good a start as we could have hoped for.

Although Henry had done amazing things in terms of securing a squad at all, there had unbelievably been no budget set aside to employ a professional coach and so that honour was also his. He's a great guy and experienced in terms of Division Three, but coaching at this level is something else. A different ball game. And expecting a guy to volunteer and fulfil this pivotal role for free had a worrying under-tone about where things might be heading. Henry would probably admit himself that the jump up from coaching Division Three (where players are either starting to work their way up or just playing for fun) to the world of the pros was an eye opener and, pretty soon, Chris Haslem and Tony Miller were taking over the reins at practice. It would be tough for these guys and frustrating all around, a lack of discipline and clear leadership was seen by some players as permission for complacency.

When the chance for some time away came along (a short break to Milan with Midnight Madness to take part in a tournament to celebrate 25 years of the 'Air Force One' basketball shoe), I jumped at it. Practices with Everton were coasting along and with the help of some of the good younger players we had such as Caleb Butler, Steve Bradley and young Anthony Purcell, we kept it competitive and had some much-needed cover when one of us main guys was injured. But the high hopes I'd allowed myself to have, buoyed by the sheer fact that Henry and the backers at Everton had managed to pull the whole thing off, were ebbing a little due to the coaching issues. Three days in Milan did me good. Time with Midnight Madness always seemed to, especially as we came home Champions; 3-0, with Marcus Knight walking away with the added honour of dunk of the tourney. We topped it off with the kind of partying you only really find at Midnight Madness and I was raring again to face the BBL.

Although he struggled early on, Tony Miller found both his feet and his conditioning halfway through the season to finish strongly. I was once again filling in at the power forward spot, something that got on my last nerve. Calvin was struggling with injuries and our African import just wasn't producing. We turned into a totally perimeter-orientated team. All our bigs, Dave, Calvin and Chris, were jump-shooters and none of them liked banging in the post. Tony Robinson was outstanding offensively but let himself down on D. It was up and down for us all. Part way through the season our ranks were increased by Richard Midgely, a white point guard from the South of England who I'd heard a lot about when he'd been doing some major work at the University of California but had never seen much of. Midge had started the season at Newcastle but settling into the role of coming off the bench behind player/coach Fab Flournoy hadn't satisfied him and his move to us came with little expectation, from me at least. We'd played against him earlier in the season and although he'd played well, I didn't think he was anything spectacular.

In a world in which camaraderie is sometimes everything and the vibe off-court can have a direct impact (positive or negative) on what happens on-court, Midge stood out. He didn't have an openly friendly nature, was pretty quiet and kept himself to himself, but on court was a different matter. Perhaps Midge said so little because he simply let his basketball do the talking. I was surprised at how good he was. I'd asked people about him before, and had always got the same answer: he was solid! They'd been right; he was an outstanding shooter, even better at finishing at the basket and was soon dominating every practice. Midge is a player with an uncontrollable hunger to score every time he gets his fingertips on that leather. It didn't help his game any going against Tony Robinson, allergic to playing 'D', although it might have helped his confidence. But in spite of his impressive skills, Midge rarely spoke to most of us and after practice would be gone in a flash. He mightn't have been big on the social interaction, but the guy could play with the best of them.

Finishing at seventh in the league wasn't exactly promising for the future but was all that could have been expected with our squad and, more to the point, our lack of coaching experience. But then my career always did seem to pull out surprises when I least expected and for only the second time as a pro, I was offered a contract extension before season was through. This time round (years of regret about the end of my Italian experience still ringing in my ears) I accepted right away and, by January, had the season ahead sorted. Unheard of!

Signing some players at such an early stage came with complications I'd not really foreseen. In addition to the season extension I'd signed, a couple of other guys had signed deals which secured them at the Tigers for the next three years. And when word got around (as it always does), there were some hard feelings. Other players who felt they were worthy of extensions (and in my opinion were right) hadn't been approached and it soon caused a rift within the team. It was especially difficult for Dave Aliu, a home-grown talent who'd had a solid year averaging around 16-points per game, and who hadn't been approached at all. It was tough. There was no way I could expect anything like a three-year deal at my age, but some decisions I was really pleased about: John Simpson was a player similar to me who lacked a little self-belief at times, he'd also been heavily under-paid at Chester and it was great to see him rewarded at last. It always struck me when I saw a player with flat-out game who held himself back by doubting his ability, too close to home probably, I always tried to get John involved in Midnight Madness and was convinced he'd make the top-ten no problem. But I had never managed to convince John of this.

I was looking forward to the 2007 season, despite the sense of dread that it might be my last. Over the summer, Henry had officially stepped-down and Chris Haslem had suggested Tony Garbelotto (formerly of Newcastle,

Iceland, London Towers and London United) as a potential new coach. In the sit-down meet we had, it was obvious that things were still very much open to change. One of the players who'd signed a three-year deal had already been cut and although Coach assured me that he intended to keep me and was looking forward to working with me again (Garbs had been a National Team Assistant Coach), he wasn't even beginning to entertain my requests that I not play in the four spot. I had no choice, that was made plain. Everton had four quality power forwards and that was that.

It's probably difficult to imagine the security that a contract established before the start of the season can bring. Most people live their lives certain of where they'll be from year to year, what they'll be doing, but even having this for a single season was a great feeling and it gave me the confidence to set about a little domestic project of my own: gardening. When I was a teenager and all I wanted to do was play ball, my dad would guilt-me into doing jobs at home in return for his commitment to our sport. The most dreaded job was 'cutting the ivy'. We had a lean-to shed at the back of our house which was so covered in ivy that a couple of times a year it seemed about to take over the house and, at these times, dad would make Gid and me get up there and cut it all back. I hated it. Since then I'd managed to avoid doing anything 'homely' (what with never having really had a home) and so when I offered to sort out and turf Yasmin's garden, I had no concept of quite how much I'd committed myself to. By lunchtime of day one I got a concept: too much. That place was like a jungle; nettles and weeds about 4' high and in danger of making me throw up backwards when I realized how much work I had to do.

As a workout it was great; countless hours traipsing back and forth with bagged-up nettles and then transporting round the back the eight tons of soil which had been dropped off at the front of Yasmin's gaff. It was also an exercise for me in mental toughness. I hated this kind of manual labour but, having promised to do it, knew I just had to get the job done. Not all on my own mind, I'm not daft. I recruited my boy Sean McKie and Reece (Yasmin's son) and one day even two local tough-necks who agreed to help for some money for ciggies. There was a moment to relax and then the turf came, resting up like Kilimanjaro at the front of that tabernacle and the whole transporting process started again. It was the first time I'd ever 'built' something and when the job was done, I stood back and felt serious pride in what I'd achieved. It had taken me the best part of a month (and a considerable amount of Yasmin's money, who'd been, as ever, putting in major hours in her own job) and had taught me something else; a kind of simple pride in a job well done. As a person who's lived his life as part of a team, a sole effort seems so alien, but I allow myself little props for it when I look out on that garden and it led me to thinking maybe life beyond a team was something I'd cope with after all.

When first practice rolled around, it was clear that Coach Garbelotto had spent his summer doing some serious recruiting. With four guys already in place: me, Chris Haslem, Richard Midgely and John Simpson, he'd also managed to add a true BBL Legend, Tony Dorsey, to the squad. Tony has had an amazing career; he shot from his Division Two college all-guns blazing, a guy on a mission to prove his worth feeling that people looked down on players who hadn't been in Division One. And with this passion fuelling his game, he'd since gone on to dominate English ball for many years in the early nineties before moving on to a great career in Belgium and Israel. Returning to England, he'd spent the previous season securing some silverware for Guilford Heat and was now with us, all 38 years and one bum knee of him.

The Tigers was a true vets team; good for practice but less good for court-time and the team's budget. Our Americans were Andre Smith from North Dakota State; Wyoming's Marcus Bailey and Josh Gross from the IBL. As well as James Jones (Jeff's son); former Leverkusen baller Chuck Evans and 2008 playoff finals MVP Olu Babalola, from Clemson University and Newcastle Eagles. Olu is a beast, a total freak of nature, 6'6" 280 lbs and still cat-quick. He doesn't only have a nice 3-point shot and serious handles, to top it all, he's an outstanding defender and ambidextrous. We were seriously stacked. Our five players who came off the bench had all been starters on different teams the season before and so things were looking good.

It was back to my old stomping ground for pre-season when we travelled to friendlies in Holland and Belgium, facing Chris Finch's (Great Britain Coach) team from Mons as well as a Dutch squad. Andre Smith was beginning to show a few glimpses in practice against the slower, bigger Chris Haslem. But after the Mons game, there was much talk that the coaches were doubting whether they'd even keep him: kind of funny in hindsight as 'Dre went on to totally dominate every practice and league game. He became The Man. Despite his youth and his constant joking around, 'Dre was actually really old-headed. Not bad for 23 years of age.

Things weren't only improving for Andre but also for me as I was now finally running some three spot, at least until the inevitable happened: Dorsey got injured and I was sent inside again, against 6'8" Andre, man-mountain Olu, and Chris Haslem who was an inch shy of 7'. It was hugely frustrating for me. I'd just got my outside rhythm and now Dorsey would be out for three months and, by then, I'd have certainly lost it again. But I did what I always did, got on with it, kept versatile, helped in no small way by the fact that we spent most of the season dominating the league. In January we won the National Cup, beating Plymouth by a record-breaking 50-point margin. I'd been on the sidelines with Coach's preferred player Josh Gross taking up the slot but now, with Josh out due to suspension, I was to start at the wing spot. Months and months of two-a-days running the four spot in every practice and then off the bench to start on the wing in a Championship final: Mr Versatility.

I always tell young players that patience is as much a part of basketball as silky-moves. Even if a player feels he's earning his minutes in practice, there will still be times when Coach just goes with someone else and the key to being a great baller is not only realizing this but also staying focused, ready to seize an opportunity when it arrives. The chemistry in our starting-five had been non-existent. The other guys just didn't gel with Josh, so what should have been a weakness with him out was actually a strength and the new starting-five (with me in Josh's spot) clicked big-time. It was a great achievement for Everton (a team only eighteen months old) to win anything but to set a new record for biggest winning margin in the history of the BBL Cup was phenomenal. I'd bided my time after months on the pine and seized the opportunity when it arrived. I'd walked my own talk. But if I'd thought this performance warranted me a starting position. I was wrong. I confronted Coach about it when it was clear I was killing Josh in practice but still having to sit back and watch him play and, despite Garbs' agreement that I should be getting more court-time, the only guy with the power to change that was doing nothing about it.

I was 35 years old but thanks in part to Dave (our strength and conditioning guy), I was in great shape and I wanted to win more than I'd ever wanted it before. I wanted to secure myself one last season and then I'd retire. My fitness wasn't in question. A renewed focus on weight-training had ironed out the niggles of the season before and the highly professional schedule we had of conditioning at 9am followed by a two-hour practice, weight-training and a break before another practice in the evening meant that I was still one of the quickest on the team and could still perform any dunk. Not bad for an old codger! But I knew it wouldn't last and that, even if by some miracle it did, the players coming in under me were looking more and more like another generation and so I made up my mind: one more season after this and Mr. Versatility would be hanging up his jersey.

Although we'd had a great season, just like in Den Helder, we were pipped at the post by a familiar foe: Newcastle, who overtook us in the league and beat us in the play-offs by 3-points. It was a great send-off for Midge who dropped 36-points and retired to California. But a disappointing one for Andre who, despite being the league's dominating baller, missed the chance to play as the death of his father meant he returned to the States. His record as league leader in points, rebounds and 3-point percentage speaks for its self and he's still doing some major work, now out in Turkey. What Newcastle seemed to have (just like Amsterdam) was a core group of players (especially Americans) and a consistent coach who stayed with the squad. Both factors made a solid base for home-grown players to be built around. I had no idea whether Everton would take any lessons from this and look to keep consistency in the squad for the new season, but was quietly confident I'd done enough to justify one more season in the blue and white.

But the blue and whites were heading in a whole other direction. The one defining feature of Everton in the season ahead would be the one thing that (no matter how hard I trained) I could never now have: youth. I met with Garbs and Henry Mooney in early May and the stats looked pretty sad: a career low of 3-points per game and average minutes standing at barely fifteen, on-a-string minutes at that. Of the four older guys we'd had on our squad, three had broken down with injuries and it was a risk Coach wasn't interested in taking. I was retiring. Without preparation, without any fanfare, without the chance to shoot the ball for the last time knowing that it was for my last time. My jersey was being hung up.

Everton were looking for one last move from Mr. Versatility, though, one which would take me off the court and see me become Everton's Basketball Development Officer. It was difficult for me to see the positive side, that they still wanted me to be involved with the team; all I could see was my retirement. It was a day I knew would come but one I'd wanted to reach through my own choice, not like this. But it was the only role on offer. It would take a month or two to secure the funding for my salary (that old chestnut), but the job was definitely mine if I wanted it.

I needed some time to mull it all over. The shock of sudden retirement had stung and I needed a little space to be able to see that the money and the opportunity that Everton were offering was in fact exactly what I needed. Of course I'd always known that one day ball would be over, that one day I'd need something else, but I'd never been sure what. I'd visualized myself when retirement arrived with a little nest-egg tucked away to increase my options but that had never happened. Maybe this was what I was meant to do. I accepted the job offer and, whilst I waited for news of the funding, spent my first summer not working out and scrimmaging down at the Amaechi Basketball Centre. Usually I'd be down there kicking-it with the bunch of guys who frequented the facility that John Amaechi had been instrumental in founding, a place I'd have died to have had back when I first found ball in Manny. I'd spent countless hours there with guys like Stefan Gill, Adam Slater (also a talented website and book-cover designer!), Andrew Thompson, my old boys Yorick and Sean, Alan Metcalfe, Callum and James Jones, Nick George, Menelik Watson, Liam Johnson, Steve Gayle, and my one of my best friends James Smith, guys who, like me, lived to ball.

I had always expected that when I did finally hang up my boots, I'd be doing it knowing that I couldn't ball anymore. But I still knew I could and so it was difficult to accept that this was it. I focused on the future, on the new job with Everton and all the stuff that this would open up, and waited for the call. And then I waited. And then, whilst in London with Yasmin visiting her sister Jan, I took a call from Everton's GM. There was no job. At least there was no job now, no funding for one. It was a role they fully intended to have, in the future, and when they did have a Basketball Development Officer they wanted it to be me, in the future, maybe, when they got some funding. In the mean time there was nothing. The deal was over. Oh, and one other thing, the car they'd been loaning me to tide me over until the job was secured: they'd be needing that back too.

A Mad, Mad World

In 1999 a guy by the name of Nhamo Shire came up with a unique idea to provide young people with an opportunity to divert their energies away from the kinds of shenanigans that might land them in trouble and towards something more positive instead. Concerned about rising levels of gun crime and gang violence, and inspired by the passion he'd seen for street-ball, Nhamo devised a format of amateur tournament which England had never seen before. He rented a local sports hall, brought along a boom box, had his missus hook-up some good Jamaican scran[xvi] and invited kids from the area to come in and ball all night. It was an opportunity for kids to come in and hoop; to socialize and stay out of trouble: to encourage them to put down the weapons and pick up the Spalding. Nhamo, completely unassuming and filled with good intention and a love for basketball, had no idea he was in fact birthing a monster.

By the time Midnight Madness (as it developed into) came to my awareness, it was already in its sixth summer and was fast becoming THE event of the British basketball year. I'd heard some chat about it a couple of times and everyone who mentioned anything at all about Midnight Madness raved about it. But it had kind of passed me by until, in 2005, one of my best friends, Mike Martin, had asked me whether I wanted the chance to go to New York and play with a UK All-star team. Of course I did, that was exactly the kind of thing I wanted to do. Mike gave me the lowdown, outlining the idea of this tourney which had been devised by one of his closest friends, raving about Nhamo, about how we should meet: Midnight Madness, Mike assured me, was something else. As exciting as it sounded, it would be the next year before I could have a taste of it for myself. For now, summers were (as they had been for ten years) all about the National Team. I needed to concentrate on fulfilling my ambitions with them.

The following summer with the English National team having returned triumphant from Melbourne with a Bronze Medal each for our troubles, the team ceased to exist. We'd gone out on a high and the powers that be had decided to fold the team and re-launch it, re-vamped as a Great Britain squad who, with a much-needed increase in funding, would focus on preparing for the 2012 London Olympic Games. I stepped out of the England squad and into Nhamo's mad, mad world.

It was good timing for me. Although representing England had given me some of my greatest basketballing memories (and some of my most fun times), I'd decided before to going to Melbourne that it was time to call it a day. I'd given the team ten years service and they'd given me something I'd never dared to dream I'd win, a Commonwealth Medal and the honour of representing my country 77 times. In 2009, 77 was the most caps gained by an active player; all the other guys with more caps had retired. I stand at an overall 7th all-time in number of National Team caps. Our leading-ever player is, of course, Ronnie Baker, a great guy with over 130 International caps to his name. It had been a long time and a lot of commitment and apart from anything else, I was 33. Not exactly what you'd call a whipper-snapper any more.

National Team commitments had been the main-stay of my summers since I'd graduated from Wright State and become a pro and most of any summer break I had would be taken up keeping in shape for England responsibilities whilst trying to sneak in a couple of weeks partying, catching up with my old mates Stateside. With such commitments gone, there was a huge gap in my summer holidays and the last thing the remains of my career (or for that matter my health) needed was the opportunity to spend more time kicking-it in the States. I needed something to fill the time and also to fill in for the huge highs and challenges that had come with my International career. Enter Midnight Madness.

I'd been really impressed by the whole idea of Midnight Madness from the moment I'd heard about it and even more impressed once I'd attended one of the qualifying events. Talk about an eye-opener. It was like I'd had my head buried in the sand all these years. Like a crowd-bound air-ball, the whole street-ball phenomenon had passed me by completely. In my defence, International ball had swallowed up the past ten summers and before that, even the thought of kids balling together on street courts was completely alien. Basketball isn't like soccer, you can't just set a court up like you can a pitch, using jumpers for goal-posts. At the very least you need a proper hoop and when I'd been growing up in England, hardly anyone even knew what basketball was let alone how and where to play it. Since then, there'd been a revolution.

The tiny event that Nhamo had thought up and developed along with his right-hand man, Jackson Gibbons, had been rapidly picking up speed. A man of vision, Nhamo had conceived this unbelievable (and unbelievably simple) idea which had turned into a mammoth annual event. It works like this: Midnight Madness is essentially a knock-out tournament, a national competition which pits ballers from throughout the country against one another, from Street to Elite, to battle it out to discover, and sometimes uncover, the UK's Top Ten Ballers. Anyone can enter. Nhamo and his crew hold a series of qualifying events in venues throughout the UK, from Glasgow all the way down to Plymouth. Although open to any player, entrants are separated across two courts, one for the Elite (pre-seeded players, invited to take part) and the other the Show N' Prove, open to anyone prepared to come and present his or her skills in a bid to make it from nowhere across to the Elite.

Each player registers online for free and receives a uniquely numbered Midnight Madness vest, which allows them to be tracked through the contest with their stats being recorded on a computerized system as they progress. At each event, play begins at 8pm and from then until midnight, players do whatever they can to show their skills on the Show N' Prove Court. Scouts line the courts and a lucky couple of dozen or so players are selected to come and play against the big boys; the Elite players who aren't required to play their way through the early stages as they've usually come with a proven rep', and tended to be either England Internationals or guys back home for the summer from their US college.

At midnight the main event starts. Ballers who've made it through so far pick their own squad of five players. They give their numbers into an official who writes the teams on a whiteboard in the order they come over until the list is pretty much touching the floor. Two teams are picked at random to start and winner stays on. It's as simple as that. A game lasts 10 minutes and a team wins by being the first to score 7-points (with a 3-pointer being worth 2- in the scoring system). Reach 7- points and your team stays on court, lose and boy you've got a long wait to get back on, one of you needs to leg-it over to the whiteboard and get your team written back up. By now there's gonna be at least ten teams before you, so this is where tactics come in: you either stick with your own squad or, in most cases, the better players will jump ship and get recruited by some other team higher up on the board who might have only three or four names down and are just waiting for an Elite player to find themselves on a losing team so they can recruit them and strengthen their squad.

So how does an individual actually win? Well this is the really unique bit, a system devised by Nhamo which he calls 'Ball Without Bias'. On the surface it's a street-ball tournament but in practice, Midnight Madness is really geared to unearthing the best all-round players and those guys who play smart as a team. Each player is individually awarded points which are recorded on laptops by the volunteers who line courtside. You get 5-points if your team wins a game, then individual positive points for steals, assists, blocked shots, made shots and rebounds. You get negative points for turnovers, missed shots, fouls and for a team loss. Teams battle it out 'til dawn. Only the strong survive and as the night progresses, the level of competition isn't a player's only challenge as they also fight the tiredness and hunger that only balling through the whole night can bring, and often frustration too.

To put it plainly, the team that strings the most wins together and manages to stay on the court is going to have its players qualify. Only ten people qualify from each satellite event to go forward to one of the two regional qualifier tournaments (one in London, the other in Birmingham, Manchester or Nottingham) to attempt to qualify for the ultimate Midnight

Madness finals in London, from which the top players will be crowned and will head off Stateside to represent the best of British street-ball. A team of England Internationals normally dominates these events. Usually finding they're pretty unbeatable if they stick together and play team ball, and generally being just too big and too smart for your average wannabe baller. But occasionally a decent squad will give them a good run for their money and knock them off. The highlight of the night tends to come when two super-teams, both with International players, clash. One team stays on and the other (no matter who they are or what kind of rep' they might have) goes to the back of the queue to just wait alongside everyone else.

By 6am the place is in carnage, with some of the country's fittest athletes strewn about bloody knackered. Scores are tallied up and the top ten individual scorers get an automatic bid to the regional qualifiers. The phenomenon of Midnight Madness is so great, the ultimate prize so impressive, that if they miss a spot, some players will travel all over the country in a bid to still qualify. If a good baller fails to make the top ten at the London qualifier, he'll go to Milton Keynes or Liverpool to try to make it through. The ten satellite qualifiers result in twenty Elite players still standing (the top two finishers from each of the ten events), half play in the London regional and the other half in the Northern.

The atmosphere at Midnight Madness events is unbelievable. The crowd is noisy enough to rival my old stomping ground 'The Pit' and the events have a real sense of party about them with live DJs and plenty of entertainment. The format of the regionals is the same as in the satellites and the chance still remains for people to get selected from the Show N' Prove courts to be promoted to the Elite. From here, there will only be ten players selected: those with the highest scores at the end of the night. They will make it through to the huge finals night at the end of August. And it really is huge. In 2009, the finals at Wembley drew a sell-out crowd of 5,000 crazy street-ball fans. It really is one of the best atmospheres I've ever witnessed at any basketball event, anywhere, and when Busta Rhymes performed his set there, those fans lifted the roof of that tabernacle!

The twenty players who've impressed the crowd and racked up the stats are now separated into two even teams, they're kitted out with a load of Nike freebies (including boots), and battle it out in an single 40-minute game. The format's the same in that the top ten players at the end of the game will be those with the highest individual scores. Who makes it is who performs best, not necessarily whose team has won. It might be six players from the winning team and four from the losing team. Whatever it is, it'll be the best players the UK has: and, as Pierre Henry-Fontaine once said, they'll all be *'hustling for the same piece of cheese.'*

My teenage dream of getting to the States in order to build myself a basketball career wasn't unique then and it still isn't now. Getting into a US college remains by far the best way for a young guy with talent to make it big. It wasn't an easy thing to achieve in the early '90s and it still isn't. Getting a spot on the final Midnight Madness team isn't only a way to guarantee respect from your balling peers, it's also a chance to play in the States and (for younger players) a chance to get scouted. The team spends a week in America representing the UK against US sides in a series of games and pretty much having the time of their lives.

2006 was my first year as a Midnight Madness baller and I had no idea that, before long, Nhamo would tell me, *'There is no question that your name and game are cemented in the Midnight Madness hall of fame'.* In '06 the prize up for grabs was a trip to Chicago and although I was definitely after a slice of the Chi-town action, the whole experience of even competing in this crazy atmosphere was kind of a prize in itself. I made it to the finals at Crystal Palace and was gutted to have finished 11th overall, leaving me just outside of the top ten ultimate team. I'd returned to Manchester and a few days later Nhamo phoned me to explain that one of the top ten had turned out to be ineligible due to NCAA rules: *'So how would you like to come to Chicago?'* There was only one answer: 'Meow!' One of the best phone calls of my life. I was already smiling because I was lying next to a beautiful woman (Yasmin). But now I was grinning from ear to ear. All those late-night qualifying tournaments, forcing my 33-year-old body to keep on playing 'til 6am had paid off.

I headed down to Seven Oaks in Kent the next day to meet up with the team at a basketball camp being held by Luol Deng. Our two-day preparation would begin with a game against Loul's staff team that night, followed by as much training as we could squeeze into that tabernacle before jetting off to Chicago. That opening practice game was really fun. I'd heard a lot about Loul, he's 6'8", tough in the post with some silky 10' turnarounds in the paint. I could tell the summer meant he wasn't in the same shape he'd be in during the season but still, guarding him for most of the game, I couldn't defend some of his moves. He hit a few big shots down the stretch and we lost by around 7-points.

The winning team coach from finals night was Sam Stiller and the next day he conducted a series of really intense drills for us. Sam's a great guy, really philosophical, something I admire more and more the older I get, and I was looking forward to him coaching us through to Chicago. He led us through two very hard long practices and it was clear from the start that going to Chicago would be an amazing experience. We'd do loads of cool stuff, but we weren't going for a holiday, we were going to win. There would be one final line-up change before we flew out, a last-minute authority issue with one of the top ten which, after a vote between staff and players, saw the guy in question being sent home and the door now being wide open for Germayne Forbes to step through into the squad. Germayne was an England teammate of mine. He's a class player who can flat-out stroke it, with a consistent 3-point shot and a cunning way of lulling you to sleep, only to hit one in your face or shake you with a nasty cross-over and then drain one in your mouth. At Midnight Madness events, the man was a legend. And it goes without saying that a call to come to Chi-town wasn't something he was about to pass up.

The trip was impressive on all angles. As well as the team, Nhamo and Jimmy Rodgers (a veteran and much respected coach from London), we were accompanied by a Nike representative (sponsors of the trip) and by a TV crew who were capturing every move for a documentary which was being made about the Midnight Madness phenomenon. As well as time practicing and representing in a number of games, there was time to enjoy a few treats: one being a tour of the Chicago Bulls' stadium by England's rising star and Jimmy Rodgers protégé Loul Deng, who was carving a career for himself in the NBA playing for the Bulls. Times were good, the hotel was nice and I roomed with my boy, Liverpool's finest, Dave Aliu.

With the arrival of our first game came the realization that we were well and truly on someone else's turf now. The game was to be played in a gym on the west-side of Chicago. We were greeted on the door by a security guard who told the guys on our team wearing hats that they had to remove them before he could let us into the gym. What? He needed us to help him out. There was no way, he explained, that he'd be able to protect us from the gangs in the gym (who determined where your loyalties lay by the way you wore your hat) if we went in risking it all with hats on. Holy Shit, I thought, this is deep. Pretty deep; the lesson for wearing your hat the wrong way might come etched on a bullet.

We hadn't come here to get shot, we'd come here to play ball and as Nhamo liked to remind us all, we brought the UK's reputation with us. I started the game and we went back and forth. We were pretty much tied after the first-half in which Marcus Knight really shone for us; then enter the ringer! At the start of the second-half, some guard shows up from nowhere and just drops off our point guards. No one could guard him and he was single-handedly the factor which meant we lost the game. We still managed a nice joke though: I was being guarded by a 6'4" guy who'd come straight out of the Boston Celtics summer league team and was hawking me all over that tabernacle as they full-court pressed us. As I brought the ball down court he was really pressuring me, but of course had no idea I used to be a point guard as I was playing in the four spot. As I got to the 3-point line, I really felt him breathing all down my neck, thinking I couldn't take the pressure and that he was about to rip me. Ok, I thought, Ok, and I gave it to him. I put the ball quickly through my legs with my right hand and then dribbled really fast behind my back twice: he was wobbling. My quick cross-over finished him off and forced him to attempt an aggressive reaction which made him slip and fall flat on his ass, hard... He should've known better; I was wearing the No.1 uniform; a sure sign I'd grown up idolizing 'Penny' Hardaway. The home crowd went crazy, laughing, and saying *'oohhhhh shiiitttttt!!'* It was a sweet move and made me laugh a lot. There's nothing like a bit of on-court jokes. But we'd still lost. We weren't quite a team yet and even though there were only around 7-points in it, a loss was a loss and was also not what we'd come to Chicago for.

We went back to practice hard the next day with a three-hour session which was only forced to conclude when Germayne accidentally broke the ring with a reverse dunk. For our second game we travelled to the east-side of Chicago to face the team of a tough guard who played for North Carolina. We weren't warned about any potential gang warfare and went on to play some great team ball, with some especially great defense courtesy of Steve Ogunjimi and Dru Spinks. It was Midnight Madness's first win on US soil and it felt great. The hard work from Coach Stiller's practices was paying off and we celebrated with a nice team meal.

The third and final game made Midnight Madness history. In Nhamo's words it was simply: *'Right people, right time, right occasion.'* It seems a little ironic now, as it was also a game I almost missed. As the team piled into our two hired mini-buses I shouted to a couple of the guys to tell the driver to wait as I had to go to the shop and, in the confusion of who was travelling with who, the message didn't get relayed and the damn team left me at the hotel. Both thinking I was on the other bus, they took off and I came back out of the shop to an empty street. I couldn't believe it and, after a couple of unsuccessful calls to cell phones that were either unheard in bags or not working, I went back to my room. I didn't know the gym we were playing in, let alone how to get there, but after twenty minutes of restlessness in my room, still in my game uniform, I decided to wander back down to the lobby and came face to face in the lift with Germayne. I started to say 'So you finally came back for me then –' but Germayne looked baffled *'Nah, we came back for my boots, I forgot them.'* Germayne had no idea I was missing and by the time we made it to the facility in the hood, an almost-missed game was the least of our worries.

This place was way, way in the hood. There'd have been no way I'd have found the place even with an address and the decent-sized crowd already there was looking like they had the potential to get kind of volatile. In the short time since our second-game win, we'd managed to build ourselves a reputation. They'd had some good players but we'd beaten them in their own hood and word had spread that this team from England had some ballers and could flat-out play. This last team, determined not to go down the same way, had drafted in re-enforcements.

There was a pair of 6'8" monsters on the inside that made Dave and Darius Defoe look kind of under-nourished; a tiny guard who was playing big time pro over in France, Pro A; as well as a 6'8" three-man who played at Loyola and was on the Nike Battleground DVD where Lebron James hosts New York V. Chicago. He was naughty. I guarded him and he hit me with three or four great pro moves. We got exposed in the second quarter and were down big. They dominated us at every position. It looked like we were in for a really long night.

Coach Sam Stiller, who'd built his own pro rep' as one of the best shooters in the English game, gave us the speech of his life. We were a team who'd only been together for five days, who were down 20-points early in the first-half of a game in a really hostile environment, but still he truly believed in his heart that we would win. We were also a team who'd been built under Nhamo's mantra: 'I. Don't. Lose', and so we were already accustomed to thinking big. It was really inspirational stuff from Coach, a guy with plenty of talk to support his players and bring out their very best. We kept our composure and, driven by his words, Germayne and I started stepping-up. The third quarter was The Forbes Show. He came down and hit four straight shots with a guy in his face. Three of them were 3-pointers. It was great to watch, he really shone, showing both his coolness and class. We were biting into their lead but they held it off and were making some big plays of their own.

Enter Dave Aliu. Not really having found himself in Coach Stiller's rotation, Dave's court-time had been limited. But coming into the game in the fourth quarter, he did what he does best; rained three huge 3-s back to back and single-handedly blew the game wide open. Thirty-four seconds left and we were within 5-points. Personally it'd been a good game. Coach

Stiller is exactly the kind of guy who brings out the best in me. My self-belief rockets when I sense someone else's faith in me: *'Del has a rare gift to unify his team, not in a forceful way but through his composure, timing and his ability to lead by example.'* And it made the trip all the sweeter to feel that my style of play and interaction was not only understood but appreciated: *'Delme had an effect on his teammates that made them play unselfish basketball. We share a language beyond space and time. A language that speaks loud in a quiet voice above all things finds a way. The strong alone can pass through the procession of life, but strength lies in gentleness.'*

I'd played the whole game and so I was in a good rhythm, scoring consistently in each quarter. I had two 3-s in the fourth; one of which was huge as it came at the point when there remained just seconds on the clock. Dean Williams had come off a pick and roll and Germayne was guarded, so he hit me on the deep wing and I nailed it. Putting us within a point at 104-105. A couple of free-throws were missed by them which led us nicely into the game's (the trip's) finale. We broke the press, I dribbled down the court, got doubled and found Dave Aliu. He threw a great dime to Dru Spinks, who hit a tough lay-up with three-seconds left, and won us the game.

We went ballistic. It was such an emotion-filled victory. We'd come to represent the UK and were going home 2-1 in the series as Champions. I'd finished the game with around 23-points and 10 boards and had had the time of my life. It's only right that last words go to Nhamo Shire, Midnight Madness would be nothing without him. If you ever get hold of the documentary of the trip, it's worth a watch if for nothing else than the grin on Nhamz' face at the end. He sums the trip up best: *'We OWN Chicago right now!'*

Another Shot

So what's next? Because there has to be a 'next'. Even sportspeople who retire with Jordan's money, Beckham's fame, are looking for 'next'. There's a lot of life past 36 and it needs filling....

At some point between Everton's phantom job offer and the truth coming to light, something in me had silently clicked. A quiet acceptance. I'd stopped working out like I used to and, without conscious thought, accepted retirement. It wasn't like I had nothing. A couple of years before, I'd started my own basketball club for kids in Widnes and, thanks to a grant from Halton Youth Bank, was able to cushion my disappointment about how things had turned with Everton by taking nine of my young players to Laszlo Nemeth's Eurocamp in Cumbria where I was going to coach. It was just what I needed. This is a great camp. I'd coached there before and it had always been a pleasure. I'd find myself inspired by the youngsters I'd see there, by their dedication, and their pure out-and-out damn near rude love for the game would breathe something through me and take me back all those years to the Leeds Camp where I'd been just like them, so full of hope, so full of hunger.

Some players would stand out right from the off, like I'd done to Dean all those years ago. One such player was Michelle Turner, a slight 15-year-old at the time, who was competing alongside the boys as there weren't enough females to warrant their own conference. When I saw her take to the court for the first time I kind of winced; fearful of how much she'd be man-handled. But boy was I wrong; that kid has GAME; a point guard with serious skills and composure, along with a toughness which you wouldn't expect from such a young girl. I'm happy to go out on a limb for her: she was probably a better player than I was at the same age. You need to watch out for her, I'm sending her all the luck for the career than undoubtedly lies before her.

Camp rejuvenated me but, in spite of the attempts of other coaches and campers to convince me it was too soon to retire, I knew it was over. I wasn't going to play in the BBL again. But what was I going to do? I'd been building up a little business part-time since I'd been back in England, coaching in schools and running my own club, but it wasn't enough to support me: I needed a proper job. As part of my involvement with Everton I'd been running a Tuesday night session at Toxteth Sports Centre for kids who'd been involved in knife crime. There'd been some difficulty securing the kids a coach whom they respected enough to work with but we seemed to be getting along pretty well now and it felt good to be involved in something which was helping kids to move away from all the negatives and the violence around them. I'd seen enough of the heartache of gang-violence through the tragedies which had touched some of my Manny boys. And it was here one night that I took a call from a guy I didn't know at all, a call which would end up opening a whole other series of doors for me.

I'd been working the day before doing a coaching session for Jeff Jones at Manchester's Burnage High School when I'd got chatting with the school's P.E. teacher, Matt Weadle. Ball remains a small world and I already knew Matt as the coach of Newi Nets a Division Two side based in Wrexham, North Wales. Matt and I had been joking about my unexpected retirement. He'd said *'Well, you could come and play for us this season'* and I'd joked back 'Show me the contract and we'll talk.' The next day Andrew Donaldson called and it turned out it hadn't been a joke after all.

Andrew Donaldson is arguably Britain's most enthusiastic man. He's certainly England's. A successful businessman and entrepreneur, he'd spent the previous two seasons as lead sponsor of Chester Jets and had broken away to focus his energies on the kind of lowly Nets whom he was working with in partnership with Warrington Wolves Rugby League team, a massive side based a couple of miles from Widnes. As founder of one of the northwest's biggest storage companies, Andrew was looking for his next challenge. You'd call it a hobby but for a man with such drive, a hobby is a pretty serious business. He had a couple of youngsters under his wing,

Rabah, and Max, who were playing at Newi and he wanted me to play there too. He was offering me a job. Essentially the same job Everton had 'offered' but that it was real and came with the added clause that he wanted me to play. Funny how things turn out: all that time spent trying to get away from the limitations of growing up in a town obsessed with Rugby League and now it had come full-circle. In a roundabout way, Rugby League would after all be a part of my life and my career. If I still had a career. Andrew's determination was immediately obvious, he wanted this team to go places and he wanted me to help get them there.

It was crazy how this whole thing came so completely out of the blue. A career in pro ball prepares you for precisely no other job once inevitable retirement catches up with you, and I'd been reluctantly planning a Supply Teaching comeback; something that was more a necessity than a serious stepping stone towards anything more promising. Promising was exactly what Andrew's offer seemed to be and, with nothing to lose, I signed a contract with him and found myself training again, this time across the border at Glyndwr University. When Andrew introduced me to the team on the first night, he told them how serious he was about contending for the title this season and as he did, I spotted a familiar face; Usman Baba, one of my boys from all those Amaechi Centre summers. Ten minutes into practice it was clear that Andrew's determination wasn't the only thing we'd need to get us through the season; I'd let myself go a little physically, but mentally even more so in terms of the mind-set required to perform at the kind of level I was accustomed to performing at. It felt like it was going to be a long season.

I decided to treat the whole experience as a transition stage. I wasn't coming out of retirement, just taking a side-step towards securing my alternative future. I helped Matt out a lot with coaching and focused on the development side of ball. I was busy off the court coaching in Warrington schools, promoting my boss's brand 'Big Storage' and the Warrington Wolves. Although based in Wrexham, the Wolves connection meant there was an agreement to play five games in Birchwood, Warrington, and it felt good to be back in my own area, promoting ball to young local kids. Since I'd returned to England, I'd been on the lookout for the next potential player. I'd been quietly developing a new dream: helping a young baller to take their game to the States, just like I'd done.

In spite of our disappointing season, only managing to finish seventh, I'd surprised myself by racking up some great shooting stats. In spite of my less-than-pro fitness level, I led the league in something which had been the Achilles heel of my career, 3-point shooting, at 56%. As a team we'd tried our best but faced some tough competition, especially in the form of Durham Wildcats who dominated all season and gained promotion.

After a couple of months of the by now almost boringly inevitable funding issues, my role with Warrington Wolves is officially secured. A new team has broken away from Newi Nets, we're Warrington Wolves Foundation Basketball Club. And so this season, following in the tradition of some pretty weird and wonderful characters, for the first time ever, Head Coach will be me, Mr. Versatility. We need to work our way up, a brand-new team like us starts in Division Four. But then Division Four's the perfect place to start. From there the sky's the limit, isn't it?

Do I still like to play? Retirement or no retirement: I will always be a baller. Basketball has pumped through my veins for the majority of my life. It doesn't just go away and I guess it never will. After all, why would I want it to? Could I have lived this life without it?

So what of regrets? Well, I could fill a book with regrets, but I've tried not to. All too often, significant figures in my balling life have said it could've all been so different; with better advice, with different support, but then this has been life, hasn't it? Sometimes ball became so caught up in financial issues that it was difficult to touch the initial passion I'd felt. Laszlo Nemeth once told me, *'all the acknowledgements you will get for your loyal service will last much longer than just petty cash'*. It took a long time for me to realise how right that wise man was. I used to think basketball was all there was. It was when I began to learn that life is all there is that I really grew.

And what of dreaming the dream, was it worth it? Hell, yeah. Every second. Every heartbreak, every basket, every wrong move, every rebound;

everything. I still have dreams, ones that matter in a different way now that I've found another chance for them, another shot. It's less about me now and more about the new generation of Mr or Ms Versatilities. If this life has taught me anything, it's taught me how much I have learned and how I might now pass that on. My goal is to teach this new generation to never be defined as just a basketball player, just a shooter, just a rebounder: all those 'justs' are inevitably just too small. Teach them to work until they're good at everything; to concentrate on their weakness more than on their strengths. Above all, to teach them to treat people with respect, to teach them that the ultimate baller doesn't have to sacrifice honour and humility to achieve his goals.

And what about family and homeliness and domestic things? Well that lawn I slaved over is still weed-free. I'm settled in Manchester with Yasmin, trying to continue Oz's legacy by being the best step-dad I can be to Yalkin and Layla, being a mate to Reece. Would I like to have biological kids of my own? Definitely. Am I destined to remain unconnected to anyone genetically related to me? I hope not.

And what about belonging? What about all that 'find your father' stuff? Well, that day, Jos Wolfs had never been more right in his life, and the older I get the more the need for that knowledge grows. I'd thought that the dream would secure me a place in which to belong and it did. But the belonging we find within ourselves is the only one which truly matters, which truly lasts. Through all those years, through all those highs and all those lows, I was looking for the one thing which still eludes me. He's out there, somewhere...